Stop Blaming Mothers *and* Ignoring Fathers

HOW TO TRANSFORM THE WAY WE KEEP
CHILDREN SAFE FROM DOMESTIC VIOLENCE

DAVID MANDEL

CREATOR OF THE SAFE & TOGETHER™ MODEL

Stop Blaming Mothers and Ignoring Fathers:
How to Transform the Way We Keep Children Safe from Domestic Violence

Published by Legitimus Media, Canton, CT

Copyright ©2024 by David Mandel. All rights reserved.

No part of this book may be reproduced in any form or by any mechanical means, including information storage and retrieval systems without permission in writing from the publisher/author, except by a reviewer who may quote passages in a review.

All images, logos, quotes, and trademarks included in this book are subject to use according to trademark and copyright laws of the United States of America.

Paperback ISBN: 978-1-7351645-3-3
Hardcover ISBN: 978-1-7351645-4-0

FAMILY & RELATIONSHIPS / Abuse / Domestic Partner Abuse

Cover and interior design by Asya Blue Design, copyright owned by David Mandel. Comic illustrations by Awele Emeli at https://www.aweleemili.com/.

While I hope this book will lead to transformational change and increased health, safety, and well-being for families, improved systems, and better professional practice, it is intended for informational purposes only and does not represent any specific guidance or recommendations for anyone's professional or personal situation. If you are a survivor, please seek the support of friends, family, and qualified professionals. If you are professional, please exercise your own judgment, seek out professional supervision and support as necessary, and be faithful to the legal, policy, and ethical mandates of your profession and your agency.

Except where otherwise indicated, all quotes, dialogue, and cartoons in this book represent conversations or composites of conversations based on my best recollections. The transcripts of interviews with practitioners and survivors have been edited for clarity and brevity. Any case examples are composites, and/or the identifying details have been modified to protect the privacy of individuals involved.

QUANTITY PURCHASES: Schools, companies, professional groups, clubs, and other organizations may qualify for special terms when ordering quantities of this title. For information, email business@safeandtogetherinstitute.com.

All rights reserved by David Mandel and Legitimus Media.

Printed in the United States of America.

DEDICATIONS

This book is dedicated to Ruth, who is my partner in life, work, family, and fun; to my children, who teach me love and humility every day; to my dad, who showed me what it means to be a mensch; and to my mom, who loved me every day of my life.

I also dedicate this book to all the mothers and children who have suffered a domestic violence perpetrator's abuse and had that abuse compounded by the failures and abuses of systems; to all the fathers whose parenting was ignored by systems and who wanted help to be a better father; and to all the professionals who are striving to be better at their job every day.

NOTE

The author and publisher acknowledge that First Nation Peoples are the Traditional Custodians and the first storytellers of the lands on which we live and work. We particularly want to honor the Tunxis, on whose land this book was written. We recognize the damage of colonization and the need for continuous work to repair those harms. We honor First Nation Peoples' continuous connection to Country, waters, skies, and communities. We celebrate their stories, traditions, and living cultures; and we pay our respects to Elders past, present, and emerging.

CONTENTS

Foreword v

Preface ix

Introduction 1

Chapter 1: Why Does She Keep Choosing Him over Her Children? 7

Chapter 2: Blaming Mothers, Ignoring Fathers. 19

Chapter 3: Challenging Professional Myths About Domestic Violence 39

Chapter 4: The Myth of the Child Witness 49

Chapter 5: The Myth of the Domestic Violence Incident 78

Chapter 6: The Myth of Failure to Protect. 117

Chapter 7: The Myth of Perpetrator Accountability 162

Chapter 8: The Myth of Parental Alienation 200

Chapter 9: The Myth of Trauma-Informed Practice 228

Chapter 10: Critical Components and Principles: A Common Language 270

Chapter 11: Developing Evidence for the Model 309

Chapter 12: Honoring the Voices of Survivors and Practitioners 320

Chapter 13: Change Starts Now. 344

Acknowledgments 353

Glossary 356

About the author 362

The Safe & Together Institute's Offerings 363

About the artist 364

Endnotes. 365

FOREWORD

It is a pleasure and a privilege to have been invited to write the foreword to this long-awaited book by David Mandel. As someone who has worked with David for many years, it is wonderful to hear David's thoughtful, informative, and irrepressible enthusiasm coming through on every page. This is not an academic book, nor is this the Safe & Together detailed training manual. It is the voice of David coming through in the writing to talk through the principles and practices of Safe & Together, as well as the poignant moments and stories that continue to inspire and drive the desire to create progressive change. It tells the story of the paradigm shift required to ensure a safer, more effective, and more accountable practice when children are living with domestic and family violence.

Many myths and distortions have found their way into our current legislative and practice frameworks. Unfortunately, this has meant practitioners have become stuck in organisations and practices that are not fit for purpose. They often know that they are blaming mothers for circumstances beyond the mothers' control and that children are not any safer following their interventions. However, there is no map or framework to provide alternative pathways that are easily understood by those practitioners and by their colleagues in other organisations (such as mental health, substance use, housing, family services, and justice).

The Safe & Together Model, with its clear set of Principles and Critical Components, provides the opportunity to develop a shared language that facilitates collaboration between organisations with different cultures and priorities. Time and again, I have seen experienced practitioners from the child protection and family violence sectors marvel at the changes that occur for the families they work with when they have a shared foundation for practice through the Safe & Together Model and training. The articulation of this framework and its explication in this book through case examples, graphics, and cartoons will offer practitioners a shared framework through which they can refresh and reflect on their own work.

While the book is all about organisational and practice development using the Safe & Together Model, the other framing that is woven through the book is that of social justice. Practitioners and managers are invited to examine constantly the ethics of their practice and whether they are aligning themselves with the most vulnerable members of society and making a stance against violence, abuse, and oppression. They are urged to consider whether their practice replicates the abusive practices of the perpetrator, thus contributing to the secondary abuse of child and adult victim survivors. This is a book for those practitioners and managers who are currently uncomfortable and distressed by a mismatch between their values and their practice. It provides a pathway to align core values of social justice with their work through attending to safety and well-being in the context of structural disadvantage. It is not an easy road. However, there is inspiration in collaboration when people with shared values work together to change their organisations and create a context in which abusive behaviours are able to be challenged. Those who are most vulnerable experience support and can find allies who can stand with them as they navigate complex service and justice systems, providing hope that change is possible and that safer ground can be found.

I was interested to come to the end of the book and to see that adult survivors, those with lived experience, are provided with a voice. A number of these survivors are also practitioners, a group whose knowledge is both professional and personal. Their testimony points to the value of the Safe & Together principle of partnering with the nonoffending parent and challenges the failure to protect myth.

FOREWORD

A further valuable insight from adult survivors lies in the recognition that the person using violence and abuse (usually fathers) should never be invisible to helping professionals. Their behaviour should be mapped and documented. While accountability is emphasised, so is acknowledgment that fathers generally do not disappear from the lives of their children. Wherever it is safe to do so, engagement with their motivation to change and their potential to contribute in a positive way to the functioning of the lives of others in their family can be explored. This is part of the paradigm shift described in this book, which brings invisible men into the professional's frame of reference and discusses the skills and approaches practitioners need to make this change possible.

My own experience across five research projects with David Mandel is that the Safe & Together principle of pivoting to the perpetrator is the approach that practitioners find most valuable. Generally, we do not train practitioners to work with men, let alone with men who use violence. Once the core Safe & Together training has been undertaken, the guidance in the Perpetrator Pattern Mapping Tool provides the refresher—the map that step-by-step ensures that the tactics of abuse and their impact are identified and recorded. Complex practice is made accessible. This speaks to the author's many years of practice experience, which he has synthesised to a few key principles and critical concepts. These form the foundations for effective, efficient, ethical, and safer practice with children living with domestic violence.

I would highly recommend that you read on! You will not be disappointed.

Cathy Humphreys
Professor of Social Work, University of Melbourne
Melbourne, Australia
February 2023

PREFACE

Every day, children and adults suffer at the hands of a loved one who chooses control over connection. Their trust and love are betrayed. Their lives are bent and broken, sometimes irrevocably, through violence, control, and manipulation. Every day thousands of professionals labor to help these survivors, working inside systems that are flawed in myriad ways—especially in how they ignore fathers and blame mothers when it comes to the question of domestic violence and children.

For almost forty years, I've dedicated myself to the seemingly quixotic goal of ending male violence against women and children. When I started, my professional work was focused on helping individual men change, holding them accountable for their violence and abuse in one-on-one sessions and groups. Eventually, I realized the skills and experiences I had gained through that work could help a range of professionals from other sectors to better intervene with men using violence against their loved ones. No longer was my focus on "fixing" men. I became focused on fixing systems. I wanted *all* professionals who worked with families, not just "men's behavior change facilitators," to challenge, support, and hold accountable men who violated, hurt, and abused their family members.

Eventually, my efforts to repair systems expanded to encompass better partnering with survivors around the safety and well-being of their children. Partnering was based on the assumption that survivors were almost always actively working to keep their children safe, and it was the role of the professional to identify these strengths, validate them, and collaboratively plan—as partners—with the survivors to improve their situation. This concept became central to my work on numerous levels. I encapsulated my thinking into the concept of domestic violence-informed systems and practice. I developed the Safe & Together Model as a theory and practice that could aid professionals to be better allies to adult and child survivors and to focus more on perpetrators as parents.

My experiences across multiple systems shaped my thinking and the Model. What started with an intense focus on child protection grew to embrace other sectors such as mental health, substance misuse, specialist family violence, family court, health visitors, and law enforcement. Transformational efforts came to include tackling cutting-edge issues such as police officer-involved domestic violence, the relationship between mother-blaming and worker safety fears, and perpetrator manipulation of systems.

In the last fifteen years, I've built a global organization dedicated to changing the lives of professionals and families from New Zealand to New Mexico, from Sydney to Singapore, from London to Lincoln. I have poured myself into creating the Safe & Together Institute, collaborating with my team members so we could impact as many people as possible. If you've picked up this book, you understand this drive toward action. My hope in writing this book is that it will further accelerate the positive change I see resulting from the Model's implementation.

The last few years have brought major personal changes. After years of working at the intersection of domestic violence, fatherhood, and children, I finally became a dad. Ruth, my partner in life and work, trusted me to co-parent her three amazing children. As a "new" father, I hungrily lapped up every experience, from playing catch to attending school concerts and to helping with math homework. Our constant conversations—about Ruth's experience as a child and adult survivor of family violence and about my experiences from work—inspired our podcast, *Partnered with a Survivor*. All these experiences, professional and personal, influence what is reflected in this book.

My journey has been one of hope, persistence, and collaboration. I started my journey around gender-based violence in university, where

I started to listen to and learn from the experience of women I knew personally. I was inspired to action by other men who had committed themselves to ending male violence against women. I've been supported along the way by people who believed in me, people who gave me a chance to try out new ideas. Each opportunity helped me learn more about how to make systems more responsive to the needs of adult and child survivors.

Along the way I've been energized by the feedback of survivors who, after learning about the Model, thanked me for reflecting their lived experience back to professionals. I've gained confidence from practitioners who have told me the Model prevented them from quitting, out of frustration and loss of faith, their chosen career. My commitment to my path has been strengthened by social workers who reported "feeling smarter" and better prepared to help families after a Safe & Together Model consultation. I've been blessed with research partners, colleagues, and staff who have been there every step along the way—building, learning, and creating together.

Every day, many of us who are dedicated to ending domestic violence are confronted by fears of failure or that we aren't doing enough. We question how much difference we may be making. Our failures feel very concrete and visible: The survivor who remains in danger despite our best efforts. The perpetrator who isn't willing to change regardless of interventions. The children who still face fear. Yet our legacies are so much bigger than our obvious failures. What we don't see and cannot see is the powerful, rippling, positive impact of our actions. We often don't see how our words of positive validation to a survivor are an important part of her journey to safety and freedom that comes to fruition years later. We miss how the "failed" intervention with a perpetrator planted seeds of change that eventually manifested into meaningful change. Our legacies include our influence on our present-day colleagues and future generations of children we will never meet.

I hope that reading this book will help you strengthen your own legacy of change, one that you may never fully appreciate but that still gives you meaning and hope and changes the lives of people, now and in the future.

INTRODUCTION

This book is a deep dive into the concepts, practices, and, indeed, myths that have shaped mother-blaming, father-ignoring domestic violence policy and practice. It is also about the approach that has been overturning this outdated, harmful paradigm across the globe. The Safe & Together™ Model and its associated practices represent an implicit challenge and critique to the dominant, often deeply held, ideas that shape our culture and the response of systems to domestic violence and children. In the book I refer to these deeply held ideas as "myths," by which I mean problematic or incomplete understandings that are not in alignment with the lived experience of adult and child survivors. For each myth, I set out the problems and how the Safe & Together Model offers solutions to those problems. Myth by myth, I dismantle cultural misconceptions and professional terminology, centering an approach that focuses on the behaviors of perpetrators and the realities of survivors.

I also tackle the gender paradox of domestic violence-informed practice: how the best response to domestic violence requires an objective behavioral assessment framework that works regardless of the gender of the perpetrator and survivor. At the same time, that framework needs to name and deconstruct gendered expectations around parenting to achieve full accuracy and effectiveness.

The Safe & Together Model contains a suite of tools, practices, policies, and concepts designed to stop professionals and systems from engaging in practices that blame mothers for the impact of their male partners' behavior on their children. These interventions often create more hardship, pain, and danger rather than increasing safety and freedom from fear. Eschewing mother-blaming, the Model guides professionals to "pivot to the perpetrator," focusing on the perpetrator's behaviors as the source of the harm to child, partner, and family functioning. Making this shift requires connecting the dots between low expectations for men as parents—which is the source of the practice of ignoring fathers—and mother-blaming attitudes and practices. By raising expectations of men as parents and increasing the focus on perpetrators as parents, the shift changes how professionals in a variety of systems interact with survivors. The idea is that if you stop ignoring the role, good or bad, that fathers' behaviors play in families, you are better able to help mothers, children, and even fathers.

This is not an in-depth "how to" book about the Safe & Together Model. Since the Safe & Together Institute trains and teaches on the Model all the time, and since you can access the Model's tools through multiple platforms, I wanted to offer a "look under the hood." What are the problems the Model is trying to solve? What is the thinking behind the Model? What influences and ideas drive the Model? What are survivors and practitioners saying about the Model and its impact? Because the Model really comes alive in action, you will also walk away with concrete, specific things to reflect upon and actions you can take right now. Whether you are a practitioner or a survivor, this book is designed to help you.

Throughout these pages, I take you on a journey that I hope will include many familiar landmarks. You may recognize yourself in the conversations or actions I describe. These moments of recognition may feel uncomfortable at times—or they may feel incredibly validating. My advice, in those moments of possible discomfort, is to remember that our thinking and practice is shaped by *systems*—educational, cultural, and bureaucratic. We've been encouraged and trained to think through specific lenses or told to practice in specific ways. Use this bigger view to counter any blame or shame you might feel for practices that you would do differently today. Understanding the forces that shape your practice can make it easier to act differently once you see things differently.

This book is divided into three sections. The first chapters serve as an orientation to the book, including its major theme: blaming mothers and ignoring fathers. The middle section covers the six myths that the Model challenges. The final few chapters will help you better understand the Safe & Together Model, the impact it's having, and how to take action using the Model as your guide. Throughout the book, I highlight the voices of survivors who have been helped by the Model and practitioners who have championed its implementation. The Model is nothing without the practitioners who apply it, nor can its effectiveness be truly measured without hearing from survivors impacted by professionals' use of the Model.

Why a Focus on Mothers as Victims and Fathers as Perpetrators?

This book's title speaks to a tight focus on domestic violence perpetrated by fathers (see the glossary for the inclusive definition of fathers) against mothers. However, the Safe & Together Model doesn't just apply to heterosexual couples or the most common scenario of male perpetrator and female victim. The Model's pattern-based behavioral approach has proven useful in every possible relationship scenario. including female perpetrator against male victim, same-sex relationships, and instances when one or both of the partners are trans or non-binary.

The Model recognizes that men, women, trans, and non-binary people can be violent and controlling. Domestic violence occurs in same-sex and straight relationships. Nor does the Model fail to recognize that women can and do perpetrate child abuse and neglect. At the same time, gender-neutral language, when discussing domestic violence and children, glosses over crucial facts. While the declaration that *all lives matter* is true, it also doesn't capture the critical reality and unique dynamics of structural racism and targeted violence directed at Black lives. Similarly, a gender-neutral, sexual orientation-neutral, *all victims matter* approach

3

does not equip us with the tools to challenge the structural dynamics of gender-based violence and the gender bias of our current systems' dominant response to domestic violence and children—a response where the behaviors of fathers who choose coercive control are often ignored or minimized and the mothers, who are working hard to parent and protect in the context of those behaviors, are blamed.

There are multiple reasons why we need to differentiate between men's and women's domestic violence perpetration. Men's use of violence against women is more associated with physical injury than women's use of violence against men. Injury can be viewed as a reasonable indicator for the presence of fear and control—if the perpetrator can injure you, you are more likely to feel threatened, afraid, and controlled. This is consistent with data that shows that men's physical violence is more likely to be embedded in a wider pattern of coercive control.[1] Coercive control is a critical lens for helping us fully assess harm to children. Finally, differing expectations of men and women as parents make it misleading and disingenuous to talk in a gender-neutral manner. Using the term "parent" obscures what may be the most critical issue we need to confront if we want to increase child safety and well-being—low standards for men as parents.

Coercive Control

Throughout this book, I talk a lot about the concept of coercive control, so it's worth spending a little time here setting out where the term originated and how identifying and responding to perpetrator patterns of control is central to the Safe & Together Model. Evan Stark defines coercive control as "a pattern of behavior which seeks to take away the victim's liberty or freedom, to strip away their sense of self. It is not just women's bodily integrity which is violated but also their human rights."[2] Stark made the case as early as 2007 that domestic violence should not be categorized as a series of individual incidents of physical violence. He argues that systems should be approaching domestic violence as a pattern of behavior by the (usually male) perpetrator against the (usually female) victim and her children. For interventions to be meaningful and effective, they need to seek to ameliorate the harms caused by these ongoing patterns of controlling behavior.

Throughout the book you will read the term "perpetrator pattern-based approach." This is the foundation of the Safe & Together Model. The Model integrates the concept of coercive control into the heart of its pattern-based approach. You will see how important it is to not just focus on bruises and other physical injuries but also the way the perpetrators' behaviors (and the responses of systems) entrap survivors, limiting their freedom and their choices. The concept of coercive control, and its comprehensive behavioral assessment lens, is central to the understanding of the myths and the solutions to mother-blaming, father-ignoring culture.

Who Is This Book for?

This book has a number of audiences. It's for anyone who is interested in the intersection of domestic violence and children. It's for practitioners like me, who are fierce advocates for adult and child domestic violence survivors and who are deeply passionate about system change. It's for anyone who believes we need to stop ignoring fathers but without sacrificing the safety and well-being of women and children. Mostly, though, it's for anyone who has been critical of the current systems' response to domestic violence and who dreams of a time when those systems are better allies to adult and child survivors. Whether you are a child welfare practitioner, domestic violence advocate, probation officer, law enforcement officer, judge, therapist, or addiction counselor, there is something here for you. Hopefully, this book will reshape your thinking about domestic violence survivors as mothers, domestic violence perpetrators as fathers, and domestic violence systems—from law enforcement to mental health providers to home visitors—as responders to both.

I know this book can transform your individual practice. But more than that, I want you to use this book and the Safe & Together Model to become a champion for a new paradigm addressing systems handling domestic violence cases involving children. I want you to use it to change your agency and how you collaborate and interact with your colleagues in other systems. By the time you finish reading this book, I want you to be confident that applying a perpetrator pattern-based approach can make you more successful in your work.

> *I want you to become a change agent—advocating for an end to mother-blaming and a new approach to men as parents.*

This book is also for adult domestic violence survivors. I want you to feel validated in your experiences of abuse, including the ways that systems' responses have supported and hurt you. I want to arm you with the ideas and words to demand better from practitioners, many of whom want to help but have been constrained by outdated concepts and tools. I want this book to help your voices be heard. I particularly want this for survivors from the margins, who experience multiple forms of victimization based on gender, race, class, sexual orientation, and other factors. For these survivors, freedom from domestic violence is only part of the story. As survivors from the margins have taught me, efforts to address domestic violence that ignore other forms of oppression do not reflect their realities and needs.

While the problem is domestic violence and its impact on children and families, the goal is changing society so it's more just, safe, and equitable. The ultimate goal is ending family violence; ending gender-based violence, misogyny, and sexism; and ending racism and other forms of oppression intertwined with violence in the home. At times I've felt like we're all tilting at windmills—the problem is so massive. Change is hard, but this book will equip you with ideas and actions you can use immediately and over the long term to accelerate the transformation of your practice, and through your practice, transform society, culture, and the lives of families.

CHAPTER 1

Why Does She Keep Choosing Him over Her Children?

I was introduced to the problem of mother-blaming and father-ignoring in one of the earliest conversations I ever had with a child protection social worker about domestic violence and children. It involved a worker who was confused, frustrated, and blaming a mother despite her knowledge of the perpetrator's patterns of entrapment, surveillance, and control through fear and violence. She blamed the mother for visiting him in prison with their baby although she knew he had orchestrated, from prison, a heinous sexual assault against the mother using a third party. Even though the training session I was leading was specifically intended to educate workers on strategies for engaging perpetrators, I was being asked to turn away from the perpetrator and explain a victim's decision-making.

Even with me directing her attention onto the continuing danger, the worker resisted contextualizing the mother's decision-making. She was unable—or unwilling—to shift her perspective to consider that the mother's decision might be a rational, self-protective response to his escalating pattern of abusive behavior and to the failure of the systems' intervention to make her safe. Visiting him in prison with the baby was likely a desperate attempt to placate him, feign loyalty, assess his mood, and stave off any further danger to herself and her child.

However, when I pointed all this out to her, the worker would not, or could not, shake off her focus on the mother's choices. She appeared baffled as to why the mother wouldn't accept the agency's financial support to relocate thousands of miles away to live with her parents. When I questioned her about the mother's thoughts on the plan, the worker said, "The mother says it won't work because her parents and his family live only a few houses away from each other in that same town." Even when I pointed out that the proximity of his family would give him access to her new location and make the plan unsafe, the worker continued to express frustration and concern about the mother's choices. Her attitude and words were laden with judgment, culminating in the accusation that this was a mother who was failing to protect her child.

Despite my attempts to pivot the conversation to the person who created the risk—the perpetrator of the violence—*the worker couldn't take her eyes off the mother.* To the worker, the mother's choices were to blame for the danger to the child. The perpetrator's behaviors were a background blur, practically invisible, not relevant to how she discussed the case, and not viewed as a context for the mother's decisions. The worker's biggest worries were not about the father's omnipresent pattern of control and violence—but about the mother's choices.

This conversation was my introduction to the culture of mother-blaming that was, and still is, the dominant paradigm in domestic violence cases involving children. Accusations such as "Why does she keep choosing him over her child?" are just one of the many expressions of blame focused on domestic violence survivors who are mothers. Repeated over and over in different countries, and with professionals from diverse sectors, I've heard statements such as this:

> She let him back into the house, despite there being a court order.
>
> She keeps making babies with him.
>
> She doesn't understand the impact of the domestic violence on her children.
>
> She's just going to keep choosing abusive partners.

> If it was that bad, she would have left sooner.
>
> Now that they are separated, domestic violence is no longer an issue. Why is she trying to keep the children from him?

All these conversations and statements have two things in common. First, the domestic violence survivor—usually the mother—is being scrutinized for what she did or didn't do to protect her children. Her choices are measured by a one-size-fits-all yardstick of protective actions that boil down to leaving and ending the relationship as the only right choice. Calling the police, going to a refuge, getting a court order, or engaging in services sometimes can be seen as steps in the right direction. But if the violence persists, so the thinking goes, the only acceptable answer is to leave and end the relationship. No matter how many other creative strategies the survivor develops to reduce the risk to the children, no matter how hard she is working to protect her children, little else, from the perspective of professionals, seems to matter.

The second, interlocking commonality is how consistently violent fathers' responsibility for harming the children is ignored. Families come to the attention of the police and child protection because of a father's choice to be violent to the child's mother, but all the activity and attention will center on the mother's real and imagined problems, particularly her parenting, relationship choices, substance misuse, and mental health. In many cases, the violent father may never even be interviewed by a social worker. The perpetrator's abuse is not framed as a parenting choice. Everywhere, including the criminal justice system, the perpetrators as parents and the connections between their behaviors and the harm to the children are all but invisible in day-to-day practice. This has been defined by Cathy Humphreys and Ravi Thiara as "absent presence," which means the perpetrator, even when he is out of the home and not engaged by social workers, still is a force to be reckoned with.[1] He is present in the trauma symptoms, the disrupted family functioning, and the continuing fear. Cathy Humphreys and others, in a later article titled "More Present Than Absent,"[2] argue that "fathers who use violence are actually more present than absent in the lives of children (and women), even following separation." The study

CHAPTER 1 : WHY DOES SHE KEEP CHOOSING HIM OVER HER CHILDREN?

further highlighted the "problematic fathering that many children experienced, both before and after separation . . . and the very high levels of child abuse and poor attitudes to both women and children."

> *I often say that a father is a father, whether they're present or not . . . my mother was a survivor of domestic violence, and even when my father left the home, he was still my father. He was an absent father, but he was still my father. I knew he existed. I knew he wasn't coming around. I knew what I had seen. I knew what I had heard. He was just the father that caused harm and a father that's not there. And fast forwarding, when I'm advocating for fatherhood support and services, I often say not only is this a father, whether they're present or absent, but they could potentially reunite and reunify as a family. So he becomes the father again in the home or he could father another child of his own. So, he becomes a father again. Or he could remarry someone who has children. So, he becomes a father again.*

—Eloise, independent consultant, child-adult survivor, US

Mother-blaming requires ignoring fathers' choices and responsibility for the harm their behaviors created.

My early discussions with social workers revealed how much they knew about mothers' trauma histories but how little they knew of the specifics of actual behaviors of the perpetrator. They could describe how many abusive relationships the mother had been in but not how many past partners the perpetrator had abused. They could recite, from memory, the perceived faults of the mother and the services she was offered. But they could not describe the perpetrator's pattern of behavior, how that pattern impacted the survivor's parenting, or how the pattern related to the problems the children were experiencing. Many couldn't even describe factors indicative of high levels of danger or the dynamics of control and entrapment. They knew little or nothing about whether a particular perpetrator was a danger to professionals or others beyond the immediate family. Digging even deeper, it also became clear that most workers couldn't answer questions about the role of culture, power, and privilege or how domestic violence intersected with issues such as substance abuse and mental health. The practices associated with blaming mothers and ignoring fathers were, and still are, hiding in plain sight.

These attitudes and approaches are as prevalent now as they were when I first started to experience them over twenty-five years ago. Individual practitioners were not making up these practices themselves. They were following the contours of the terrain laid out for them by laws, policy, tools, and culture. What I see now, and saw repeatedly then, is the same practice equation. It was like professionals everywhere were reading from the same script. For child protection practitioners, it looks something like this:

Identify domestic violence
as an issue in the family.

Expect the survivor, usually the mother,
to agree to ensure that the children will not
be "exposed" to the violence.

Refer her to domestic violence counseling
to gain insight into the domestic violence
and its harm to the children.

Expect her to call the police, get a court order,
or leave for refuge.

Remove the children into care if the mother fails
to act according to the prescribed formula.

Turn a blind eye to the potential for post-separation
or family court abuse by the perpetrator.

Fail to hold the perpetrator to account
as a parent every step of the way.

CHAPTER 1 : WHY DOES SHE KEEP CHOOSING HIM OVER HER CHILDREN?

The "checklist" may look slightly different for professionals in other sectors. In family court it might include items such as "ignore domestic abuse perpetration as a relevant post-separation issue" and "allow perpetrators to use accusations of *parental alienation* to continue controlling their ex-partner and children." Mental health and addiction practitioners might add that the court should "treat symptoms, ignore the cause." In criminal court, we would see almost complete blindness to the perpetrator as a parent. The unfairness of this relentless focus on the mother's actions, and what it means to survivors when practitioners and systems shift that focus to the person doing harm, is articulated well by a practitioner in Australia and her client:

> *A mother was informed that we recognize her strengths and actions to keep her children safe and acknowledge that her partner's choice to use violence was not her fault, nor her responsibility. She burst into tears, saying that no one else has ever said this to her throughout years of receiving services from child protection, family support, and family violence case management. She told us,*
>
> '*After twenty years of living with a person who is physically and emotionally abusive to me, an absent father, an abusive father, this is the first time that a service has engaged with him to hold him accountable. Until now, he has gotten away with it in the shadows, while I take the blame.*'
>
> —Karen, child and young person practice lead, Australia

The unfairness of these practices is obvious. But they are also inefficient and ineffective. Many practices wrongly identify the source of the danger as either the decisions made by mom, or the relationship dynamic. Not seeing the perpetrators' behaviors and choices as the danger is more likely to lead to poor, harmful, and costly decisions. Here is the problem laid out in three questions:

- How can we effectively address the safety and well-being of children impacted by domestic violence if we are ignoring (and not intervening with) the parent whose behaviors are the source of the harm?
- How can we effectively partner with the survivor around the safety and well-being of the children when we are blaming her for what the other parent has been doing?
- How can we help children if we can't correctly identify how their problems, like anxiety or delayed development, are connected back to the violence and abuse a parent is perpetrating in the home?

All of these experiences made me realize that a new approach was needed. It was an approach that did the following:

> provided an ethical, efficient, effective, and safer environment for all involved
>
> helped professionals gather more accurate, objective, and comprehensive information around the harm domestic violence perpetrators' behaviors created for children
>
> paid attention to the role fathers played in family functioning and gave mothers full credit for their wide-ranging protective efforts
>
> created partnerships between professionals and survivors around their shared interests in child safety and well-being

> centered the perpetrators' behaviors and choices—not the survivors'—as the cause of the harm to the children
>
> sought actively to keep children safe and together with the protective parent, the domestic violence survivor

The driving idea behind the initial creation of the Safe & Together Model was that child protective services could do a better job accomplishing its core mission—providing for the safety, permanency, and well-being of children in domestic violence cases. I believed that a perpetrator pattern-based approach would be more efficient and effective than the failure to protect approach that had been the dominant child protection response to domestic violence.

Given the high correlation between domestic violence and child maltreatment and the association of domestic violence with child mortality, I saw the Model as a "win-win" solution. [3] [4] [5] [6] For the family and communities, it would mean more children remaining with protective parents in their communities. For survivors it would lead to greater safety and freedom and validation of their experiences. It would mean more focus on perpetrator parents, increasing the potential for more accountability and more interventions to help them become better, safer parents. It would mean safer, healthier children who would have a greater chance of leading happy, successful lives. For practitioners, it would mean very difficult jobs might become a little easier, safer, more rewarding, and more aligned with their values. For agencies, it would mean that they would see better practice, fewer tragedies, and cost savings associated with fewer unwarranted removals of children.

How do we achieve these very attractive outcomes? By fearlessly tackling the gendered expectations of men and women as parents. In the next chapter, I explore the implications of expecting less from men as parents, the dangers of ignoring fathers, and the importance of recognizing that fathers' choices and behaviors matter. I also lay out how focusing on mothers' protective efforts can be a game changer, a critical force for ending mother-blaming, and a transformational key to how we keep children safe from domestic violence.

CHAPTER 2

Blaming Mothers, Ignoring Fathers

When I shared the title of this book with my brother, whose career has spanned being an academic, a journalist, and a book author, he asked me, "Is this book about mothers or fathers?" I said "Yes." Expectations of men and women as parents are intimately connected. Entire sectors ignore or minimize the positive and negative impact of fathers' behaviors on their children and partners. The importance of fathers' choices on family functioning is not reflected in how systems interact with families. Not only does this mean that assessments of families are lopsided and inaccurate; it also means when something goes wrong with children, *mothers are often held exclusively responsible—unfairly*.

For the title of this book, I deliberately chose not to use the words "survivor" or "abuser." I consciously chose to refer to "fathers" and "mothers." Any real progress in the area of domestic violence perpetrators as parents requires a complete rethinking of how professionals, systems, and society approach *all* men as parents. Early in the twenty-first century, we still have strongly differing ideas about the behaviors associated with mothering and fathering. And these differences have consequences for how our systems respond to domestic violence where children are present.

These differences are quantitative and qualitative. They are quantitative in terms of how much time we spend thinking about women's versus men's behaviors toward their children. A quick internet search for "fathering" returns more than two million results. A search for "mothering" produces almost five times that number, at upward of ten million. A qualitative search of both these words tells us a lot about what behaviors we associate with mothers and fathers. Top-level definitions of "mother" include the words "protective," "caring," and "kind." Common definitions of "fathering" are missing adjectives related to behavioral qualities. "Fathering" is primarily associated with the procreative role of men.

We Expect Less from Men As Parents

This "hot take" on gender expectations provided to us by the internet is just a tiny reflection of the wider day-to-day attitudes, values, beliefs, and behaviors that translate into lower expectations for men as parents than for women. In society, it's present whenever anyone refers to a father "babysitting" his own child. Expectations of many religions and communities are that women will be the caretakers of children and keepers of the home environment. It's reflected in global social programs such as home or health visitors who are designed to promote maternal and infant/child health and well-being but almost universally ignore the role of fathers in the lives of their children and partner. These types of programs are only one example of how services and systems reflect a worldview that boils down to thinking that fathers' behaviors and choices are not relevant to outcomes for children and families—except when it comes to supporting the family financially.

Many of these attitudes, beliefs, and values are codified in the education, training, and practices of practitioners who work with families. Very few social workers take a university course that educates them on men's parental development. Similarly, most social workers learn their craft by working with women and children, not men. My very informal, but large sample survey of professionals all over the world found that around 10 percent of social workers and other professionals have any formal training and education in working with male populations. This means that around 90 percent of professionals working with families have little to no formal experience and training in understanding the impact men's behaviors have on family functioning or how to engage them as parents .

CHAPTER 2 : BLAMING MOTHERS, IGNORING FATHERS

At the micropractice level, low expectations for men as parents shape every aspect of family engagement. For example, social workers almost always ask mothers, not fathers, if the child is medically up-to-date. Social work forms and processes heavily emphasize the "primary caregiver"—universally understood as the mother in heterosexual couples. Low expectations for men are evident in the pages of family assessments, where there is typically barely any mention of the impact of fathers' choices and behaviors on children.

This means that many systems are bulging with professionals, working every day with families, who have little to no skills, knowledge, or confidence in engaging and intervening with fathers. From a practical point of view, their understanding of "family" often equals "mother and children." To this day, I assume that when professionals mention they are working with "the family" or they have a program "for families" that they mean they are working with women and children—and usually my assumption is proven accurate. This gap is often invisible to practitioners who are deeply steeped in the culture of gender double standards.

I once acted as a consultant for a community initiative that was seeking to improve outcomes for children and families by providing stable housing. Those leading the initiative had asked me to help them with their domestic violence interventions. As part of the needs assessment, I asked if they needed any training in family engagement skills. They said they did not. Their team was very skilled in family engagement. I probed a little further: "Does this include engaging fathers, including violent fathers?" They laughed and one of them said, "Oh no. We don't know anything about working with fathers." Their definition of family, and therefore family engagement, excluded fathers .

> *Low expectations for men as parents shape every aspect of family engagement.*

CHAPTER 2 : BLAMING MOTHERS, IGNORING FATHERS

Ignoring Fathers Has Profound, Harmful, and Dangerous Implications

The effect of the widespread practice of ignoring the importance of fathers and the impact of their behaviors on child, partner, and family functioning is cumulative. The collective blindness has profound, harmful, and dangerous implications when it comes to violent and abusive fathers. If social workers lack the skills, confidence, knowledge, and institutional mandate to assess and engage nonviolent fathers (the majority of fathers), then how confident, skillful, and knowledgeable will they feel when it comes to assessing and engaging violent fathers?

Therefore, we cannot be surprised when workers say that "it's just too hard" to engage violent fathers or when they claim to not be able to find them. I used to think this attitude could be explained by the very real challenges of working with domestic violence perpetrators. Now I've come to believe it is just as much, or even more, a reflection of the noteworthy absence of the following elements related to working with violent fathers:

> formal education and training
>
> support for worker safety
>
> supervision around working with violent fathers
>
> organizational mandates to work with domestic violence perpetrators as the source of the harm to children

It doesn't need to be this way. In one US-based project[1] that I was involved with, where child protective services trained and supported social workers and expected them to find and engage domestic violence perpetrators, they were able to make at least one contact with the perpetrator during the first thirty to forty-five days of the case opening in approximately 73 percent of the families.

When there is limited or no intervention with the perpetrators as parents, all the responsibility for harm to children and any poor family functioning is placed on the survivor. This can lead to punitive, adversarial approaches to protective survivors—survivors being compelled to take actions that increase their danger and their children's danger; unnecessary removal of children by child protective services; dangerous and destructive custody and parenting time decisions by family court; flawed and incomplete interventions by addiction and mental health practitioners; and other harmful decisions by professionals and systems.

I believe we will never be able to hold violent fathers fully accountable for their behaviors until we stop ignoring how *all* fathers' choices and behaviors, good and bad, impact their families.

> *It really feels like it should be such a no-brainer that we're aiming to hold fathers to the same parenting standards as mothers.*
>
> —Emma S., specialist family violence adviser, Australia

Stop Ignoring Fathers—but Not at the Expense of Mothers and Children

The idea that we should stop ignoring fathers is going to sit uncomfortably with some and be saluted by others. If you believe, as I do, that societies have not yet shaken off their patriarchal roots, then the idea of focusing more on fathers may sound like pouring gasoline on an already-raging fire. The fear here is that more attention on men equals more power for men. For others, the response to this approach will be "it's about time." Some of these people would say that mothers are already favored over fathers. Some of them might be advocates for marginalized communities, where men's roles in families have been devalued and attacked through systemic racism and colonization. Others may genuinely feel that fathers' behaviors and choices need more attention.

I wholeheartedly understand the worry that more attention to fathers could equal less power and freedom for women. Any whiff of movement in this direction is antithetical to my values. At the same time, I respectfully disagree that greater attention to fathers, depending on how it's done, is automatically harmful to women and children. In fact, by definition, to be measured as successful, interventions with violent fathers must have positive outcomes for the safety and well-being of women and children.

It is important to acknowledge that many social and policy initiatives related to fathers and families downplay or ignore the relevance of domestic violence. These efforts can be divided into two broad categories: fathers' rights and fathers' involvement. Fathers' rights efforts promote fathers' claims to equal custody and access in divorce. Father's involvement efforts are often focused on promoting the role of low-income and marginalized fathers in the lives of their children. Father's rights efforts systematically ignore the quality of fathers' parenting and are actively dismissive of concerns related to fathers' domestic violence and the physical and sexual abuse of children. Fathers' involvement efforts often reflect a world view that fathers' involvement with their children is always positive, again missing any assessment of the quality and safety of a man's parenting. If we are to stop ignoring fathers, we must be prepared to objectively assess their statements, their behaviors, and the impact of both on their children. We need to skillfully and carefully listen to what they are saying and doing—or not saying and doing. We need to use a behavioral lens to examine fathers' positive and negative contributions as parents and partners.

> **"***Perpetrators aren't necessarily the authority on the truth.***"**
>
> —Emma S., specialist family violence adviser, Australia

CHAPTER 2 : BLAMING MOTHERS, IGNORING FATHERS

Father involvement efforts often are attempting to repair the damage of structural racism and colonization. That damage has been caused by the societal patterns denying men from minority groups the same rights and privileges offered to men from the dominant culture. While it is imperative to correct the history of racist and colonizing attitudes and policies that have impacted fathers from minority families, let's state the obvious—all fathers, just like all mothers, are not automatically a positive force for their children. Any blanket advocacy for fathers' involvement in the lives of their children can gloss over real danger. When the quality of fathers' parenting is not considered, increased harm may be the result. An abusive father may be brought back into contact with a family that fled his abuse in the interests of "father involvement." Fathers with histories of violence may have been given unfettered custody of children they have harmed. In these instances, in the name of fatherhood, the state facilitates perpetrators' destructive access to the adult and child survivors.

For me, putting fathers back into the picture of families requires an approach that avoids the pitfalls of both men's rights and father-involvement movements. Fathers, abusive or not, *do* matter to children and families. And finding the right way to support minority fathers' role in families is critical from a social justice perspective. You cannot heal families and communities traumatized by colonization, the Stolen Generations, mission schools, slavery, and Jim Crow if you ignore fathers. At the same time, you cannot ignore domestic violence perpetration and its impact on the social and cultural connection of children and families. The resolution of this tension rests in a focus on fathers' behaviors and choices.

> **There is a subtle but crucial difference between saying "fathers matter" and saying, "fathers' choices and behaviors matter."**

A behavioral approach to fathering seeks to answer, in all families, the following questions: How have the fathers' choices and behaviors impacted child, partner, and family functioning? Or put another way, what has the father done or said that has strengthened or weakened the functioning of the family? It operates from a premise of equality—that children benefit when we have similar expectations about men as parents as we do about women as parents. Here is just a tiny sample of the questions about a family that might be included in this approach:

> What does the father do or say to support the relationship between his children and his partner?
>
> How does the father demonstrate to the children, through his behaviors, his respect for his partner?
>
> What kinds of statements and behaviors does the father engage in to create a nurturing and stable home environment?
>
> How have the father's behaviors and choices created or contributed to the family's current problems, such as homelessness or children's behavioral issues?

> *"I've had practitioners who have said to me 'I didn't know how to work with men, but now I've got a starting point. Now I know the kinds of questions to ask.' It's so powerful."*
>
> —Karen, child and young person practice lead, Australia

These questions are not a replacement for similar questions about the mother's parenting. They are only shared here to demonstrate a pathway for ending the invisibility of fathers in families in a way that avoids being simplistic or reinforcing patriarchy. A behavioral approach to assessing fathers' roles in families is objective and adds tremendous value to the work with families.

The focus on behaviors changes everything. Discussing fathering behaviors automatically moves away from father's rights arguments, which are often justified based on shared DNA with little attention to parenting behaviors. Those behaviors need to be factored into any case work, whether a father is absent or present and regardless of whether the couple is still living together or still in a relationship or not. *A father's avoidance of service or engagement with professionals does not mean his influence over the family's functioning should be forgotten or invisible.*

In the family court of Australia, family violence and child experts trained in the Safe & Together Model are able to use targeted questioning to hold fathers accountable.

The focus on behaviors changes everything.

> *What the Model does is allow us to ask some follow-up questions to really make the perpetrator more accountable. For example, 'If you couldn't control your anger in that situation, can you tell me what that means? What should I take from that about your ability to parent if you have such little control of your emotions?' It puts the focus on responsibility and doesn't allow those kinds of generalizations from perpetrators to be brushed aside. It gives us permission to ask some follow-up questions when someone says, 'No, I didn't do that.' We're trying to delve a bit deeper, qualify some of the deflections, and bring it back to the person that we're talking to—and I think that's really good.*

—Joanna, senior family court child expert, Australia

Behavioral exploration of fathers' roles in families accomplishes a lot when it comes to domestic violence:

- It improves screening for the presence of domestic violence in families. Whenever you ask mothers behavioral questions—such as "How does the child's father demonstrate that he respects you to the children?"—you are likely to increase disclosures around domestic violence.
- It improves outcomes for professionals and families by creating a framework for connecting the dots between the pattern of abusive behaviors and their impacts on the functioning of the children, partner, and family. This is especially important since so many issues—such as children's medical care, overall home environment, and day-to-day care of children—are generally seen as the responsibility of mothers. For example, a behavioral framework can help us explore the connection between the perpetrator's pattern of behavior and a child's missed days of school.
- It contextualizes the mothers' parenting choices. Increasing standards for perpetrators as parents helps us better understand how their behavior is shaping the behavior of the survivor as parent. For example, if a doctor tells a mother that a child needs more "tummy time" to improve the child's gross motor skills, but the perpetrator doesn't want "his" child on the floor, then the mother may be blamed for the child's lack of developmental progress. A focus on the perpetrator as a parent can help us unravel his role, putting the mother's behavior in context.

An approach stressing that fathers' choices and behaviors matter to child, partner, and family functioning is one that also helps systems create a stronger rubric for accountability. A behavioral lens helps you assess whether an agency should do any outreach to a father who hasn't seen his children in five years or whether to combat an abusive father's argument that his past violence to his child's mother is irrelevant to a court's decision about custody and access.

This behavioral approach to fathers, which operationalizes higher standards for men as parents, is one of the transformational concepts that underpins the Safe & Together Model. Throughout this book, it is one of the major themes that is woven into every chapter. It is central to the deconstruction of every myth in this book and to building a new practice paradigm.

The need for this new paradigm is illustrated by the words of a survivor in Scotland who said that her social worker, who was trained in the Safe & Together Model, advocated for her in meetings with child protective services. These meetings were called every time the abusive father of her children did something wrong, and the survivor's social worker kept reminding the child protection practitioner that the perpetrator was not actually there at the meeting, noting, "You are blaming her for this. You have called a meeting for it, knowing full well he's not going to turn up for it."

The Limitations of "Empathy" and How It Leads to Mother-Blaming

It's not every day you see a social worker buried under a pile of coats by her peers. I was watching a training exercise for new social workers that was intended to help them feel empathy for domestic violence survivors. Each coat, which had been piled on one by one, represented a different barrier to leaving an abusive relationship. This included the following: lack of affordable childcare; not having enough money for the deposit on a new apartment; police who didn't arrest the perpetrator; and the perpetrator's threats against anyone who helped the survivor. The theory behind the exercise was that by helping social workers understand the barriers to leaving that are experienced by survivors, it would lead to the end of victim-blaming by child protection workers. The activity carried the strong message that blaming a survivor for not leaving an abusive relationship is unfair, which, of course, we know to be true.

Domestic violence educational activities, like this "coat" exercise or the more common "walk in her shoes" exercise, where participants are invited to experience the world through the eyes of a survivor, are powerful methods to help participants understand and empathize with the day-to-day reality for women experiencing violence. They raise awareness, revealing the impact of the abuse and also the challenges, threats, and dilemmas associated with system responses. The hope is that empathy will inspire action. When the audience is the general public, the actions might be donations, volunteerism, and support for a loved one who is being abused. For professionals, the hope is that it will spur greater empathy, reduce victim-blaming, and lead to referrals to domestic violence services.

Teaching empathy has been a mainstay in the domestic violence education playbook. Unfortunately, over the years, I have watched passionate, skilled advocates flummoxed as the "empathy strategy" crashed against entrenched mother-blaming in systems focused on children. Faced with information about the myriad barriers survivors encounter when attempting to leave an abusive relationship, child protection and other professionals would make statements such as this: "If she can't keep herself safe, then she can't keep her children safe."

Teaching empathy for domestic violence survivors has not worked as a transformative strategy for ending victim-blaming, especially in failure to protect practice. In fact, teaching empathy has often backfired, and spectacularly. Empathy as a strategy to end victim-blaming often has increased professional frustration and anger, and it has even created more victim-blaming. Even if you disagree with victim-blaming practices, it is easy to empathize—and I use this word purposefully—with the frustration of social workers. On the one hand they have been told by some that it is unfair to expect a survivor to leave the relationship when she is facing so many barriers, but on the other hand they have not been offered alternative pathways to achieve their mission of child safety. A focus on greater empathy for survivors leaves social workers empty-handed from a practical point of view, so they end up returning to the familiar and easier path to get their job done, justifying it with a statement like this: "I know I shouldn't blame the victim, but my job is child safety. I must act to protect the children. Working with the victim mother is *familiar* and what I'm expected to do."

The failure of empathy strategies, in many ways, probably comes as a surprise. The conventional wisdom is that empathy is a dependable doorway to prosocial action. This may be a myth. Paul Bloom, in his book *Against Empathy*,[2] writes that greater empathy does not guarantee positive changes in behavior. In fact, he points to research that suggests that attempts to increase empathy can actually increase judgment and blame when we identify the person or group as "less than" or "other." Mothers who are domestic violence survivors may be one such group. Sexism, misogyny, and racism may contribute to low opinions of domestic violence survivors. As a result, education that focuses on feeling the survivor's pain of entrapment can work against creating constructive partnerships. Education designed to create more empathy for survivors because of the barriers they face in leaving an abusive relationship may backfire. Instead of producing compassion, it may increase judgment and blame. This may be especially true when paired with information about how bad domestic violence is for children. Conventional wisdom suggests that if we can raise awareness about how domestic violence harms children, it will lead to better support for adult survivors. The opposite may be true. The actual effect might be increased empathy for child survivors and increased negative feelings toward adult survivors.

If Not Empathy, Then What?

So if empathy is not the best strategy for improving the way professionals interact with survivors, what is? I've already outlined the first strategy: Higher expectations of men as parents will lead to increased accountability for fathers causing harm. Increased accountability for perpetrators as parents will reduce the negative scrutiny of mothers. When we look for connections between an abusive father's controlling behaviors and a child's behavioral problems, we are less likely to blame the child's mother for not being able to control her children.

more > ACCOUNTABILITY FOR ABUSIVE FATHERS

less < MOTHER-BLAMING FOR SURVIVORS

The second strategy is improved behavioral assessments of survivors' protective efforts. This requires recognizing how higher standards for women as parents makes many of the survivors' protective efforts invisible to others. Higher standards for women as parents lead professionals to measure survivors' protectiveness primarily by a set of dramatic and drastic protective efforts such as leaving the relationship, going into refuge, or calling the police. Those actions involve major changes in housing, employment, and other aspects of day-to-day living. While such efforts can be protective, they don't work for all survivors, and they do not constitute the bulk of what mothers do day in and day out to protect their children.

This narrow view of protective efforts sustains and promotes mother-blaming. By only acknowledging survivors' protective efforts when they leave the abuser or involve the criminal justice system, the courts, or mainstream domestic violence services, we guarantee that most women will be judged as "failing to protect" their children. This can create double jeopardy for marginalized survivors who have legitimate reasons for not engaging mainstream services or systems. For instance, First Nations survivors in countries such as Australia, the United States, Australia, Canada, and New Zealand—where there are devastating documented histories of genocidal removal of children—may have great reluctance in calling law enforcement or even mainstream domestic violence services for fear of having their children unfairly removed.

A focus on identifying, validating, and documenting mothers' full range of protective efforts offers an alternative pathway to improving the response of systems to the survivors. It creates a solid foundation for partnering with survivors. *Seeing survivors as active in the realm of protecting their children is the bridge to partnership.* This is the direct opposite of a failure-to- protect culture, which uses high standards for mothers as justification for punishing mothers for not meeting the narrow, cookie-cutter definitions of protection used by professionals and systems.

Widening out the assessment of survivors' protective efforts—beyond the obvious safety efforts such as calling the police—to include efforts to promote and maintain children's well-being helps us capture all the day-to-day labor of mothers in the context of domestic violence. Survivors develop active strategies, such as not leaving their children home alone with the perpetrator or placating the perpetrator by giving in to his wishes so he's less likely to ruin a holiday celebration or a child's birthday. These efforts take too many forms to name. One example is a survivor cooking the perpetrator's favorite meal so that he doesn't disrupt family dinner with verbal or physical violence. Another is a survivor intervening with the perpetrator, risking violence to herself in order to shield her children. And there's the instance of a survivor snuggling with her children on the couch, comforting them by watching their favorite movie after the perpetrator goes to sleep.

Survivors persist. They persist—in the face of abuse, control, and disruption—in maintaining the day-to-day routines and rituals of the family that are so important to children. Keeping the children on track with meals, hygiene, school, medical appointments, and bedtime rituals are all part of what matters to children. It is almost always the survivor parent, the mother, who is making sure these routines persist, even in the face of violence and control.

Identifying the full spectrum of the nonoffending parent's efforts to promote safety and well-being of her child is one of the Safe & Together Model's Critical Components. Throughout this book, this theme will be woven through all the chapters. Mother-blaming cannot be challenged without this fuller understanding of what constitutes protective efforts.

CHAPTER 2 : BLAMING MOTHERS, IGNORING FATHERS

> ❝*Just the way this Model is laid out doesn't allow you to ignore a father.* ❞
>
> —Carol, advocate, The Domestic Violence Project, US

The "Three Planets" Challenge—Tackling the Flaws in Systems That Work against Mothers and Embolden Abusive Fathers

To underline the necessity of addressing gender expectations in order to change systems and keep children safe, I close this chapter with a reference to the pioneering work of UK author and academic Marianne Hester.[3] In her work on mothers, parenting, and domestic violence, she analyzes the experience of survivors with multiple systems (child protective services, family court, and criminal justice) through the unexpected yet powerful imagery of different planets.

By referring to each system as a planet with its own "assumptions and practices," Hester, along with her colleague Lorraine Radford in their important book, *Mothering Through Domestic Violence*,[4] underlines the reality that each system has its own set of rules, requirements, and purpose. Each planet has conflicting and sometimes diametrically opposed expectations of adult survivors. For example, family court prioritizes collaboration and shared parenting even in situations with a history of extreme abuse, control, and violence. The same mother may be involved with a child protection agency that expects her to keep the children from the abusive parent, even in defiance of family court orders. Criminal court wants the survivor to be a "good witness and victim"—making reports to law enforcement, following court orders, and providing testimony to support prosecutions. These contradictory rules place survivors and their children in impossible no-win scenarios and embolden perpetrators' control, especially because of their ability to manipulate systems and professionals.

Despite their differences, the rules of all the planets depend on gendered expectations of men and women as parents: low expectations of men as parents and much higher expectations of women as parents. None of these systems are known for using a perpetrator pattern-based approach, defining domestic violence as parenting choice, or providing robust assessments of survivors' protective capacities. Gender double standards are a unifying (in a negative way) force across the planets. Equalizing out gendered parenting expectations, across all systems, is the key to transforming the dynamics that harm survivors and empower perpetrators.

Hester and Radford describe the necessary solution, which aligns very well with the Safe & Together Model approach. They point to two necessary steps: 1) a unified approach across the separate "planet" areas and 2) acknowledgment of the processes of gendering that are situating women as culpable victims. It's not enough to coordinate services or increase the flow of information between systems. In fact, more coordination and more information flowing, when it is shaped by gender bias, may increase the harm done to survivors by systems. Real change requires a new paradigm and new ways to operationalize more equal expectations of men and women as parents.

In the following chapters, I will show that the Safe & Together Model's perpetrator pattern-based approach doesn't just offer transformation to child protection agencies. It also offers change to diverse sectors such as family court, criminal court, and beyond—to nonstatutory sectors such as addiction and mental health. But beyond its ability to shift practice in individual sectors, it offers the potential to create a consistent approach across sectors so that survivors are no longer trapped between conflicting expectations, and perpetrators are no longer able to manipulate these differences to their advantage.

CHAPTER 3

Challenging Professional Myths About Domestic Violence

I've never been a "myths and facts" kind of person. As a disciple of experiential education, I've often found the "myths and facts" domestic violence educational approaches simplistic and pedantic. So, it struck me as a bit ironic when I started thinking about the concept of myths as I was planning this book. I found myself considering "myth" from the perspective of the definition in the Encyclopedia Britannica. This definition states that **every myth presents itself as an authoritative, factual account, no matter how much the narrated events are at variance with ordinary experience.**

The myths I was interested in exploring were not the common public misconceptions about domestic violence like "it doesn't happen in wealthy communities" or "substance abuse causes domestic violence." I was interested in the ones that guided professional practice—the ones that our systemic responses to domestic violence are built on and still stand fortress-like today. In many ways, the Safe & Together Model was developed as a challenge, critique, and correction of these myths. In this book, I'm attempting to explain how to bring these myths back down to earth, out of the realm of the authoritative professional voice, into better alignment with facts and the ordinary experience of adult and child survivors.

The Six Myths

Together we will explore six key myths or concepts. The myths are:

1. the myth of the child witness
2. the myth of the domestic violence incident
3. the myth of failure to protect
4. the myth of perpetrator accountability
5. the myth of parental alienation
6. the myth of trauma-informed practice

These myths reflect some of the most powerful ideas that drive policy, law, and service delivery. They dominate the conversations of professionals with one another and with adult and child survivors. They shape how courts intervene with and create accountability for perpetrators. They present themselves as definitive, when, really, they only capture a portion of the lived experience of families. Their hegemony hobbles our abilities to listen to the voices and experiences of children. They blind us to opportunities for partnering with survivors. These myths cripple our capacities to intervene with perpetrators as parents.

The Six Myths summarized

The following tables are a summary of the myths, how they act as the dominant paradigm, the problem with those myths, and then the Model's dismantling of each of those myths.

CHAPTER 3: CHALLENGING PROFESSIONAL MYTHS ABOUT DOMESTIC VIOLENCE

MYTH OF THE CHILD WITNESS

THE MAIN MESSAGE: The primary way to understand how children are harmed by domestic violence is seeing and hearing incidences of physical violence

How It's a Myth (or at Odds with Lived Experience of Survivors and the Needs of Professionals)	An Example of How the Model Innovates to Challenge the Myth
• Fails to name the person creating the harm • Fails to capture the significance of the parent as perpetrator • Does not account for low expectations of men as parents • Does not assess for the wider range of perpetrator behaviors that harm children • Does not reflect wider patterns of coercive control • Ignores how perpetrators actively target children and use them as tools against the other parent • Assumes children are passive witnesses • Does not account for the overlap of domestic violence and intersectional violence that children experience • Is overreliant on a psychological approach to harm • Struggles with describing the impact to infants and other nonverbal children	• Highlights the active choice-making and responsibility of the person choosing to act abusively • Acknowledges the significance of the parental role of the person acting abusively • Accounts for the gendered nature of our expectations of parenting by men and women • Is inclusive of how both child maltreatment and partner abuse are often part of one person's pattern • Is inclusive of coercive control and how harm is transmitted along multiple pathways and is much broader than psychological impact • Assesses how children resist and respond to the abusive parent's behavior • Integrates an understanding of harm that encompasses intersectionalities and structural violence • Offers multiple pathways to the assessment of harm even for preverbal and nonverbal children

MYTH OF THE DOMESTIC VIOLENCE INCIDENT

THE MAIN MESSAGE: The systems primarily organize their responses to domestic violence around isolated incidents of physical violence

How It's a Myth (or at Odds with Lived Experience of Survivors and the Needs of Professionals)	An Example of How the Model Innovates to Challenge the Myth
• Does not focus assessment on patterns of behavior • Is generally not inclusive of coercive control • Silos adult-to-adult violence from child abuse and neglect • Makes it harder to see the loss of liberty and entrapment generated by the perpetrator's pattern and the role of others in the entrapment • Reinforces racial stereotypes around violence • Promotes misidentification of survivors as perpetrators • Ignores strength and cultural privilege differences associated with sex and gender • Plays into ideas that abuse is " a temper problem", the result of an "escalating argument" or a "loss of control" • Makes sexual assault invisible in the discussion of domestic violence	• Is inclusive of all forms of abuse and control; considers behaviors of the perpetrator across different relationships and situations • Considers the perpetrators' violent behaviors in the context of other abusive and controlling behaviors including violence outside the family • Keeps the focus on the perpetrators' underlying control and entitlement thinking; puts the abuse into context of pattern • Considers the perpetrators' direct abuse and neglect of children and identifies the multiple pathways to harm for the children • Includes perpetrators' active manipulation of systems and how systems' functioning can contribute to entrapment • Is sensitive to privilege and vulnerabilities related to different factors, including racism, homophobia, transphobia, colonization, and other structural forms of oppression • Includes an analysis of how a bigger, stronger person often can use these attributes to be more controlling; the social context of patriarchy gives men certain advantages when it comes to control and violence • Focusing on patterns of coercive control reduces the likelihood of attributing domestic violence to "a temper problem" or other misattributions

CHAPTER 3: CHALLENGING PROFESSIONAL MYTHS ABOUT DOMESTIC VIOLENCE

MYTH OF FAILURE TO PROTECT

THE MAIN MESSAGE: Domestic violence survivors are responsible for what their partners do to the children

How It's a Myth (or at Odds with Lived Experience of Survivors and the Needs of Professionals)	An Example of How the Model Innovates to Challenge the Myth

• Is inefficient, ineffective, unethical, and unsafe based on:
 	
  • a gendered and racist expectation of men and women as parents
 	
  • an incomplete understanding of the adult survivors' protective efforts
 	
  • the flawed assumption that the mother's "insight" into the impact of domestic violence on her children automatically makes them safer
 	
  • the wrongful focus on the relationship between the parents or the survivor's choices, instead of the perpetrator's pattern of behavior, as the source of harm to children in domestic violence situations
	• Holds mothers and fathers equally responsible for children's safety and well-being
	
	• Operationalizes the accountability for perpetrators as parents by identifying the perpetrator's behavior as the source of the harm to children
	
	• Recognizes that survivor "insight" does not automatically create safety
	
	• Uses a wider definition of protective behaviors and considers the role of system failures, culture, and perpetrator actions undermining the efficacy of survivors' protective efforts
	
	• Contextualizes survivors' decision-making back to the perpetrator's pattern of behavior
	
	• Replaces failure to protect with partnering
	
	• Centers child safety and well-being
	
	• Combats racist and colonizing practices of penalizing survivors

MYTH OF PERPETRATOR ACCOUNTABILITY

THE MAIN MESSAGE: The dominant interventions with perpetrators are focused on court-ordered separation and carceral approaches to accountability

How It's a Myth (or at Odds with Lived Experience of Survivors and the Needs of Professionals)	An Example of How the Model Innovates to Challenge the Myth
• Makes definitions of accountability and intervention strongly correlated with criminal justice interventions • Ignores or pays little attention to perpetrators as parents • Reinforces patterns of colonization and structural racism in responses to domestic violence • Fails to offer survivors a range of ways to improve their situation beyond leaving or calling the police • Ignores structural problems with the carceral approach; for instance, high suspected rates of police-perpetrated domestic violence • Ignores accountability in other systems such as family court and child protective services • Ignores engagement strategies and other forms of interventions	• Believes accountability starts with and is enhanced by a common language and framework • Focuses on perpetrators as parents • Creates multiple avenues for intervention and different vectors of accountability • Puts greater emphasis on meaningful, sustainable behavior change as a goal and measure of success • Listens to adult and child survivors' definitions of accountability and change • Recognizes the value of perpetrator healing and change for the sake of families and communities • Starts with the premise that fathers' choices and behaviors matter to child, partner and family functioning • Acknowledges the importance of microaccountability efforts

MYTH OF PARENTAL ALIENATION

THE MAIN MESSAGE: The concept of parental alienation can appropriately be applied in domestic violence cases

How It's a Myth (or at Odds with Lived Experience of Survivors and the Needs of Professionals)	An Example of How the Model Innovates to Challenge the Myth
<ul><li>Has limited definitions of perpetrators' patterns of behavior</li><li>Fails to operationalize ongoing dynamics of coercive control in custody and access matters</li><li>Uses gender bias in its application</li><li>Has low standards for fathers making it difficult to assess them as alienating through their abuse</li><li>Relies on dominant risk assessment frameworks that are focused on adult danger and that neglect full assessment of harm to children from perpetrators' patterns of behavior</li><li>Has a heavy emphasis on collaborative coparenting even in cases of coercive control</li></ul>	<ul><li>Offers an objective, neutral, behavioral approach to domestic violence assessments</li><li>Uses a perpetrator pattern-based approach helps connects the dots between the domestic violence and the harm to children</li><li>Uses a behavioral approach to assessing protective efforts that is transparent and factual and is contextualized back to the perpetrators pattern</li><li>Helps identify patterns of post separation coercive control</li><li>Gives attention to postseparation behavior patterns, protecting courts and professionals from being manipulated into collusion with perpetrators</li><li>Challenges the weaponization of survivors' addiction and mental health</li><li>Helps identify situations in which there is a protective parent and a parent who is causing harm to children, which helps align court decisions in support of the protective parent's efforts and statutory mandates for child safety</li><li>Identifies connections between perpetrators' behaviors and survivors' mental health and addictions issues, including interference with recovery and treatment</li><li>Applies collaborative coparenting standards to perpetrators as parents to improve assessments and accountability</li></ul>

THE MYTH OF TRAUMA-INFORMED PRACTICE

THE MAIN MESSAGE: A mental health framework dominates the understanding of the impact of domestic violence on survivors

How It's a Myth (or at Odds with Lived Experience of Survivors and the Needs of Professionals)	An Example of How the Model Innovates to Challenge the Myth
• Does not lay out how different issues of domestic violence, substance use, and mental health interact with each other • Has language that often glosses over the importance of different permutations of complex, intersecting issues • Does not account for the different ways that perpetrators' behaviors impact functioning of children, adult survivors and family • Leaves out many of the behaviors associated with coercive control as they don't fit within the trauma definition • Does not address how coercive control is currently interfering with or shaping lives of clients (everything is not "post" trauma) • Fails to assess for acts of resistance and protection • Identifies trauma histories and substance misuse in perpetrators as the cause of their violence and abusive behavior • Decontextualizes survivors' diagnosis and treatment from the perpetrator's pattern of control	• Uses an intersections versus a laundry list approach to complexity • Expands impact beyond psychological and trauma effects to all areas of functioning affected by perpetrators' coercive control • Assesses dynamics of coercive control, actions taken to harm children, and their relevance to current safety, functioning, diagnosis, and treatment • Names the person who has caused the trauma and his actions to help increase accountability for perpetrator as parent and to reduce victim-blaming • Acknowledges the role of gender in shaping narratives of accountability, dynamics of entrapment, and the differential response of systems to men and women as parents • Looks at past patterns, current coercion, and future danger • Believes that a trauma history is not an excuse for abusive behavior; there needs to be a clear focus on behavior change, not just trauma healing; true trauma healing cannot happen without the cessation of the perpetration of violence.

THE MYTH OF TRAUMA-INFORMED PRACTICE (cont'd.)

THE MAIN MESSAGE: A mental health framework dominates the understanding of the impact of domestic violence on survivors

How It's a Myth (or at Odds with Lived Experience of Survivors and the Needs of Professionals)	An Example of How the Model Innovates to Challenge the Myth
• Does not encompass how perpetrators use mental health and substance use allegations as weapons against survivors, including complete fabrication of problems • Fails regularly to identify how structural and intersectional forms of violence compound trauma from domestic violence	• Understands the perpetrators target systems and practitioners as part of their coercive control • Articulates that wider dynamics of oppression, like homophobia, racism and colonization, need to be factored in to the understanding of trauma resulting from domestic violence

While the chart separates out the myths, they often work together to reinforce one another—in a type of negative synergy. For example, both the myths of failure to protect and the myth of parental alienation rely heavily on the myths of the domestic violence incident and the child witness. The myth of trauma-informed practice rests heavily on the myth of the domestic violence incident. The myths of perpetrator "accountability" and parental alienation are deeply intertwined. Together these myths form the hidden infrastructure that supports mother-blaming and father-ignoring. These myths, "unbusted," stand in the way of keeping children safe from the behavior of domestic violence perpetrators. No real progress can be made in changing systems and improving the responses of systems to families until these prevailing ideas are challenged and new policies and practices replace the old, outmoded ways.

Many of these myths started their lives as deservedly celebrated breakthroughs in hard-fought battles against domestic violence. Others, such as parental alienation, have been victim-blaming from their conception. But over time these terms and concepts have become unexamined jargon, ideas, and terms that are often used by frontline professionals without critical reflection. They have become the "truth," often crowding out survivors' realities. They reflect dominant paradigms and cultural power dynamics. The myth of perpetrator accountability contributes to the over-policing of different marginalized groups.[1][2][3] The dominance of the myth of the child witness reflects how the psychological paradigm, with its emphasis on symptoms, diagnosis, and treatment, often pushes aside other realities and perspectives on domestic violence. Parental alienation is a highly gendered tool used to blame survivors for protective behaviors. Failure to protect isn't just a framework for protecting children; it is an instrument for punishing mothers for the behavior of fathers.

Reading Chapters Out of Order

Now that you've gotten the introductory chapters out of the way, you do not need to read the rest of the book chapters in order. You certainly can, and I've tried to lay them out in an order that makes sense—for me. But everyone's needs are a little different. For example, for those of you who are not familiar with the Safe & Together Model, you may want to jump next to chapter 10, which is titled "A Common Language." This chapter will give you some background information on the Model's development that may help you understand the references to the Model in each of the myth chapters. If you are curious about the effectiveness of the Model or want to connect to the voices of practitioners or survivors, first, go to the "Results" and "Voices of Survivors and Practitioners" chapters. If you are action oriented, your first stop may be the "Change Starts Now" chapter. Because of the work you do or a specific interest, you may be drawn to a particular myth chapter first. Go for it! While one myth chapter occasionally references another myth chapter, they stand pretty much on their own merits.

CHAPTER 4

The Myth of the Child Witness

What if I told you that the child witness to domestic violence is a myth? What if I said that it left out some of the most important aspects of harm that perpetrators cause children? How would you react if I said that we've turned a blind eye to the limitations of this concept, how it can work against adult survivors and even sometimes helps tip the scales of the response of systems in favor of perpetrators of abuse? What would you say if I could offer you a much more comprehensive way of considering the harm to children from domestic violence that encompasses "witnessing" but goes much further in its ability to help us partner with survivors, support children, and hold perpetrators accountable as parents?

This chapter examines how the child witness lens, which focuses on *seeing* and *hearing* as the primary nexus between domestic violence and harm to children, is a potent yet incomplete approach to understanding domestic violence and child harm. The chapter will explore some of the key tensions and challenges associated with the myth. It will finish by outlining how the Safe & Together Model offers some better ways to organize how we approach children and harm.

Deconstructing the myth of the child witness is not intended to minimize the significance of seeing or hearing acts of violence perpetrated by one parent against another, a sibling, or another family member. In fact, the goal is exactly the opposite—to give us the language and framework to better articulate the full ranges of harms experienced by children and more tightly tie them back to the person choosing coercive control. I propose a broader paradigm for assessing and documenting child harm that can reduce victim-blaming, create stronger alliances across sectors, and ensure that children's best interests are truly at the center of our public policy, private sector services, and judicial decision-making.

The Myth of the Child Witness

The Power, Presence, and Ubiquity of the Child Witness

When you imagine a child witness to domestic violence, it's likely that some version of the following comes to mind:

- The sobbing child on the couch, watching the father punching the mother
- The fearful child on the stairs listening to the father yell, scream, and degrade the mother
- The distracted child falling asleep at school after being kept up all night by the father's violence to the mother
- The scared child hiding under the bed, in the closet, or out on the street, escaping the violence and chaos of home
- The brave child comforting a younger sibling

These images reflect the searing reality for many children witnessing domestic violence. The powerful, and often life-long, effects of seeing and hearing physical violence by one parent against another cannot be overstated.

One can draw a straight line between these evocative, painful images and the public response to domestic violence and children. Much of our domestic violence policy and practice is built on this idea of the child witness: the child who sees, watches, and observes—the child who is present when the violence is occurring in the home between the adult caregivers. For example, the United Kingdom Domestic Abuse Act 2021 says that a child is a victim of domestic violence if the child "sees or hears, or experiences the effects of, the abuse." [1] Scotland's Domestic Abuse (Scotland) Act 2018 recognizes children as direct victims of domestic abuse and the impact on them of coercive control.[2] In Australia, the Family Violence Protection Act 2008 includes provisions to protect children from "behavior by a person that causes a child to hear or witness, or otherwise be exposed to the effects of family violence as defined in the Act.[3] In the United States, over twenty-six states and territories have laws that define child witnesses to domestic violence. Some definitions use a very basic standard: actions "committed in the presence of or perceived by the child." A 2006 UNICEF report estimated that between 133 million and 275 million children around the world witness frequent domestic violence each year.[4]

The literature on domestic violence and children is overflowing with papers on the child witness or the common alternative phrase "children exposed to domestic violence." Videos, posters, and other educational materials are punctuated with images of the terrified and cowering child witness. Entire policy initiatives are launched, ground-breaking legislation is passed, and services are designed based on the idea that the harm of domestic violence is transmitted to children through their little (or not so little) eyes and ears. When society peers into homes with domestic violence, what tugs on its heartstrings are children—fragile, innocent, and vulnerable—at the mercy of the outsized force of adult violence.

The concept of the child witness is intimately tied to the prevailing understanding of trauma. The heavy focus on the traumatic impact of domestic violence, in return, reinforces a focus on incidents of physical violence and the tightly associated child witness approach. According to The National Child Traumatic Stress Network (US), a traumatic event is a "frightening, dangerous, or violent event that poses a threat to a child's life or bodily integrity." Also included in the definition of what can be traumatic for a child is "*witnessing* (my emphasis) a traumatic event that threatens life or physical security of a loved one." [5]

When professionals develop programs or make decisions related to children and domestic violence, it is the concept of the child witness that heavily influences those efforts. Trauma counseling and trauma-informed group work for children exposed to domestic violence are common interventions. The groundbreaking and influential Adverse Childhood Experience (ACE) study[6] identifies exposure to violence against a child's mother as more prevalent than a child's experience of direct psychological or physical abuse. This, and subsequent studies, and the correlation between childhood trauma and adult health, has spawned a cottage industry of initiatives around trauma-informed care using the ACE data as a justification.

When it comes to courts, judges make decisions related to custody and access that are heavily shaped by the idea of "witnessing" domestic violence as the primary nexus or connection between domestic violence and children. There is a strongly embedded belief that once the relationship between the parents is over, the children are no longer at serious risk for witnessing any domestic violence. The view is that with the dissolution of the relationship and the fact that parents no longer share a home, the risk of witnessing melts away.

Many services for adult survivors are crafted as a response to the danger of physical violence, prioritizing leaving and related support. These interventions are understood to also protect the children from further witnessing of the violence. Funding for direct services for children often takes a back seat to services for adult survivors with the assumption that helping the adult survivor stay safe from physical violence is the main way to prevent further child exposure.

Child protection practitioners assess children for their proximity to the "the zone of danger." In interviews they ask questions about children's experience of seeing or hearing violence in order to make decisions about removing children. If the child is asleep, too young to be interviewed, or not at home when the violence occurs, even when the violence is heinous, child protective services is often stymied in its assessment of child harm.

Law enforcement officers who are attending incidents of violence can have a similar focus on child "witnessing" as the main source of harm to children. For example, the International Association of Chiefs of Police, with the assistance of the Yale Child Study Center, has targeted the response of police officers to children exposed to violence, especially domestic violence.[7] These efforts focus on immediate effects of seeing or hearing violence and the role law enforcement officers can play in those critical moments after an incident of violence.

The powerful and important concept of the child witness, with its associations with trauma and physical violence at the hands of perpetrators, forms the substrate of the majority of domestic violence policy and practice as it relates to children. It provides a road map for service delivery, court responses, and other interventions. It is a powerful approach that has positively changed the lives of many children exposed to domestic violence. And yet, as important as the concept is, it is still only a partial reflection, a fragment of the full harm experienced by children at the hands of domestic violence perpetrators.

The Need to Go Beyond the Jargon

I started getting an inkling of the limitations of the child-witness approach to domestic violence and children during my earliest conversations with child protection social workers. Workers taught me how they were constantly running up against barriers in assessing and documenting the impact of domestic violence perpetrators on children:

Worker: *Their child is preverbal, so we can't interview them, so we don't know how to document the impact.*

Worker: *Everyone is telling me the children didn't see the incident, so while I'm worried about them, I cannot document the impact on them.*

Worker: *Our legal team says we cannot move forward with the child protection case because the children were not in the "zone of danger."*

Each statement represents the long shadow cast by the concept of child witnessing over the day-to-day practice of those entrusted with being the last line of defense for children in our communities. These daily conversations with frontline workers really taught me how the concept of child witnessing was often an impediment to actually naming the harm children were experiencing at the hands of domestic violence perpetrators. The concept of *witnessing* often narrowed the assessment lens to focus on a child's verbalization of what that child saw—and perhaps felt—rarely venturing into the fertile, and often directly observable, terrain of functioning and behavior.

The concept of "child witness to domestic violence" and the closely related concept of "children exposed to domestic violence" have almost a complete monopoly over the conversation about domestic violence and children. An internet search on any given day yields hundreds of thousands to millions of results related to children witnessing or being exposed to domestic violence.

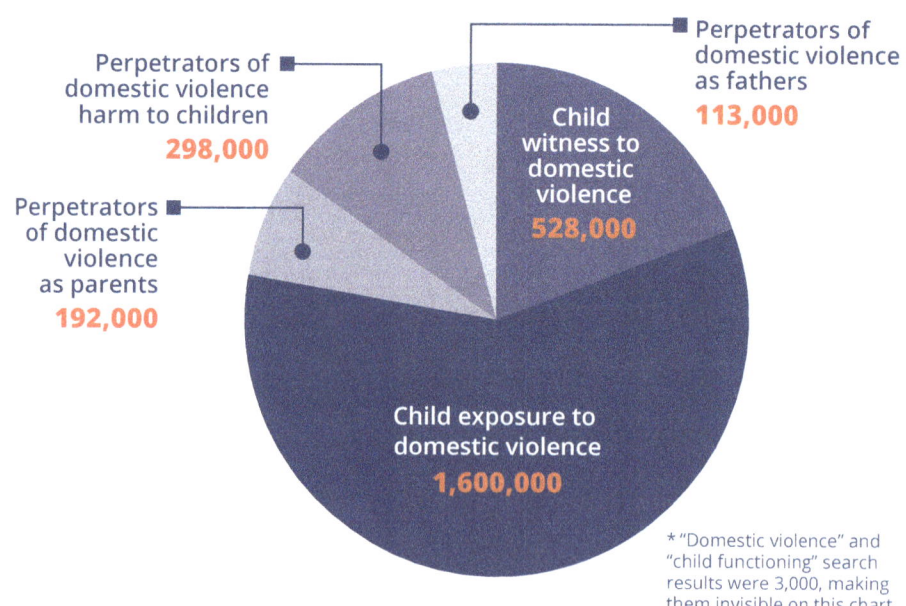

INTERNET SEARCH RESULTS FOR SCHOLARLY ARTICLES USING THE FOLLOWING TERMS

- Perpetrators of domestic violence harm to children: **298,000**
- Perpetrators of domestic violence as parents: **192,000**
- Perpetrators of domestic violence as fathers: **113,000**
- Child witness to domestic violence: **528,000**
- Child exposure to domestic violence: **1,600,000**

* "Domestic violence" and "child functioning" search results were 3,000, making them invisible on this chart.

CHAPTER 4: THE MYTH OF THE CHILD WITNESS

The terms "child witness" and "child exposed to domestic violence" have become jargon, or standard phrases, in the lexicon of professionals in domestic violence and related areas. Used without much reflection on limits or appropriateness, jargon is attractive for its perceived efficiency, offering a convenient shorthand for complex and important phenomena. At the same time, jargon can also obscure, misdirect, and even lie to us about reality. Jargon can also fool two people or groups of people into believing they are referring to the same phenomena while they have different understandings of what the term means.

These misalignments and misconceptions can have a profound effect on the decisions and behaviors of professionals at all levels, and these, in turn, can have sometimes catastrophic effects on the lives of families. For example, when I say, "A child witnessed the violence," am I referring to the child's presence in the room when there was physical violence? Am I including the child's hearing the days and hours of emotional abuse leading up to the violence? Am I referring to the child's conflicting feelings of confusion, relief, and fear associated with the experience of going to a refuge after an incident of violence? Does the phrase encompass the child's sadness related to missing the abusive parent? Does it include all the ways the coercive control associated with the violence shapes the child's daily life? Does it help you connect the child's homelessness to the violence perpetrated against the mother?

When you read the phrase "the child was exposed to domestic violence," what do you picture? Is it the same as what I meant? Do you know who perpetrated the violence? Do you know the pathways to harm? Do you even know the exact nature of the harm to the child? Do you know how it changed the child's life? The parents' lives? The siblings' lives? Do you have a feel for how it intersects with other forms of violence the child is experiencing, including community violence, racism-driven violence, or other forms of abuse?

These phrases and concepts need examination and reflection of how they are constructed, what they teach us, and how they operate in the world. An examination of how they may help or hinder our work with families and, maybe most importantly, our communication with other professionals will add to our practice, not detract from it. Let's take a closer look at what's missing.

What Does the Myth of the Child Witness Leave Out?
- The perpetrator of the violence
- The parental role of the perpetrator
- The gender of the perpetrator
- Coercive control
- Children as targets and tools
- Children's resistance and resilience
- Impact of intersectional forms of violence
- Most impacts besides psychological impacts
- The effects on infants

The Missing Perpetrator of the Violence

The phrases "child witness to violence" and "children exposed to violence" teach us, through their construction, to ignore the perpetrator. In each phrase, there is no actor who is choosing to engage in the violence, making it harder to develop a narrative of accountability. So in the case of male perpetrators, it reinforces ignoring fathers' influence and impact on families. The language implies that the perpetrators' actions are inevitable and not controllable, like the weather. The absence of a subject and the passive phrase construction are subtle yet powerful invitations to turn away from the perpetrator. This opens the door to both mother-blaming and the mutualizing of responsibility between the perpetrator and survivor. Compare this to the following phrases: "domestic violence perpetrators' harm to children" or "the harm to children from perpetrators' patterns." The last two phrases name the person and the harm.

The Missing Parental Role

The absence of the perpetrator takes on greater significance when we recognize that the perpetrator, the person who chooses violence, is usually in a parental caregiving role. This means that this person is a) betraying their duty of care and b) using their trusted, intimate knowledge and their role as a parent to supercharge their ability to create damage on so many levels. This isn't a stranger doing harm. It is a person who has a legal and moral responsibility to protect this child. Even when it is a boyfriend or non-biologically related person, the law usually recognizes some level of legal caregiving responsibility for any adult in the home who has regular interactions with the children.

The nonstranger relationship offers insider access to a child's inner emotional life and to the child's day-to-day routines, relationships, and activities. The perpetrator knows the child's likes and dislikes, desires, and fears. Access also means more practical levers for control and more reach into different aspects of a child's life to do damage. Caregivers often have access to children's public and private spaces, whether it's a football pitch or a bedroom. Their violent and controlling behavior is not the behavior of a stranger, where there is no special expectation of trust. Feelings of betrayal, disappointment, hurt, lack of trust, and lifelong fear of intimacy are just a few of the potential effects generated by the perpetrator's role as parent.

The phrase "child witness" hides the domestic violence perpetrator's intimate placement in the lives of those children and the violation of the trust children place in the perpetrator as a parent. By ignoring this relationship, the myth of the child witness makes it harder to fully connect the harm back to the person causing it and harder to emphasize perpetrator accountability as a parent.

Whenever our language doesn't guide us toward the perpetrators, their behaviors, and the parental nature of their role, it encourages the narrative that the harm to the children is the responsibility of the mothers, obscuring the reality that domestic violence perpetration is a parenting choice.

No Perpetrator Equals No Gender Analysis

When we talk about child witnesses, not only do we make the parental responsibility of the person using violence invisible, but we also make it harder to explore the gendered aspects of family violence. In the world imagined by the child witness myth, a child is a witness regardless of the gender of the perpetrator. It doesn't matter if you say that "the couple engaged in domestic violence" or that "the mother hit the father" or that "the father hit the mother," the children are the witnesses to the violence either way. This absence of gender attention might not matter if our expectations of mothers and fathers were the same, but they aren't. In a world where we have much higher expectations of mothers than fathers, the gender-blind language of child witness is a gateway to mother-blaming and ignoring fathers. Alternatively, language that names the person causing the harm makes it easier to tackle gender double standards.

CHAPTER 4: THE MYTH OF THE CHILD WITNESS

Missing Coercive Control

Seeing and hearing violence reigns supreme as the main pathway for assessing child harm. While the connection between seeing violence perpetrated by one parent against another and a range of trauma symptoms is well documented, the concept of the child witness locks in the moment of violence as our primary vantage point for understanding how children are harmed by domestic violence perpetrators' behaviors. If the child wasn't in the room or didn't hear violence, professionals are often at a loss for assessing the child's harm experience.

The myth of the child witness fails to fully reflect the concept of coercive control, with its diverse pathways, beyond seeing and hearing, to child harm. Instead of assessments focused on incidents of physical violence, a focus on coercive control can reorient the assessment lens toward wider patterns of behavior that limit survivors' freedoms and ability to control their own lives. Physical violence becomes one of many possible behaviors and one that can be completely absent in some of the most severe cases of coercive control.

From the vantage point of coercive control, it is easy to see that a large chunk of perpetrators' actions falls outside the paradigm of witnessing violence. Off the top of my head, I can think of many examples of behaviors, often associated with severe patterns of abuse, that fall outside the mainstream thinking about child exposure. In one home, the social worker observed a lock on the freezer. When queried about this, the mother said, "He thinks the children and I eat too much meat." In another home, control was exercised over the movements of family members inside the home, using tape on the floor to indicate how family members should move through the house. In a third, the perpetrator repeatedly threw out all the children's school supplies and sports equipment to undermine his partner's parenting. In another home, the perpetrator took the doors off all the rooms, including the bathrooms, so no family member had privacy. Each of these examples demonstrates nonviolent yet highly invasive controlling tactics that target basic needs and autonomy—food, bodily freedom, education, and social development.

Giving primacy to a child's seeing and hearing physical violence makes it harder to practice from a more comprehensive coercive-control perspective. Most of the behaviors associated with coercive control do not involve physical violence, so therefore they fall outside the dominant paradigm of witnessing and trauma. Without a child assessment pathway that includes—but goes beyond—incidents of physical violence, we cannot truly see and hear children's full lived experience of harm from domestic violence perpetrators.

> *The myth of the child witness, on many levels, has been a hindrance to appropriate responses. The witnessing is only one aspect, but not looking at those multiple pathways of harm is a hindrance. Child protection workers have always been very frustrated because they don't have the ability to make the decisions. They can only take notes, and it goes up the chain to decide whether to hold someone accountable. The response is often 'well, you can't show harm. There's no harm.' The policy is 'there's no harm unless there was a physical incident.'*

—Carol, advocate, The Domestic Violence Project, US

Targets and Tools

Taking their children to an undisclosed location, a father calls their mother and says she won't see the children ever again unless she gives him money for drugs.

Another father uses control over the household as part of his strategy to groom his daughter for sexual abuse.

CHAPTER 4: THE MYTH OF THE CHILD WITNESS

In another home, the father sexually and emotionally abuses his wife, physically abuses his son, and sexually abuses his daughter.

In a fourth home, a father abuses his partner while denying his disabled daughter access to support and care.

Another father tells his partner that if she leaves him, she "won't get a penny" for the children.

What these examples have in common is the children are not just witnesses. They are also *targets and tools*, part of the perpetrators' multidirectional web of abuse and control.

The primacy of the myth of child witnessing warps the conversation away from domestic violence perpetrators' direct abuse and neglect of children and their use as weapons and pawns in efforts to control the other parent. When it comes to child abuse and neglect, the numbers are clear. Research confirms a 30–60 percent correlation between domestic violence perpetration and physical child maltreatment.[8] In homes with domestic violence, children experience elevated rates of sexual abuse compared to their counterparts from homes without domestic violence. As we have already learned, domestic violence is heavily correlated with the deaths of children known to child protection.

Language like "child witness" makes it harder to hold perpetrators to account for the multiple forms of abuse they often perpetuate simultaneously.

Fragmented approaches to families are reflected in professional language that categorizes cases (and families) by the most recent reason the family came to the attention of the system. When the most recent allegation is related to substance abuse, the case is referred to as a "substance abuse case" or "neglect case" even when there are known and relevant issues of domestic violence. Separate death review processes for child deaths and adult domestic violence deaths reinforce similar divisions in thinking and practice. Whether you approach these patterns of behaviors from the adult safety or the child safety lens, it is imperative that assessments consider how one person may be engaging in multiple types of abusive behavior as part of their pattern.

Resistance and Resilience

The myth of the child witness encourages us to see children only as passive observers of the impact of domestic violence. This does an injustice to children's resilience, resistance, and choices about relationships. Children physically intervene with the domestic violence perpetrator to protect their mothers and their siblings. They call law enforcement to stop the violence. They seek help and advice from social workers, teachers, and friends. They strategize on their own or in conjunction with their mother and siblings around safety and well-being. Children have their own needs, their own assessments of safety, and their own relationships with the person who is using violence. They transfer the good and bad lessons from home to their lives at school, with friends, and into dating.

> *I am reminded of the professional colleague who shared the story of his interactions with his violent father at times he wasn't living in the home. Upon seeing his dad in their small town, the younger version of himself would run up to his dad and excitedly ask him when he was coming home. To the outside observer, he was a child who missed his father and wanted him to come home. But he was feigning excitement to elicit information. Using a sophisticated strategy, the loving child was gathering information to help him (and maybe his siblings and mum) assess and plan for the danger. Was he a passive witness to the violence?*

This image of the child as a passive recipient of the abuse is reinforced by the dominance of psychological approaches to children and domestic violence. Professionals often focus on the emotions associated with "witnessing": How did that make the child feel? How much would change if we also talked to children about what they did, what choices they made in response to abuse? Allan Wade, and the other creators of Response-Based Practice,[9] suggest that instead of focusing so heavily on feelings, we should be focusing more on actions and choices made in response to the violence. The idea is to ask adult and child survivors about what they did next after the abuse. How did they respond? What actions did they take? This kind of nonjudgmental curiosity around behaviors, instead of the psychologically oriented child-witness framework, offers rich information about both a) the harm to child functioning and b) the brave, creative actions that child survivors take to navigate danger, increase connections, and heal.

Intersectionalities Matter

The "child witness to domestic violence" lens does not actively embrace the intersectional experience of many children from historically marginalized groups. Those children experience daily forms of entrapment, discrimination, threats of violence, and actual violence based on their race, ethnicity, class, or religions. The framework of adverse childhood experiences, also known as ACE, ignores structural and institutional racism and colonization as a form of adverse childhood experience. Gay bashing, trans bashing, and other forms of violence associated with homophobia are not included either. While trauma frameworks recognize multiple forms of adverse childhood experiences, they rarely move beyond the individual or family level to the community or societal level. A true picture of a child's experience of domestic violence would include consideration of intersectional violence. This may take the form of an abusive parent who is engaging in racist abuse or racially motivated attacks by strangers. It embraces the knowledge that a child may experience compounded harm when a home is not safe because of abuse and because the community is not safe due to racism.

Psychological Impact Is King—but Maybe It Shouldn't Be

In the child-witness paradigm, psychology is king. The "child witness to violence" framework connects violent events to an emotional and psychological set of effects. The coin of the realm is the language of emotions, of the child's inner world. Research on the impact on children is skewed toward describing feelings such as fear, sadness, confusion, and stronger, more longer-term emotional states like depression and suicidality as known consequences. Policy documents frequently link the emotional effects to behavioral changes such as difficulty in sleeping, drug use, and poor academic performance.

Listening to and understanding children's interior psychological states resulting from domestic violence perpetrator behavior is essential. It is a critical but not complete perspective on harm. Emotions, mental states, and mood are not the only harms, nor are they the only way to understand changes in behavior or functioning. Our assessment gaze cannot stop at children's emotional reactions. It must be farsighted and all-encompassing. It is essential to see how the perpetrator's behaviors create concrete changes in the home environment, undermine the other parent's functioning, change the day-to-day life of the child, and change the overall functioning of the family. The language of emotions and psychology is one among many—a team player when it comes to identifying harm.

In an article on post-separation coercive control and children, Emma Katz and her colleagues outline how perpetrators, even after the relationship between mother and father ended, could still "create situations where children had to abandon their home, school, friends, routines, and local environments at a moment's notice." [10] Each loss or disruption has its own impact on a child. The cumulative impact can be devastating to a child. The language of the child witness directs us away from these other pathways to harm.

How often are professionals assessing, documenting, and reporting on the behavior patterns causing these disruptions and their life-changing effects? How would accountability, consequences, and expectations of change for perpetrators as parents improve if professionals used holistic functioning frameworks to explore the complexity of harm? The primacy of the psychological lens requires conscious efforts to expand the understanding of the impact of perpetrators on children beyond their emotional and even behavioral world to the assault on the day-to-day functioning that is one of the hallmarks of coercive control.

Infants Are Poor Witnesses

Infants, toddlers, and children with special needs are considered among the most vulnerable to harm from domestic violence perpetrators. Yet the child-witness framework, with its emphasis on identifying impact through children *talking* about their feelings about the violence, disadvantages infants, toddlers, and others who may be impossible, or at least challenging, to interview. For example, professionals may perceive a child's disability as a barrier to communication and therefore as a barrier to demonstrating harm.[11]

Considered from another angle, the child-witness approach doesn't align with the emergent science on the impact of domestic violence perpetrators' behaviors on fetuses in utero. Whether resulting from physical assault on a woman while she's pregnant or from the stress of the abuse, unborn children can be impacted by a perpetrator's behaviors. This is not usually explored in the child-witness approach.

The heavy dependence on interviewing hampers our ability to map out the different pathways to harm to infants and toddlers, such as interfering with perinatal visits, controlling the parenting of the mother, or disrupting the mother's attention to the children's day-to-day needs. In one home, the stress of the father's violence stripped the nutrients out of the mother's breast milk, leading to the baby's diagnosis by a pediatrician of failure to thrive. In another situation, a father-to-be assaulted his pregnant partner for smoking cigarettes, potentially endangering their baby—yes, that is truly crazy-making thinking and behavior. In a third case, a fathers' assault during breastfeeding caused a complete disruption in the child's breastfeeding routine—after the assault the child never nursed normally again. In each of these cases, the very real harm can be described through means other than interviewing the witness or describing the psychological impact. Professional alignment with experiences of child survivors requires a more holistic, comprehensive understanding of pathways to harm if the full experience of all children is going to be captured.

How the Safe & Together Model Innovates to Respond to the Myth of the Child Witness

Imagine this scenario:

- Mother and infant have a normal, healthy breastfeeding routine.
- Father assaults mother while she is breastfeeding, physically injuring her and disrupting the breastfeeding.
- Within twenty-four hours, the child, who had no prior issues, stops nursing.
- When presented with these facts, a judge finds that the father's violence was the likely cause of the interruption of the child's nursing and any associated developmental issues.
- The father is held accountable for this harm to his child's development.

This scenario, which is based on a real case, is an example of one of the many ways a perpetrator's behaviors can be connected to the functioning and needs of children, even infants, breaking professionals' dependence on the concept of witnessing. Whether it's the disruption of a child's nursing, interference with a child's mental health or medical care, control over household routines, homelessness resulting from the abuse, or attacks on a parent-child bond, those instances should be included in a broader approach. That broader approach should include, but go beyond, the concept of witnessing so that it will open up doorways to more accurate assessments and greater alignment of professionals with the reality of adult and child survivors.

So, if child witnessing is a myth—meaning it is not the fullest or most accurate version of the reality of the experience of children—and its dominance actually limits how we practice in alignment with the needs of child survivors, what is an alternative? An alternative would fill the gaps I have identified above. Here is a checklist of language and thinking that would better reflect the reality of adult and child survivors. The new language would highlight the following:

> The active choice-making and responsibility of the person choosing to act abusively
>
> The significance of the parental role of the person acting abusively
>
> The gendered nature of our expectations of parenting by men and women
>
> The reality that both child maltreatment and partner abuse are often part of one person's pattern
>
> The reality that harm is transmitted along multiple pathways and is much broader than psychological impact
>
> The assessment of harm that isn't exclusively dependent on collecting information verbally from children
>
> The examination of how children resist and respond to the abusive parent's behavior
>
> An understanding of harm that encompasses intersectionalities and structural violence
>
> The allowance for assessment of harm even for preverbal and nonverbal children

While all this cannot be easily embodied in one phrase, it is captured in the Safe & Together Model's perpetrator pattern-based approach. Let's take a look at how language—changed to reflect a perpetrator pattern-based approach to harm—looks, feels, and sounds compared with a child-witness approach:

- Instead of "children witnesses to domestic violence" or "children exposed to domestic violence," try using the phrase **"children impacted by domestic violence perpetrators' behaviors."**

- If we want to bring the parenting role of the domestic violence perpetrator into view, we can use this phrase: **"domestic violence perpetration is a parenting choice."**

- If we want to be more broad, comprehensive, and accurate in our assessment of harm, we should avoid saying, "Living in a household of fear and intimidation can impact a child's health, safety, and well-being." Instead, we should say, **"Living in a household where a parent engages in a pattern of controlling behavior disrupts and destabilizes daily living and can impact a child's health, safety, and well-being."**

- Instead of assuming children are only witnesses when a parent engages in domestic violence, we can always ask key questions about domestic violence perpetrators: **"What is this person's parenting behaviors?"** Or, more specifically, ask, **"Is there any knowledge or are there any concerns related to his physically or sexually abusing any of the children?"**

- Instead of siloing domestic violence from other forms of societal violence that children might experience, we can say something like this: **"The perpetrator's pattern of behavior has included**

CHAPTER 4: THE MYTH OF THE CHILD WITNESS

specific racist insults directed at the mother, who is First Nation, and their child. The child's trauma has been compounded by racist verbal assaults by classmates."

- If we want to stop ignoring fathers' roles in the lives of their children, we can say, **"Fathers' choices and behaviors, good or bad (including abuse and violence) matter to child, partner, and family functioning."**

- Instead of asking whether the child witnessed the violence, we can ask: **"How was the functioning of the child, the other parent, and the family impacted by the perpetrator's pattern of coercive control and actions taken to harm the child?"**

By shifting language, we can change professional practice because framing the problem differently requires seeking out different information and suggests different solutions. The Safe & Together Model translates this language and thinking into very specific practice tools for assessment, interviewing, documentation, and case planning. It improves collaboration by offering professionals across sectors a shared approach to the question of children and domestic violence.

The benefits of this shift are as follows:

- Increased perpetrator accountability by taking these actions:
    - Making the perpetrator visible and showing him as an active, choice-making person with a parental responsibility for the safety and well-being of children
    - Assessing for both child maltreatment and partner abuse behaviors in the same person
    - More comprehensively and accurately naming the pathways and resulting harm associated with a perpetrator's pattern

- Increasing accountability for fathers who are abusive by looking at harms to children caused by the perpetrators but often blamed on the mother—for example, missed doctor's appointments, unstable housing, truancy, and child behavioral issues
- Increased willingness and ability for practitioners to partner with survivors around the safety and well-being of their children by also taking these actions:
    - Combating gender bias, including that which is embedded in the failure-to-protect culture and including accusations of parental alienation against protective mothers
    - Preventing the unfair assignment to mothers of responsibility for children's problems through a pivot to increased accountability for the perpetrator as parent
    - Contextualizing the victim's choices and behaviors. The more accurate we are in the assessment of how the perpetrator harms the children, the more a survivor's actions to resist and protect become visible and make sense. This is essential if we want to end mother-blaming and failure-to-protect as an approach to child safety.

Moving from a child-witness approach to a perpetrator pattern-based approach has broad implications in multiple sectors. Multiagency teams, regardless of whether their area of authority is child safety, adult safety, or both, can apply this broader thinking to ensure that their assessments are more comprehensive. A US-based multiagency team that was focused on child physical and sexual abuse found that domestic violence-informed training helped them with all their cases.[12] In Australia, a multiagency triage team's use of the Safe & Together Model, when reviewing law enforcement child protection referrals for domestic violence incidents, led to almost 90 percent of the cases diverted from statutory child protection to community services.[13]

CHAPTER 4: THE MYTH OF THE CHILD WITNESS

In family court, a shift away from dependence on the child-witness myth is a necessity. A perpetrator pattern-based approach could help guide the family court in more objectively and comprehensively assessing harm to children from perpetrators' patterns of behavior. This would have the result of improving judicial decision-making and increasing accountability for perpetrators as parents. For example, in the family court of Australia, there's emphasis on looking beyond the child witnessing the violence when making assessments. A child expert in the family court said this:

"With the plainness of the Safe & Together language, we can talk about things clearly because we're really just talking about patterns, behaviors, and impacts. And that's a language that everyone can access—no matter what their background. That makes the Model quite powerful."

When we replace the narrow focus on the myth of the child witness with a broader, more accurate definition of harm, it becomes easier for the court to make correct decisions related to child safety and the child's right to a meaningful relationship with both parents. To be relevant, the concept of a "meaningful relationship" between a child and a parent who has perpetrated coercive control needs clear and rigorous expectations of how that parent will change his own behavior and heal the harm he has created for the child. The concept of "meaningful relationship" loses its validity if it doesn't encompass this. Using a perpetrator pattern-based approach, as opposed to a child-witness approach, courts can and should use the criteria such as the following when making decisions regarding parenting time and custody:

> Does the domestic violence perpetrator acknowledge prior controlling and abusive behavior as being wrong and harmful to his partner, children, and family's functioning?
>
> Has he ceased postseparation coercive control, including manipulation of systems, weaponization of the partner's mental health and addiction issues (alleged or real), finances, and any other forms of abuse?

> Is he able and willing to support the children's needs for safety, stability, nurturance, and healing from prior violence?
>
> Can he support his partner's or ex-partner's parenting and the relationship between the children and that person?

Case Example

Alison was referred to domestic violence trauma counseling. Until recently, Alison (age twelve) had lived in a home where her father had controlled her behavior and the behavior of her mother through physical violence directed at her mother; had exercised control over the household finances; and had directed persistent and severe emotional abuse at both of them. Her mother and father had been separated for over a year. Alison wanted to be in contact with her father, which was happening on a regular basis, including occasional overnight stays.

Alison was struggling with her ambivalent feelings about her father. Professionals supporting her mother felt that counseling would help Alison make sense of her feelings. The program, one of the leading ones in the area, offered a mixture of individual and group sessions specifically designed for children exposed to domestic violence. The program involved meditation, play therapy, and group educational lessons to help Alison feel connected to other children with similar experiences.

Through the program, Alison explored her worries, especially her sense of safety. The program helped her identify her boundaries and what she could do when she was feeling scared. By the end of the counseling, Alison's therapist saw improvements in how Alison discussed what her father had done, in how she felt she was not responsible for any of it, and in how she understood healthy relationships. Her mother reported that Alison had become less emotionally volatile at home and that their relationship was improving.

Let me be clear—I love the work that the therapist did with Alison and the progress that she made. This is all real and important. But there is one big gaping hole in this approach, which heavily focuses on supporting her in addressing the feelings her father's behaviors have generated: his current behavior as a relevant variable in her experience is never even explored!

The following are examples of some of the items that are often ignored or not included in system responses that are based on a backward-looking, child-witness, posttrauma model:

> **Is he engaging in any postseparation coercive control? And if he is, how is he involving or targeting Alison? What are the effects of any attempts at postseparation coercive control on the functioning of Alison, her mother, or the family?**
>
> **Has or hasn't her father taken responsibility for his past behavior and its harm to Alison and her mother?**
>
> **What is his parenting like? Is she physically safe during her visits with her father? Are there any forms of abuse he is engaging in? Is he able to nurture and support Alison?**
>
> **Can she safely share her feelings about his behavior with her father?**

In the absence of consideration of these variables, this case example problematically models the following:

- Alison taking responsibility for his behavior and doing all the work to "fix" herself
- Ignoring the role of any ongoing, postseparation behavior by her father on her mental health and healing
- Ignoring the father's responsibility for "fixing" the damage that he has created

There was an interesting study that showed that in this one particular sample of domestic violence cases where children were physically harmed by a violent father, it was the mother who took the child to get the medical care needed. We could similarly talk about all the ways mothers and children like Alison are the ones who "clean up" the emotional and physical messes created by violent fathers—even down to the level of being the ones who sweep up glass broken by the perpetrator so the toddler doesn't cut her feet. While it's naive to expect all perpetrators to be part of a child's healing, it is not naive to set that as an expectation by which all perpetrators are measured. It is common sense and reasonable and needs to be woven into our measures of change, safety, and accountability.

An abusive father who cannot be part of the solution and does not help with the healing of a child continues to be part of the problem. We should not be afraid to say that.

CHAPTER 4: THE MYTH OF THE CHILD WITNESS

The answers to the gaps created by the child-witness paradigm are not rocket science but do require a reorientation and expansion of the paradigm related to domestic violence and children. In the above scenario, the therapist needed to do the following:

1. Assess Alison's father's ongoing pattern of coercive control
2. Assess her father's overall parenting, including screening for neglect and physical, sexual, and emotional abuse
3. Assess his support for Alison's mother's parenting and Alison and her mother's relationship
4. Explore with Alison and her mother the father's history of acknowledgment of his abuse and the harm it's caused and his willingness and ability to listen to Alison's feelings and focus on her needs

The implications of any clinical approach to children and domestic violence can extend far beyond the four walls of the counseling room. If this clinician had used a more domestic violence-informed approach, the following would have been possible:

> **The child's clinician would have been able to provide documentation to child protective services or family court about how the father was (or was not) continuing to interfere with the child's safety, well-being, and healing. This documentation may have been very helpful in keeping those systems focused on the perpetrator and inoculating those other professionals from any attempts of manipulation by the perpetrator, including staving off any attempts to weaponize allegations of failure to protect or parental-alienation accusations.**

> Attention to the father's behavior might have promoted change in his behavior either through the intervention of a therapist, orders of the court, or both. This may have led to a change in his behavior that may have helped in her short-term healing and long-term well-being.

Let's extend the thought experiment a little further. Imagine that Alison's father had admitted to Alison that he was wrong about all his controlling behaviors, including the incidents of physical violence. He acknowledged to her the hurts he caused to her and her mother, and demonstrated meaningful and sustained changes in his behaviors. And finally he listened to his daughter's feelings and supported his ex's parenting and relationship with Alison. What might have been the outcome for Alison? She might not have even needed therapy! Even if this didn't happen, it would have been useful to appreciate that Alison's participation in therapy was not just a support but was also another burden she was bearing from her father's choices and behaviors—past and present! Moving beyond a child witness approach would have made positive outcomes for Alison, and other children like her, more likely.

Final Thoughts on Going beyond the Child-Witness Paradigm

Labeling the child-witness approach as a myth helps identify the gaps in the theory and in everyday practice. To end this chapter, I want to walk you through a thought experiment that illustrates how to pivot from the dominant lens of the child witness and related trauma. The following case example, which is based on an example from a major European best-practice domestic violence document, exemplifies how children and domestic violence are often addressed through policy and service delivery lenses. The example is followed by an alternative approach based on the Safe & Together Model.

CHAPTER 5

The Myth of the Domestic Violence Incident

There is a lot more to abuse than physical violence. Dramatic physical assaults, and the associated pain and suffering, are what most people think about when they hear the term "domestic violence." Physical violence by a partner—from a slap to a murder—wreaks havoc on the lives of the immediate victims and everyone around them. The individual, familial, and social costs of physical violence are steep and unacceptable. Physical safety, in and out of one's home, is a basic human right.

The association of physical violence with the term "domestic violence" (or "domestic abuse") is tight. It shapes our collective stereotypes of perpetrators and victims. The monstrous, drunken, violent husband. The cowering, submissive wife. Labels such as "battered women" and "batterer" emphasize severe violence. Public awareness campaigns seek to prick our consciences with images of women with blackened eyes. Popular tropes about physical violence in the home populate the media: the loss of control, crimes of passion, the jilted lover. There's the whispered question: "What did she do to provoke him?" And there's the self-serving defense: "How much is a man supposed to take?"

In recent years, thanks to the work of survivors, family violence researchers, and victim advocates, different aspects of domestic violence—including gaslighting, systems manipulation, and coercive control—are deservedly getting more attention. Slowly, criminal and civil laws in multiple countries are changing to reflect a more complex and complete understanding of the experience of survivors. Trailblazing academics, like Evan Stark, author of the book *Coercive Control,*[1] and Emma Katz—with her work on mothers, children, and coercive control[2]—are changing our thinking. Yet physical violence still stands as the centerpiece of much of our domestic violence work.

This chapter examines different ways that the primacy of physical violence and the associated incident-based approach can mislead and misdirect domestic violence policy and practice. The chapter will explore "sub" myths like the "escalating argument" narrative and the "loss of control" narrative as the reason for violence. I'll probe the "cycle of violence" approach and how sexual assault is often left out of the way we operationalize the incident of domestic violence. I conclude with a discussion of how the Safe & Together Model's perpetrator pattern-based approach—which links coercive control with behaviors associated with child abuse and neglect—can challenge these myths and help us intervene with perpetrators and partner with survivors.

> *As much as victim advocates have tried to evoke and articulate harm beyond bruises, blood, and broken bones, the incident of physical violence remains the symbolic heart of domestic violence.*

Primacy of the Domestic Violence Incident

The centrality of physical violence is woven into the fabric of diverse systems. Child protection workers assess whether children were within a "zone of danger." In medical settings, screening protocols prioritize the incident of physical violence. The common screening question for domestic violence—"Are you safe at home?"—translates into this: "Are you at risk of physical violence?" Courts, whether criminal or civil, lean heavily on physical violence in their decision-making. Stay away orders often depend on evidence of recent physical violence or threats of physical violence. Lack of reports to the police or medical evidence of injuries is often used to "disprove" allegations of domestic violence in family court or other judicial settings.

The fields of psychology and counseling, which are influential in the response to domestic violence, rely heavily on trauma theory, which is strongly weighted toward violent events. While experienced practitioners and researchers understand that chronic nonviolent abuse can create trauma symptoms, trauma theory strengthens the primacy of physical violence in the minds of most practitioners. Other forms of neglect and chronic patterns of control hover at the periphery, getting less attention. Despite concerted efforts to widen the definition of abuse, it turns out that policy, practice, and the popular imagination are still dominated by the idea that domestic violence equals an incident of physical violence.

> *The domestic violence incident is so harmful because the assumption is if law enforcement or the system got involved around this incident, it must be the most severe one. This is not even close to true for many families. So it means we may be missing a whole bunch of other stuff that cumulatively causes damage*
>
> —Beth Ann, S&TI faculty, independent consultant, US

CHAPTER 5: THE MYTH OF THE DOMESTIC VIOLENCE INCIDENT

The Myth of the Domestic Violence Incident

Because it is an incomplete roadmap for systems and practitioners who want to effectively respond to adult and child survivors and domestic violence perpetrators, the domestic violence incident cannot remain at the center of professional policy and practice. Please don't misunderstand me—physical violence is a critical aspect, and often an overriding element, of the dynamic in domestic violence. It cannot and should not be ignored. But it is not present in all scenarios of coercive control. Even when it is present, it is not always the biggest concern of a survivor. Many survivors will openly express that it's the emotional and psychological abuse that is worse for them than the physical violence. Other survivors will talk about the devastating impact of emotional abuse and threats made before, during, and after incidents of physical violence. Survivors often tell us that their concern for the physical, emotional, and psychological well-being of their children can be more important to them than a push or even a more severe physical assault. Even when physical violence is part of the pattern of abuse, professionals are not making the connections between the physical violence and entrapment, deprivation of liberty, and changes in the family functioning. We are prone to missing important realities for survivors when the image of the drunken, violent brute looms larger in our psyches than the gaslighting whisperer who, with precision and forethought, targets the reputation of the survivor with friends, family, professionals, and even her own children.

Paradoxically, the myth of the domestic violence incident can even encourage us to empathize with the perpetrator of violence and ignore or blame the survivor. When domestic violence is viewed through the lens of isolated incidents of physical violence, it is easier to fall into a narrative of justified, provoked violence. This can be seen in how often the media titillate the public with news reports using the narrative of the enraged jealous husband who lost control because he was cheated on—or the despondent, suicidal father who murdered his children because he was denied custody. Rarely is the story told through the lens of a wider pattern of entrapment and control. This makes victim-blaming easier and often emboldens other perpetrators to feel justified in their own acts of violence.

Equating domestic violence with physical violence can stop us from asking the right questions about change and accountability. **When the focus is on physical violence, perpetrators are free to continue nonphysical forms of manipulation and coercion with impunity.** In these ways, theories such as the cycle of violence or trauma initiatives, which use the myth of the domestic violence incident as their foundation, can inadvertently and unconsciously make it harder for us to be the best allies possible for adult and child survivors and hold perpetrators fully accountable.

Perpetrators' Goal Is Not Violence; It's Control

When I ran men's behavior change groups, the men were almost always referred to the program for an incident of physical violence. I always thought that one of the main goals of my job was to make the problem "bigger" in their minds—to get the men to see that their hurtful behaviors were bigger than physical violence. I wanted them to identify the wider range of problematic behaviors, and the associated sense of entitlement, used to control their partners and their children's actions, feelings, and thoughts. I wanted them to stop all their attacks on their partners' self-determination, safety, and satisfaction—not just stop being physically violent.

In these groups, I deeply listened to and learned from the men about their worldviews and expectations around behavior, gender, and life. Here are some examples of the stated and implied attitudes and beliefs:

> "I didn't want her bartending around all those men."
>
> "I get to control my partner's actions."

CHAPTER 5: THE MYTH OF THE DOMESTIC VIOLENCE INCIDENT

> "I can't trust my partner. Nor can I trust men around my partner."
>
> "I have the right to control what job my partner works at."
>
> "The fact that she's carrying my child gives me rights over my partner's body and actions."
>
> "I'm afraid, so I have to control my partner."
>
> "I feel humiliated, so I need to punish my partner."
>
> "I have the right to use violence to enforce my view of the world and my expectations."

For these men, physical violence was the tip of the spear. It was the way to enforce a broader set of beliefs and attitudes. It was a way to manage their own fears. It was just one of the ways to get what they wanted. It was not isolated from how they thought and acted in other, nonviolent ways during their interactions with their partners and others.

What I heard from the men in my group mirrored what I heard from their partners when I would check in with them about their safety. Whenever a survivor would ask about my assessment of her partner's progress in the group, I would avoid giving my opinion. My perspective on his progress was limited to my experience of him in my group. It was much less relevant than her experience of him at home. Her experience, not mine, was the one that mattered. Instead of offering my opinion, I would turn around the question: "How has his participation in the group changed things for you at home? Has he changed his behavior?" Most often I would hear about a cessation of physical violence but a continuation of emotional abuse and controlling behavior.

The physical violence propelled the involvement of the criminal justice system—arrest and a protection order. But those interventions didn't even come close to addressing behaviors like:

- ongoing financial control
- manipulation of children as a way to pressure and hurt the partner.
- separation of her from her family and friends
- manipulations of systems and threats or actual use of systems such as family court and child protective services to continue campaigns of control

> *Dealing with the myth of the domestic violence incident was important in the context of our work in the criminal justice system. We had noticed how the police and other agencies were talking about 'incidents,' which we were already talking about as a complex domestic violence situation. Right at the beginning we talked about the process of domestic violence and coercive control versus the incident.*

—Mhairi, violence against women and girls consultant, Scotland

The criminal justice system is not the only area where primacy of physical violence can create problems for survivors. When I began training with child protective services around domestic violence, I was worried that a heavy focus on physical violence and lethality markers would backfire against survivors. I knew that discussions about lethality markers and risk could suck the oxygen out of any other conversation related to domestic violence. Workers focused exclusively on preventing fatalities might miss other forms of harmful abuse. And since risk markers, such as threatening behavior, occur much more often than actual homicides do, I was worried that an emphasis on lethality would lead to unnecessary and reactive removals of their children. (I also intuitively knew that something major was missing from the conversation. I would later figure out that the concerns about risk and harm needed to be balanced off with comprehensive assessments of survivors' protective efforts, which eventually became part of the Model.)

So if we want to be allies to both adult and child survivors, if we want to be accurate and comprehensive in our assessments and planning, and if we want to increase accountability for perpetrators as parents, we must explode the myth of the domestic violence incident as the foundation of our shared understanding and response to domestic violence and children.

So, let's look more deeply into some of the ways the myth of domestic violence incident fails and locks us into approaches that don't align with the experience of survivors. This section outlines the exact nature of the problems and limitations of this focus on the explosion of physical violence, highlighting some of the limitations of the focus on physical violence.

Limitations of the Focus on Physical Violence

> The problem with the "cycle of violence"
>
> The excuse that "the argument just escalated"
>
> Loss of control and crimes of passion
>
> Consideration of rape as a separate issue
>
> Little or no focus on the children
>
> Entrapment and control considered a communal act
>
> Intersectionalities treated as if they don't matter
>
> All violence treated as equal in impact when it isn't
>
> The excuse that it is just a temper problem

The Problem with the "Cycle of Violence"

It is not uncommon to hear practitioners working with domestic violence survivors say, "I'm working to end the cycle of violence in our families and our communities." While some use the term to refer to the intergenerational transmission of violence from parent to child, the term was originally developed by Lenore Walker in the late 1970s to describe the domestic violence dynamics in couples.[3] Despite critiques,[4] Walker's theory still casts a heavy shadow across sectors, over our language, over our understanding of domestic violence, and over our practice. For example, domestic violence victims advocates, law enforcement, and mental health counselors often see themselves as helping survivors escape the "cycle of violence."

Walker's work was groundbreaking at the time. It was derived from interviews with survivors themselves, giving voice to their experiences. It was an attempt to move the conversation away from misogynistic explanations of domestic violence, which pathologized survivors as masochistic or crazy. Instead, she tried to explain the question "Why doesn't she leave?" through the psychological theory of "learned helplessness." Instead of victimization being a product of some sort of innate flaw or pathology in survivors, Walker suggested that it was the perpetrators' behaviors that led domestic violence survivors to remain trapped in a cycle of hope and hopelessness about their situation. It was a radical concept at the time.

Walker's theory describes three phases in the cycle: tension-building, incident of violence (also referred to as the explosion or acute battering), and the calm honeymoon phase. The centrality of the incident of physical violence is self-evident. The tension-building phase precedes the violent incident. The honeymoon period is what follows. Both the tension-building and the honeymoon phase are only relevant as they relate back to the incident of violence. Survivors have described "walking on eggshells" in the tension-building phase, anticipating the explosion of violence. The honeymoon phase is filled with acts of contrition, like apologies, flowers, and cards.

CHAPTER 5: THE MYTH OF THE DOMESTIC VIOLENCE INCIDENT

Despite its groundbreaking origins, the "cycle of violence" model has always felt problematic enough for me that it never really influenced the Safe & Together Model. Here are a few of the problems with it:

> **The elevation of physical violence over all other forms of abuse contradicts the experience of many survivors who report that the effects of nonphysical abuse, like gaslighting, are profound and sometimes worse than the physical violence.**
>
> **The term "tension-building" directs our attention to an impending incident of violence and away from the omnipresent dynamics of entrapment and coercive control.**
>
> **It focuses on the couples' pattern instead of the pattern of the perpetrator, suggesting that it is their dynamic that cocreates the abuse.**
>
> **It decontextualizes the behavior of the perpetrator and the experiences of the survivors from the broader cultural and institutional context. For example, there's the failure of the police to arrest, or there are victim-blaming interventions from child protection agencies.**
>
> **It completely ignores the complexity of the involvement of children or the role of family members in situations such as network-based abuse or lateral violence.**
>
> **It doesn't help us see the protective or safety strategies of the survivor, including acts of resistance.**

The language of the "honeymoon" period or reconciliation may be the most challenging and problematic. It directs us away from the perpetrator's failure to take genuine responsibility and accountability for the abuse. The "honeymoon" concept directs us away from naming the continuing coercion. For example, there is the continuous potential for violence and how it is inevitably still affecting the partner. To go even further with the last point, many of the discussions of the "cycle of violence" will talk about how the survivor appreciates the flowers, the respite, and the makeup sex. But how often is "makeup sex" really rape or sexual coercion? During a true honeymoon, there is genuine intimacy and connection. During that honeymoon phase, how free of fear does the survivor feel? Is she feeling able to talk openly about the hurt, fear, and anger she feels? Some perpetrators never apologize and never offer flowers. For some, the abuse just continues to roll on with the perpetrator blaming the survivor for the violence, pretending it never happened or claiming she is lying about what actually happened.

The language of the "honeymoon" or even the "calm" misdirects us away from the deeper experiences of continuous coercion. One practitioner observed that "breach by flowers" was very common. This is a term describing perpetrators' violation of stay away orders by delivering flowers and has often been dismissed by her colleagues as harmless. Instead, it should've been taken seriously as part of a pattern of control and manipulation—a demonstration of a disregard for consequences and limits by a person with a history of violence. The dominance of the incident of physical violence in the minds of professionals lays the groundwork for these types of assessment errors. "Cycle of violence" thinking, with its centering of the incident of physical violence, makes it harder for us to identify critical dynamics of the perpetrator's coercive control.

"The Argument Just Escalated"

The narrative that physical violence results from an escalating argument is common and misleading. The escalation label carries with it many assumptions. It implies a cocreation of the violence. It puts everyone's opinions and ideas on the same level and buries the perpetrator's unrealistic expectations and misogynistic beliefs. It directs attention away from wider patterns of control.

When we examine domestic violence through the lens of an argument gone bad, we don't pay attention to the fact that the perpetrator is justifying his behavior and rationalizing his use of control. For instance, he might say, "I don't want you to spend time with your friends because they are all divorced and will put bad ideas in your head." And that may be the starting point for an argument because the survivor might then resist this verbal attack on her right to associate with whom she chooses. The "argument gone bad" premise reframes acts of resistance to control as *shared* dysfunction.

The "argument narrative" directs us away from the individual responsibility of the person who got violent, away from his responsibility for a belief system that justifies control, and away from his own choices around his behaviors. Arguments don't just escalate. Individuals make choices, sometimes split-second choices, about how they will approach disagreements. I learned this from the men I worked with for years. Almost all of them could describe, after the fact, their underlying decision-making process behind their choices to become abusive and violent. There might be a description like this: "I was leaving, but then I turned around to 'teach her a lesson' because I couldn't let her get the better of me." His violent behavior was tied to a series of beliefs and thoughts that created a justification for his behavior, propelling him forward to violent action.

Case Example

Consider this scenario that illuminates the problem with the argument-escalation narrative.

Joe is referred to a men's behavior change program after being arrested for physically assaulting his partner, Alyssa. His story upon entry into the program is that they were arguing about her friends and the argument "got out of hand." Yes, he admits to pushing her but points out she was yelling and screaming at him and had backed him into a corner.

(Joe's admission was not complete. The police report indicated that Alyssa was badly bruised on the face, including wounds on the back of her head from being smashed against a light fixture.) He says that they were both "out of hand" that night. Now fast forward to his later involvement in the actual group, where he shares the following details about his thinking that night. He says, "I saw her wanting to go out with her friends as a sign of disrespect to me. I had already told her earlier I didn't like her friends because they were all divorced and 'sluts.' I needed her to understand that I wasn't going to tolerate her 'putting our relationship in danger by spending time with those whores.' I was calm when I told her. It was her that started yelling first."

So when Joe chooses violence as the way to enforce his perceived right or to punish his partner for daring to speak or act against his expectations, is it best to describe it as "Joe and Alyssa's argument escalated" or "got out of control"? Or is it better to describe it as "Joe engaged in a pattern of behavior, including physical violence, to prevent Alyssa from associating with friends and family?" (Spoiler alert! The latter description is more accurate and, therefore, more useful in partnering with Alyssa and intervening with Joe.)

When we think of physical violence always stemming from an escalation of an argument, we make it harder to hold perpetrators responsible for their behavior and the related harms. We make it harder for ourselves as practitioners to discover coercive control.

Loss of Control and Crimes of Passion

"I just lost it."
"I couldn't stand the idea of her with another guy."
"I loved her so much. I couldn't help myself."

A close relative to the "argument escalation" narrative is the "loss of control" or "crimes of passion" storyline. This is where the person who commits the violence or others, such as members of media outlets, frame

CHAPTER 5: THE MYTH OF THE DOMESTIC VIOLENCE INCIDENT

domestic violence as the result of "overwrought passion" or "too much love." A focus on the domestic violence incident dovetails neatly with the "jealous rage" and "loss of control" narratives. The media has used this trope extensively in the case of domestic violence homicides. The murder is framed as a "one-off" reaction to loss and grief and not connected to any other prior behaviors or forms of control.

The ideas of "losing it," "crimes of passion," and "being pushed too far" are all part of the subtle and not-so-subtle victim-blaming narratives that ask us to identify with the person using violence as being a victim, as being a good person who has been pushed too far. With phrases like "I just couldn't live without her," we are being invited to join the perpetrator in his emotional victimization and "natural" and "understandable" loss of control and his deep feelings of love and loss. This is more likely to be effective when we only focus on the incident of violence and not beyond, to the beliefs about ownership and any wider patterns of control.

Domestic violence perpetration is not an uncontrollable biological reaction. Unfortunately, the primacy of physical violence in the discussion of domestic violence incidents and the perception that domestic violence is an outburst, or an isolated incident, makes it easier for a perpetrator to promote the idea that "he just lost it." When physical violence is not seen as the logical outgrowth of the desire to control or the sense of entitlement to own another person, it makes professionals more vulnerable to manipulation or collusion. Every time we accept the "he lost it" or the "crimes of passion" narratives, we are more likely to miss wider patterns of harm and entrapment.

> *❝I think the other piece that really sticks out is the myth of the domestic violence incident. I immediately began to look for the power and control that already existed, and then I challenge the word incident again. I'm looking for the patterns and helping the survivor to identify those patterns. ❞*
> —Eloise, independent consultant, child-adult survivor, US

Rape Is Not a Separate Issue

I remember sitting in child protection meetings where, after a long discussion about a father's violence and abuse, someone would mention that the mom was pregnant again with his child. Eyes would roll and exasperated sighs would be audible in the room. The frustration was not with the violent father but with the mother who was pregnant again. There was the unspoken sentiment that there was something wrong with her for getting pregnant with this person with a history of violence. The urge to blame this mother was so powerful that it blinded everyone to the continuing power of his violence and control. His coercion was forgotten, and she was being viewed as a person who had complete control over her sexuality and reproduction, who could freely revoke consent for sex without consequence. His violence remained in view, not to give the pregnancy context but as a reason to judge her. The violence was not seen as a potential source of reproductive coercion. Instead of the information about the pregnancy opening up a conversation about rape and sexual coercion, it became a conversation about another mother who was being blamed for making poor choices that impacted an unborn child. There was zero connection being made between domestic violence perpetration, rape, sexual coercion, and the loss of bodily autonomy.

Domestic violence perpetrators regularly sexually harass, humiliate, and assault their partners. Rape and sexual coercion are the most intimate violations, often leading to some of the most severe forms of physical and emotional traumas and the most serious, life-changing consequences, like an unwanted child. In many practitioners, there is a disconnect between the assessment for the perpetration of physical violence and the perpetration of sexual violence. A confluence of factors may be at play here. For example, although sexual assault is about control and not sex, there are sex-negative attitudes—and discomfort with discussions of sexual health, consent, and pleasure—that can inhibit discussions about sexual violence. Another factor may be that we've institutionalized a separation of the fields of domestic violence and sexual assault prevention and response. In many areas, services for sexual assault and domestic violence are separate programs, with separate funding criteria and imperatives. Leaving out sexual assault from our narratives around the incidents of domestic violence makes it harder for us to understand the level of danger, the nature of the harm perpetrated against the adult survivor, and the full range of the survivors' protective efforts.

Where Are the Children?

One day he said to the children, "Come in here and watch me kill your mother." On another day, he said to her, "This is the day your children watch me kill you." A focus on incidents of physical violence can be blind to how a perpetrator is often choosing to involve his children in his abuse. I have said more about this in the chapter where I discuss the myth of the child witness, but it is important to keep in mind all the different ways that perpetrators target, involve, and impact children through their patterns of behavior. In the domestic violence incident, our first thought isn't about the children but the other adult. The language of domestic violence, with its implicit focus on the adult-to-adult relationship, makes it harder to keep children's experiences in view.

The narrative of the domestic violence incident suggests that arrest, incarceration, and other criminal court interventions resolve the danger. Those arguments often willfully ignore the ongoing relationship the perpetrator has to shared children, and through those children, his continuing access and influence on the survivor. In their 2017 paper, Bonomi and Martin [5] identify how children are used by perpetrators who are in jail awaiting trial to coerce their partner to recant. Three case examples illuminate how children are used to triangulate and pressure the survivor to change her story about the violence and abuse. In one of the examples, the perpetrator, speaking directly to his child during a jailhouse call, said, "Your mom is mean and evil. Tell her I said that. Ask your mom why she hates me. Ask her why she don't love me, why she keep puttin' me in jail." The research illustrated how successful these tactics can be. Arrest and even incarceration, while temporarily preventing new incidents of violence, did not end the use of the children as part of the ongoing pattern of control.

To hold perpetrators accountable as parents and to be able to partner effectively with survivors, we need to keep connecting all forms of domestic violence perpetration to the lives of children.

Entrapment and Control: A Communal Act

The domestic violence perpetrator never acts in a vacuum—the response of systems can increase or diminish the power of his behavior to control or entrap. As a corollary, survivors are rarely just worried about the perpetrators' behaviors. Survivors worry if calling law enforcement will lead to their own arrest or the landlord evicting her and the children. She thinks, "Will child protective services become involved and take my babies? If I leave, does my job pay me enough to keep a roof over me and my kids?" These fears are often greater for survivors from marginalized communities who face racist and colonial systems that have a track record of unequal responses. Perpetrators feel emboldened when they believe they can count on systems—such as child protective services, law enforcement, and family court—to be on their side or at least be ineffective in their response. And it's not just formal systems. The response of friends and families can make all the difference in the amount of shame or support a survivor experiences.

Risk assessment frameworks are heavily focused on the danger of more incidents of physical violence by the perpetrator. While a focus on the risks of future physical injury and death are critical, any assessment that doesn't include how systems do or don't facilitate entrapment and control is missing a key element in the experience of survivors. The myth of the domestic violence incident says we should just focus on the risk of future perpetrator violence but not the way systems and communities fail to intervene with the perpetrator and fail to partner with the survivor. In many or most instances, formal risk assessment processes do not consider the success or failure of systems interventions as a factor in the danger faced by a survivor. The myth of the domestic violence incident does not support the fullest exploration of entrapment and the role played by systems and professionals in that entrapment.

Intersectionalities Matter

If you are a Black woman, does it matter if the partner who physically abuses you is white or Black? If we only consider, in isolation, the act of violence, then no. A punch is a punch regardless of the race of the victim or the perpetrator. But if we fine-tune our lens and start considering the deeper nature of patterns of coercive control, then yes, race and the privileges or vulnerabilities associated with it may matter very much. Due to structural racism and colonization, a white perpetrator is likely to hold advantages during interactions with wider systems like the criminal justice system. A Black survivor may be more worried about how the police will treat his partner if he is Black. Fears of deaths in custody or race-based police brutality may impact a First Nation or Black survivor's decision to call the police. Overpolicing of marginalized peoples means survivors from those communities may be navigating the fear of being arrested themselves when they try to engage law enforcement for protection from their partners. These things may impact a Black woman's willingness to call the police as an act of protection.

The primacy of the incident of physical violence can make it harder to identify vulnerability and privileges associated with gender, race, class, ethnicity, orientation, and other factors that influence and shape dynamics of control. For example, the physical assault of a transgender partner may intersect with transphobia. The perpetrator's verbal abuse may include trans-specific put-downs such as the person not being "a real man (or woman)" or threats to "out" the person to employers or others. The wider dynamic of transphobia may hinder the survivor from going to a refuge or calling the police. A threat to call child protective services may have increased potency when wielded by a white abuser against a First Nation survivor, given the colonizing practices of mainstream systems taking children from First Nation parents. In these ways, all domestic violence incidents, even when they involve the same exact acts of violence, are not created equal. Our understanding of domestic violence must weave in coercive control and intersectional considerations of power, privilege, and vulnerability.

Racist stereotypes of Black, First Nations people, and other minorities as being more violent and the myth of the domestic violence incident reinforce each other. When we center physical violence in societies that have stereotyped certain groups as more violent, then we are likely to have a justification for the arrest of members of these groups at greater rates than their white counterparts. Every time we decontextualize physical violence from intersectionalities, we are standing more separate from the reality of perpetrators and survivors.

All Violence Is Not Equal in Impact

Both men and women can be violent. This is a fact. But we also know that gender matters. It is a both/and situation. Research shows us that men's violence against women is more likely to be associated with physical injury—which is not a bad proxy for fear and control. *If I can hurt you and physically overpower you, I have more ability to control and influence your choices.*

Not all violence is equal in its impact or its context. Size, strength, and patterns of behavior matter when assessing the harm from domestic violence. For example, if you have two people, and one person is 275 pounds (125 kilograms) and six feet (182 centimeters) tall and the other is 110 pounds (fifty-five kilograms) and five feet two inches (158 centimeters) tall, regardless of gender, threats of violence or actual violence is likely to have a different effect, depending on which person is the perpetrator. No reasonable person can argue that the violence is likely to be equal in force and effect. The larger person is less likely to be afraid of being overpowered, controlled, or injured by the smaller person. The smaller person, on the other hand, can be significantly injured by a larger person's physical violence. In fact, the larger person may need to use less or no actual force to achieve control over the smaller person. Grabbing the smaller person's wrist or standing in the doorway to block the other person's exit exemplify how a larger person may exert minimal force to achieve control. It's a level of physical dominance the smaller person may never be able to achieve, even with a weapon, due to her size and strength.

Now add in the fact that the larger person carries power and privileges associated with gender, race, class, or other factors. Decades and centuries of patriarchy, in many (but not all) cultures, hand men more levers for control over their female partners and a lack of consequences when they do act violently. Size, strength, patterns of behavior, and context matter. All blows are not equal in their impact.

While it is not always true, size, strength, and contextual disparities usually favor male perpetrators when they are targeting female partners. The narrative around the domestic violence incident, with its built-in primacy of physical violence, suggests we ignore this and equalize men and women's use of violence, dismissing dynamics of patriarchy, gender discrimination, coercion, and fear. Meaningful difference is dismissed with statements such as this: "Well you know they've both been arrested." Or this: "They each have court orders against the other." Without a pattern-based framework that includes coercive control and considers context, the myth of the domestic violence incident will continue to be used to obscure and increase mother-blaming and add to the ways we ignore how fathers' choices and behaviors impact their children's functioning.

Isn't It Just a Temper Problem?

The first perpetrator intervention program curriculum I taught in the late 1980s had a strong component of "anger management." It also taught communication skills and stress relief. In fact, most of the curriculum was designed around the excuses and justifications that perpetrators offer for their violence. In the popular imagination, violence is an anger problem.

So, it's understandable when domestic violence is equated with a "bad temper." The association of domestic violence with anger directs us away from seeing larger patterns of coercive control. It also offers a simplistic explanation to what is a more complex dynamic. If I have unrealistic expectations of my partner, like expecting her not to talk to her parents, then it is logical that I may get angry when I don't get compliance from my partner. If I get violent with my partner in response to my partner failing to follow my rules, then is the issue my anger or is it my unreasonable and controlling expectations?

The confusion around how "temper" fits with domestic violence may be exacerbated by the medical and mental health fields.[6] *The Diagnostic and Statistical Manual of Mental Disorders*, or DSM, the dominant guide in the United States and much of the world for identifying mental health disorders, includes spousal physical violence, psychological abuse, and sexual violence as "other conditions that may be a focus of clinical attention." At the same time, it includes the condition intermittent explosive disorder, or IED, which the guide defines as "recurrent behavioral outbursts representing a failure to control aggressive impulses."[7] While the formal diagnosis of IED requires that these behaviors not be associated with an attempt to gain control, the diagnostic criteria themselves do not require the clinician to evaluate the impact those behaviors are having on family, friends, and others. The DSM offers a nod to separating IED from coercive control. You must rule out IED if the behaviors are enacted to "obtain some tangible objective," such as money, power, or intimidation. While on paper this may sound good, it is hard to imagine that someone who engages in three or more violent incidents leading to injury to another person or damage to property in a year, or verbal tirades or temper tantrums twice a week for three months (direct from the definition of intermittent explosive disorder), is not creating fear and control in those around them.

An informal review of websites that address the topics of IED or anger management demonstrate the confusion about IED. Some sites pay little attention to how others are impacted by the person with IED. They don't even offer a clear value statement that it is not OK to be violent regardless of any diagnosis. Victims of the person with IED are for all intents and purposes invisible. Other sites, in contradiction to the formal criteria, directly connect IED and temper problems to domestic violence and even control of others. They describe behaviors that, from the point of view of the victim, would be consistent with control. For example, there's the statement that "he blows up over the smallest thing that makes him unhappy." They highlight how the behaviors make others afraid. The mixed, confusing, and unrealistic messages around IED and domestic violence create opportunities for perpetrators to hide their control and for systems to collude by accepting the diagnosis when the real issue is coercive control and broader patterns of abuse.

How the Safe & Together Model Innovates to Challenge the Myth of the Domestic Violence Incident

When I created the Safe & Together Model, I wanted to ensure that practice was guided by pattern-based, not incident-based, thinking. While survivors, domestic violence victim advocates, and researchers had been talking about patterns of abuse for decades, it has not yet become the dominant paradigm or language in many systems. For example, child protection engagement with domestic violence has been, and still is, almost always triggered by incidents of violence. This description of a conversation between a Safe & Together-trained social worker advocating for her client and a child protection social worker illustrates this well.

> *I have all the dates of incidents against the mother and children, and it took me five minutes to read out those dates. And, you know, by the end of the phone call, the social worker was just like, 'OK, OK.' And I said, 'That's what we're dealing with—you keep looking at one instance, but I've got twenty-two incidents here. That's what else is going on all the time for this mother. And you're just seeing singular incidents.*

—Catriona, independent social worker, Scotland

CHAPTER 5: THE MYTH OF THE DOMESTIC VIOLENCE INCIDENT

In most criminal justice systems, law enforcement investigates incidents of violence, not patterns of violent and nonviolent forms of control. This has only started to change recently, with criminalization of coercive control in areas such as England, Wales, and Scotland.

I also wanted the Model to close the gap between the domestic violence and child-maltreatment fields. While the data was clear that domestic violence and child maltreatment were highly correlated, practice continues to lag behind, treating them as siloed issues. Despite the awareness that one person often was perpetrating both forms of abuse in the family, systems have been acting as if they were not frequently connected.

The perpetrator pattern-based approach offers a clear alternative approach to the "myth of the domestic violence incident." Described in its most basic form, a perpetrator pattern-based approach is defined by the following two-part question:

1. What is the perpetrator's pattern of coercive control and the actions taken to harm the children and
2. What is the impact of those behaviors on child, partner, and family functioning?

While the full Model is much more complex and includes other elements, these questions are the heart and soul of the Safe & Together Model. They underpin all the Model's training, tools, and resource material. For example, when I do a domestic violence case consultation, these are the first questions I would ask. Our web-based Perpetrator Pattern Mapping Tool [8] leads with sections related to each of these questions. Whether it's the Safe & Together Institute ally guide,[9] designed to help family and friends support a loved one who is being abused, or our organizational assessment tool,[10] the individual resources available in the perpetrator pattern-based framework provide the underlying definition of the problem. The practitioners we interviewed for this book universally agreed that the Model had given them a *common and consistent language, tools,* and *framework* that enabled them to speak with women, children, men, and other professionals—with resulting better outcomes for clients.

How Does a Perpetrator Pattern-Based Approach Compare with the Myth of the Domestic Violence Incident?

	Myth of Domestic Violence Incident	**Perpetrator Pattern-Based Approach**
Is it really a cycle of violence?	"Cycle of violence" paradigm emphasizes physical violence over everything else. Focuses on relationship dynamic.	Includes all forms of abuse and control; considers behaviors of the perpetrator across relationships and different situations.
The argument just escalated.	Focuses on mutually created dysfunction and isolated incidents of violence.	Considers the perpetrators' violent behaviors in the context of other abusive and controlling behaviors.
Crimes of passion: "I love her so much."	Reinforces the "loss of control" and "provocation" narratives.	Keeps the focus on the perpetrators' underlying control and entitlement thinking; puts the abuse into context of pattern.
Rape is not a separate issue.	Perpetuates the invisibility of sexual assault as a common behavior by domestic violence perpetrators.	Assesses the full range of abusive and controlling behaviors, including rape and other forms of sexually abusive behaviors.
Where are the children?	Ignores children except if they are physically injured or are obviously traumatized by seeing or hearing the violence.	Considers the perpetrators' direct abuse and neglect of children and identifies the multiple pathways to harm for the children.
Systems' responses can increase survivors' entrapment.	Sees the incident in isolation from systems' behaviors.	Includes perpetrators' active manipulation of systems and how systems' functioning can contribute to entrapment.
Intersectionalities matter.	Wider forms of oppression are not relevant.	Is sensitive to privilege and vulnerabilities related to different factors, including racism, homophobia, transphobia, colonization, and other structural forms of oppression.
Size, strength, and context matter.	All violence is equal.	Includes an analysis of how a bigger, stronger person often can use these attributes to be more controlling; the social context of patriarchy gives men certain advantages when it comes to control and violence.
Well, isn't it just a temper problem?	Can easily and wrongly lump domestic violence perpetration into a temper or anger-problem category.	A focus on patterns of coercive control reduces the likelihood of attributing domestic violence to a "temper problem."

What Are the Benefits of a Perpetrator Pattern-Based Approach over an Incident-Based Approach?

Stopping blaming mothers and ignoring fathers requires a pivot away from a lopsided focus on incidents of violence to a more balanced focus on broader patterns of behavior. Clarifying the full extent of the problem, beyond incidents of physical violence, is necessary if we are going to hold fathers responsible for the harm caused by their behavior and if we're going to partner with protective mothers. When highly damaging, nonviolent behaviors—such as abuse via litigation or false reports to child protective services—are left out of the picture, abusive fathers are able to skirt full responsibility for the harm their choices are creating for children. Similarly, it is easier to identify survivors' protective efforts when the wide range of nonviolent threats and risks are clearly identified. When we only validate survivors' choices that protect against physical violence, like going to a refuge, we ignore and devalue all their safety planning and strategizing around nonviolent threats and potential harms.

A perpetrator pattern-based approach opens the door to a whole different set of conversations. It facilitates accountability by offering us the ability to answer this basic question: Have his patterns of behaviors changed from before, and are these changes meaningful to the survivor's safety, well-being, and freedom? An incident-based approach can delude professionals into believing that no new incidents of violence equals an absence of coercive control. Meanwhile, behind the scenes or in front of everyone's face, the perpetrator continues to engage in a wide range of controlling behaviors. Measuring change solely through the absence of physical violence can embolden the perpetrator to continue using non-physical forms of control.

> **❝The myth of the domestic violence incident is so harmful because the assumption is if law enforcement or the system got involved around this incident, it must be the most severe one. That's not even close to true for many families. So, it means we may be missing a whole bunch of other stuff that cumulatively causes damage, but we also may be missing individual incidents that caused incredible damage. The consequence of that is it allows for us to continue to ask her 'Did this awful thing happen? Just don't let this awful thing happen again.' Versus realizing that everything she does is in the context of his ongoing pattern of abuse.❞**
>
> —Beth Ann, S&TI faculty, independent consultant, US

It can also lead to a negative boomerang reaction against survivors. For example, an incident-based lens makes it more likely that professionals will be manipulated to support a perpetrator's accusations of parental alienation against a survivor. If the violence is seen as historic, and there is no attention to patterns of coercive control and harm to children, survivors' resistance to unsafe visits or custody can easily be twisted and labeled "alienation."

The perpetrator pattern-based approach transforms the significance and meaning of incidents of physical violence by widening the circle of assessment. The biggest transformation occurs when we uncouple the perpetrators' behaviors (pun intended) from the relationship. By this I mean we consider not only how the person using violence is being abusive and controlling to his partner, but also how he's being abusive and controlling to his children. We don't just look at the current household; we also consider his behavior in other households. Did he abuse his last partner? Or children in another relationship? Furthermore, a perpetrator pattern-based approach looks at abuse, violence, and manipulation targeted at people outside the immediate family. This includes friends, extended family, and even strangers. The transformation correlates the abusive behavior with the person and his pattern, not the couple or the home.

A full application of the perpetrator pattern involves asking the question: What do we know about his pattern of coercive control and actions taken to harm the children, in this relationship and others, from any available source of information—for example, police reports, child protection reports, interviews with family members, etc.?

Let's do a little thought experiment related to this. Watch your reaction to these two statements:

> John was arrested last night for grabbing his partner, throwing her to the ground, and telling her she'd "better think twice" before she leaves him.

> John, who spent years in prison for murdering his first wife after she left him, was arrested last night for grabbing his partner, throwing her to the ground, and telling her she'd "better think twice" before she leaves him.

Does having additional information about his pattern of behavior change your sense of risk and danger for his current partner? A pattern-based approach directs us to take a deeper look at the person who is causing harm and his behavior across different situations. An incident-based approach makes it more likely we will limit our view on the problem, and in limiting our view, fail in fully appreciating the situation.

Moving Beyond Incident-Based Thinking and Practice

So how do you move from a focus on incidents of violence to patterns of behavior? How do you embed pattern-based thinking into daily practice? Here are some examples of putting this into action:

> Make sure that any assessments of domestic violence start with a discussion of the *perpetrator's pattern of coercive control and actions taken to harm the children.*
>
> Connect the perpetrator's pattern of behavior to its broad impact on child, partner, and family functioning.
>
> Discuss the perpetrator's pattern before discussing the survivors' decision-making to make sure her decisions are viewed in context.

Domestic violence-informed practitioners have come up with a variety of creative ways to help survivors understand and document perpetrator patterns of behavior. A Safe & Together-trained practitioner in the United States provides this description of a method she uses with her clients as a way for them to understand the patterns and then plan for safety around this understanding:

> ❝*I create a year-long timeline with the survivor. And I'll say to her 'When something comes to mind—an act of violence or harm or embarrassment or humiliation or any of the typologies of domestic violence, whether they be physical, mental, emotional, verbal, or sexual,—I want you to just drop one word or line describing the event that took place in whatever month that was.' And so then the survivor sees the pattern. Helping the survivor to identify this pattern of power and control also supports the survivor when we are creating the safety plan, because now we know his pattern and now we know how to plan—we move from identifying his pattern to planning together.*❞
>
> —Eloise, independent consultant, child-adult survivor, US

When the focus is on the perpetrator's pattern of coercive control, survivors and professionals can work together to increase perpetrator accountability and better plan for the survivor and her children's safety and well-being.

The Importance of Centering Coercive Control

The Safe & Together Model's perpetrator pattern-based approach rests on the concept of coercive control. Evan Stark, a long-time crusader for social changes around domestic violence, defined coercive control as "a pattern of behavior which seeks to take away the victim's liberty or freedom, to strip away their sense of self."[11] The Safe & Together Model's perpetrator pattern-based approach operationalizes this concept of coercive control—bringing it into the day-to-day practice of professionals and systems.

Coercive control trains us to think differently about domestic violence. It trains us to not focus exclusively or primarily on physical violence. It trains us to think about the loss of liberty and entrapment associated with abuse. It trains us to recognize how rights and freedoms are being removed from the survivor: freedom of association, freedom of speech, freedom of safety, and freedom over her own body. As someone born in the United States, I often think of the phrase "life, liberty, and the pursuit of happiness" in the Declaration of Independence. It struck me that perpetrators' behaviors attack all three. Put another way, perpetrators attack, through their behaviors, the safety, self-determination, and satisfaction of the survivor. It is an attack on the ability to function, to freely maneuver in the world—that is both the goal and the effect of the perpetrator's behaviors. And it is through a pattern-based approach that we will most easily and effectively identify, understand, and respond to domestic violence.

When Evan Stark coined the term "coercive control," he was building upon the work of others who came before him by attempting to codify domestic violence as a human rights and liberty crime. Critical to this effort was decentering physical violence—not to ignore or minimize its seriousness but to reorient our thinking in terms of the relevance of physical violence to wider issues of entrapment and control. He wanted physical violence not just to be understood as a risk factor for dangerousness or lethality but also as a part of a wider pattern of behaviors that create entrapment. [11] This means no longer considering physical violence exclusively from the perspective of physical injuries but also from the control that flows from it. Its significance is not just in the physical injuries but the influence it has going forward. For instance, one might hear something like this: "He pushed me up against the wall and strangled me the last time I went out with friends, so it's easier and safer just to stay home." It also means considering it in connection to a wider set of behaviors, from emotional abuse to financial control, that alter how adult and child survivors function and move through the world.

The coercive control framework allows us to reorder our understanding of domestic violence, bringing it more in line with survivors' experience of being constrained and controlled by their partners' behaviors. Instead of just talking about how a perpetrator assaulted a survivor, we can now also talk about how the pattern of violence and other behaviors haves changed her work life, her housing, her relationships with her family, and the way she parents her children. The Safe & Together Model guides the practitioner to apply the lens of coercive control to their understanding of domestic violence—which is especially helpful in determining the harm perpetrators' behaviors create for child, partner, and family functioning.

The Safe & Together Model's assessment called "Multiple Pathways to Harm," or MPH, is designed to help practitioners think more broadly about how coercive control changes the lives of adult and child survivors.

The coercive control framework allows us to reorder our understanding of domestic violence...

CHAPTER 5: THE MYTH OF THE DOMESTIC VIOLENCE INCIDENT

Multiple Pathways to Harm

Years ago, I was in Memphis, Tennessee, training a group of practitioners who had been funded to test the concept that safe, stable housing reduced the removal of children from families due to abuse or neglect concerns. The team had brought me in because it recognized that many of the families involved with child protective services were experiencing domestic violence. I can still remember the moment of collective shock when they realized that their policy to evict tenants who "engaged in violence" would revictimize domestic violence survivors. The mutualizing language meant that when a resident was assaulted by a current or past partner, she would be evicted—even though she was not responsible for the violence. (They quickly committed to changing that policy!)

This example demonstrates two things:

1. How domestic violence perpetrators' patterns of behavior harm child, partner, and family functioning.
2. When systems' policies and practices do not make these linkages, survivors can suffer.

The Critical Components of the Model (jump to page 278 to view the infographic) identified elements that need to be assessed and factored into any response to families impacted by perpetrators' behaviors. The relationship between those behaviors and harm to functioning is expanded upon in the Model's MPH framework. The MPH framework is a way to increase accountability for fathers who are perpetrators as parents and to decrease mother-blaming.

The MPH framework offers a comprehensive and robust way to describe how the perpetrator's pattern of behavior harms children.

Multiple Pathways to Harm

Perpetrator's Pattern
- Coercive control towards adult survivor
- Actions taken to harm children

Children's Trauma & Safety
- Victim of physical abuse
- Seeing, hearing or learning about the violence

Effect on Partner's Parenting
- Depression, PTSD, anxiety, substance abuse
- Loss of authority
- Energy goes to addressing perpetrator instead of children
- Interference with day to day routine and basic care

Effects on Family Ecology
- Loss of income
- Housing instability
- Loss of contact with extended family
- Educational and social disruptions

Harm to Child
- Behavioural, Emotional, Social, Educational
- Developmental
- Physical Injury

The MPH framework offers a comprehensive and robust way to describe how the perpetrator's pattern of behavior harms children. Moving beyond the physical violence and trauma frameworks, it invites the practitioner into a more layered, complex, and nuanced understanding of how perpetrators' behaviors harm children. To be more comprehensive, domestic violence-informed assessments need to consider trauma and safety, impact on the family ecology, and also the influence of the perpetrator's behaviors on the other person's parenting.

This impact is often cumulative, with different effects negatively reinforcing one another. For example, when a perpetrator's behaviors lead to an eviction or force a survivor to flee with her children to a new home (temporary or permanent), it often interferes with the children's other needs being met. This avalanche of disruptions may involve education, employment, medical care, counseling, and connections with family and friends. Living standards drop for both well-to-do and financially insecure survivors. In certain situations, it could lead to deportation of family members. For Aboriginal survivors in Australia, it may impact their ability to maintain their children in their traditional communities. Survivors from small immigrant communities may be forced away from their familiar neighborhoods and community support.

Once you have an idea of the patterns of behaviors—not just arrests or child protection involvements but actual behaviors, statements, and actions—it becomes easier to see and talk about the impact of those behaviors on child, partner, and family functioning. What's different in the lives of family members because of those behaviors? How many days of school were missed? How many forced moves were there from one housing situation to another? How often did they need to leave their community or country to be safe? What income was lost? What connections with friends and families were weakened or broken? How has the partner's parenting been impacted by the perpetrator's behaviors? How has she been prevented from being the parent she wanted to be? How has the relationship between the adult survivor and her children been weakened and transformed?

> *I had a lightbulb moment with the domestic violence-informed language and Multiple Pathways to Harm. And as much as it was a lightbulb moment, it was also so obvious, and made me think—why did I not see it like that before?*
>
> —Debbie, practice development coordinator, Scotland

A rigorous application of the MPH framework helps connect an abusive father's behaviors to the harms and hardships he causes his partner and their children. Unaddressed gender double standards around parenting means that disruptions or problems with the basic needs of housing, education, and medical care are laid at the feet of mothers, even when they have been caused by a father who chooses violence. Mothers are expected to get the children to medical appointments even when their doctor is now two bus rides or an hour car ride away instead of around the corner. It is her job to find a way to get the children there or find a new doctor. It is her job to manage the children's behavioral issues, even when they have been caused by the perpetrator's behavior. Not only is she expected to fix these issues, but she is also often blamed for the children's problems in the first place, with comments like, "Her parenting deficits are the reason why the children are having behavioral issues."

The MPH framework offers practitioners the language needed to assess how an abusive father caused or contributed to problems with children's day-to-day needs being met. Once you have this framework, mapping it is straightforward. You can consistently ask these questions:

> **How has the perpetrator's behavior caused or contributed to X problem (housing, truancy, mother's loss of employment, missed doctor's appointments)?**
>
> **How did the perpetrator's behavior help or hinder the resolution of X issue?**

These types of questions, and their answers, allow us to increase accountability, but maybe more importantly, they stop us from misidentifying the source of the problem. A mother may not have any trouble maintaining safe and stable housing for the children except that her partner has sabotaged and undermined that ability. A mother may not have any trouble parenting her children except that her partner has attacked and undermined her relationship with her children. The MPH framework helps connect children's harm back to the perpetrator, contextualizes the victims' decisions, and helps set expectations for behavior change. It's also useful for what it highlights and rejects—untimely or wrongly targeted discussions of the survivors' trauma history and misogynistic blame laid on mothers for male partners' choices. This is all very different from the myth of the domestic violence incident.

Final Thoughts on the Myth of the Domestic Violence Incident

One of the great strengths of a perpetrator pattern-based approach is its utility in situations where both parents are identified as being abusive. When both parents have been arrested, there are cross allegations of abuse, or both parties have stay orders against them. In that situation, it is easy for professionals to default to mutualizing the abuse, thinking of them both as perpetrators. This is one of the effects of a domestic violence incident-based approach—one arrest for violence, even when the violence is in self-defense, can lead people to treat that person the same as someone who has been arrested multiple times with multiple partners.

CHAPTER 5: THE MYTH OF THE DOMESTIC VIOLENCE INCIDENT

This can be avoided by asking this question: *"What is each person's individual pattern of coercive control and actions taken to harm the children?"* Focusing on each individual's behavior pattern, in most cases, quickly makes clear who the primary aggressor is and whose behavior patterns are having the more significant impact on the family's functioning. In other circumstances, there may not be enough information to determine if there is a primary aggressor, or it becomes clearer that the violence is situational and not part of a larger pattern of coercive control. Starting with an objective behavioral lens, the perpetrator pattern-based approach has much greater diagnostic sensitivity to varying scenarios than an incident-based approach.

I was once presented with a case where I was told by the practitioner that both parents were violent. I used this method to guide the case consultation. My behavioral questions helped fully lay out the father's pattern, including threats of gun violence against the social worker, multiple severe physical assaults against the mother, abandonment of the mother and their two children after a car accident, and directly observed threats to sabotage her case plan. The only concrete instance of the mother acting violently was her jumping on his back when he tried to take the license plate off her car. Committed to a full exploration of the mother's pattern, I asked the practitioner if there was anything else the mother had done as part of her pattern of control. This was the conversation:

> **Me:** So, what else, besides jumping on his back, did she do that was part of a pattern of violence and control?
>
> **Worker:** She threatened to take him to court for child support.
>
> **Me:** That's her legal right, so I'm not sure if that would be considered a threat in the same way. What else?
>
> **Worker:** I know she is doing more.

Me: **What is she doing or saying that is making you suspect that?**

Worker: **I don't know anything specific, but I'm sure she is doing something else.**

So, I'll ask you the same question I asked everyone in the room that day: Are his pattern and her pattern of violence the same in importance and impact?

By considering each person's pattern separately, in this case and many others, it became clear that their patterns were drastically different in their severity and context. It also became clear where the worker appeared to insert a subjective opinion without any facts to support it.

In other cases, this same approach has identified women as primary aggressors against men and also helped sort out the primary aggressor in same-sex relationships. Dependence on the myth of the domestic violence incident is one of the major reasons that professionals fail in their alignment with survivors and are vulnerable to manipulation by domestic violence perpetrators. To fully partner with adult and child survivors, professionals need to consider the wide range of behaviors associated with coercive control and actions taken to harm the children. This is how we keep children safer, stop ignoring fathers and blaming mothers.

CHAPTER 6

The Myth of Failure to Protect

I've participated in hundreds of cases involving domestic violence across different cities, states, and countries, and there can be a sameness to the conversations—a consistency that reflects shared values and beliefs around domestic violence, children, and gender expectations. The systems' go-to expectation for survivors is almost always the same—end the relationship with the perpetrator. The belief that leaving an abusive relationship is the only real way for mothers to protect their children is the heartbeat of the failure-to protect culture. Everything short of leaving is considered failing to protect your children. Its rhythm drives child protection practice and provides a strong backbeat to practice in many other sectors. Even domestic violence advocates sometimes cannot escape its highly gendered pulse.

Even when you include a few other "right" behaviors, such as calling the police or going into refuge, domestic violence survivors' protective efforts are judged by a very narrow set of criteria. When professionals perceive a survivor is failing to act according to these predetermined standards, she is often labeled, formally or informally, as failing to protect. Many of my conversations with social workers over the decades have gone something like this:

CHAPTER 6: THE MYTH OF FAILURE TO PROTECT

In each example, leaving is the answer. In each example, mothers who don't leave are at risk for being seen as failing to protect.

The Myth of Failure to Protect

Why the Failure-to-Protect Approach Is Inefficient, Ineffective, Unethical, and Unsafe

The term "failure to protect" refers to a type of neglectful maltreatment in child protection. In criminal law statutes, failure to protect may be a crime. But in order to really understand the influence and impact of failure to protect as a concept used against domestic violence survivors, it is best to understand it as a form of culture expressed through a set of informal customs or informal practices. These customs or unwritten laws add up to a culture of failure to protect that is embedded in child protection and other systems. It is expressed, in big and little ways, throughout the interactions of professionals with one another and with the family. Failure-to- protect culture appears in everyday professional practice. It's there in these cases:

> Whenever a case presentation starts with the statement that "the big issue is that the mom keeps going back to him" instead of the statement that "the danger here is from the dad's violence"
>
> Whenever someone says that "she let him back in the house" without ever exploring the dynamics of coercion or the failures of systems to hold the perpetrator accountable
>
> Every time a practitioner focuses more heavily on the survivor's trauma history instead of the perpetrator's coercive control as the key issue related to domestic violence
>
> Every time a mother's addiction or mental health gets more attention than a father's violence

CHAPTER 6: THE MYTH OF FAILURE TO PROTECT

It's just there embedded in almost every interaction touching domestic violence and children, and like a slow drip of water on one side of a balance scale, eventually all the small interactions add up, turning the formal and informal judgments of professionals and even family members against her.

On paper, failure to protect refers to the gender-neutral concept that a parent can and should be held responsible for failing to act to prevent harm to a child at the hands of another person. Advocates for children believe that failure to protect is an essential tool for the protection of children. It is not enough for parents to be liable for engaging in acts of *commission*, such as physical or sexual abuse, that threaten a child's safety and well-being—they must also be held liable for acts of *omission*, failing to act when they should have to protect their child from harm. Criminal and civil consequences for these "sins of omission" are designed to increase pressure on parents to prioritize their children's needs over their own and to punish them when they fail to act in the state's definition of the child's best interest.

In real life, failure to protect is a highly biased, commonly used weaponization of motherhood against domestic violence survivors. Failure to protect is much more likely to be applied to mothers than fathers.[1][2][3] Differing expectations of mothers and fathers is such a powerful force that in some instances alleged crimes of omission may be given more weight than crimes of commission. For example, mothers of children who have been physically abused and severely injured by their male partner have received longer criminal court sentences for their failure to protect than the perpetrator received for committing the violence. Investigative journalist Alex Campbell[4] found numerous cases that illustrated this point. In one example, a father who'd broken multiple bones in his daughter's body received two years in jail while the child's mother was sentenced to thirty years for failing to intervene. In most of these cases, the mothers were also victimized by the same person who abused her child. Some US states allow lengthy criminal sentences, up to life in prison, for failure-to-protect types of crimes.

Failure to protect has been and continues to be child protection's axiomatic, primary reflex to cases involving domestic violence. Child protection systems, which have made mothers the focal point of child protection interventions for decades, fervently—and often slavishly—apply the failure-to-protect framework to solve the genuinely complex and real problem of domestic violence perpetrators' behaviors to children. Failure to protect offers a seductive solution. Drawn in by perceived simplicity, case workers engage the parent that the system is more familiar and comfortable with—the mother. They hold her responsible to get the child and herself away from someone who is dangerous to both her and the children—regardless of the impediments placed in her way by the perpetrator, unsupportive cultural attitudes, economic barriers, biased systems, and well-intentioned but poorly prepared professionals.

Instead of being the best approach to domestic violence and children, it is a myth that needs to be questioned and challenged and, I believe, ultimately discarded as a tool for keeping children safe. It is neither reflective of the reality of families nor the best approach for professionals. It is inefficient, ineffective, unethical, and unsafe. Gendered in its application, it often creates more problems than it fixes. The myth of failure to protect needs to be confined to history in favor of innovative approaches that center on the responsibility of the perpetrator as parent. It needs to be replaced with partnering with, instead of blaming, survivors.

A perfect example of failure-to-protect culture: Some US states even allow for the prosecution of a parent who "allows" a child to watch the parent suffer the abuse.

CHAPTER 6: THE MYTH OF FAILURE TO PROTECT

In this chapter, I describe how failure to protect is a set of customs or culture that is the quintessential expression of ignoring fathers and blaming mothers. I outline four pillars of failure-to-protect culture. We also look at how failure to protect is an inefficient, ineffective, unethical, and unsafe way to approach the intersection of domestic violence and children.

> **Inefficient:** it creates unnecessary barriers to accurate assessments and to partnering with the protective parent around her children's safety and well-being.
>
> **Ineffective:** it focuses on the wrong person.
>
> **Unethical:** it creates unfairness in its gendered application and the way it blames and harms already marginalized mothers.
>
> **Unsafe:** it creates danger for families and workers.

Finally, I show how the Safe & Together Model shines a light on what really works to protect children by shifting the focus back on domestic violence perpetration as a parenting choice.

The Four Pillars of Failure-to-Protect Culture

The four pillars of failure-to-protect culture lay out the underlying beliefs and values that undergird the informal customs and practices. By understanding them, we have a greater chance at dismantling this harmful approach and replacing it with a cultural practice much more beneficial to workers and families.

- **Pillar 1:** Gendered and racist expectations of men and women as parents
- **Pillar 2:** An incomplete understanding of the adult survivors' protective efforts

- **Pillar 3:** The flawed assumption that the mother's insight into the impact of domestic violence on her children automatically makes those children safer
- **Pillar 4:** The wrongful focus on the relationship between the parents, instead of the perpetrator's pattern of behavior, as the source of harm to children in domestic violence situations.

Let's look at each one in turn.

Pillar 1—Gendered and Racist Expectations of Men and Women as Parents

Early in my career when I was training child protection workers about domestic violence perpetrators, I would talk about how they could develop case plans that would set expectations for behavior change for perpetrators. Often, a variation on the following conversation took place:

It was clear that they had no built-in, automatic sense of accountability for fathers like they did for mothers. These conversations were part of my initial introduction to failure-to-protect culture, where violent fathers are ignored and survivor mothers are held accountable. These discussions introduced me to the awareness that most of the practice around failure to protect is not written down. Only a tiny proportion of failure-to-protect practice is guided by written law, policy, or guidance. Eventually it became clear that failure to protect is about *culture* and *unwritten rules*, or customs, and those rules are shaped by wildly differing expectations of motherhood and fatherhood.

> *Failure to protect and mother-blaming is rooted in gender inequality and misogyny.*
>
> —Beth Ann, S&TI faculty, independent consultant, US

Failure-to-protect culture rests on and contributes to a highly gendered view of parenting. Mothers' behaviors are heavily scrutinized, and male caregivers' choices and behaviors are almost completely invisible. A gendered response to families is not a new practice. In their thought-provoking review of child protective service's response to domestic violence across decades, Cathy Humphreys and Deborah Absler, in their 2011 article "History Repeating: Child Protection Responses to Domestic Violence,"[5] identified a hundred-year pattern of social services "disciplining women/excusing men." Their work and the work of others—such as Julia Krane, Lorraine Davies, Simon Lapierre, and Kris McDaniel-Miccio—outline the highly gendered focus on the duty of women to be the fierce protectors of their children. In addition to being gendered, failure to protect is also colonized and racist. The parenting of mothers from First Nation, Black, and other minority groups is more likely to be judged. Historical and current views that marginalized women are "less than" white women means that their parenting is already suspect even before they are scrutinized as domestic violence survivors.

These beliefs aren't limited to laypeople. They are often deeply held by professionals who are making assessments and decisions that fill in those fuzzy areas left wide open by the lack of detail in (sin-of-omission) statutes and policies. I've witnessed professionals justify failure-to-protect practice by invoking metaphors comparing ideal mothers to "a momma bear protecting her cubs," fiercely protective and willing to go to any lengths to protect their children, including putting themselves in harm's way. I remember one female professional saying to me, "If that was my child, I would be willing to jump out of the second story of a burning building to save her." The message was clear: If a mother is not engaging in superhuman acts of protection that might endanger her own life, sacrificing her life for her child's, then she is guilty of "failure to protect." I've rarely heard anyone articulate the alternative view, that of course we can't expect her to act in ways that are likely to increase the danger to her or the children.

On the flip side, I have rarely heard professionals express the same level of emotion toward the obligations of fathers to stop hurting their children. Strong emotions are usually reserved for the behavior of mothers. For example, during a conversation with a social worker, I heard her express strong anger and frustration with a survivor who was "lying" to her about her domestic violence victimization. When I asked if she felt the same level of anger at the perpetrator for engaging in the violence in the first place, she responded with awkward silence. Gently, I said, "Do you think your anger at this mother has any impact on her willingness to talk to you about what is happening?"

Pillar 2—An Incomplete Understanding of the Adult Survivors' Protective Efforts

Mona Eltahawy, the brilliant Egyptian-born feminist writer, outlines in *The Seven Necessary Sins for Women and Girls*[6] the global unwritten rules of patriarchy and how women and girls need to fight them with anger, profanity, lust, and other "sinful," rule-breaking behaviors. Patriarchy defines the *unwritten rules* of behavior for women and girls (and men and boys). At its core, failure-to-protect culture is an expression of patriarchy. It is about professionals, family, and friends (everyone else but the mother herself) defining how a woman is supposed to act when her partner is being abusive to her, the children, or both. None of these definitions is codified in law or administrative policy—but the definitions still profoundly shape practice.

> *Obviously, failure to protect has run deep in child protection work for a long, long time. We decided to pivot to the perpetrator—the person who's the source of harm. I think that's a big change for child safety. I was a domestic violence worker before, and we demonized child protection for their stance on failure to protect, you know. That's why we didn't like them. We didn't talk to them because we knew that was wrong. Mother-blaming has sexism and misogyny at the heart of it.*
>
> —Emma R., domestic and family violence principal project officer, Australia

Spend any time working around professionals in the area of domestic violence, and you will hear mothers who are domestic violence survivors evaluated through the lens of two major questions:
- Does she have *insight* into the impact of the domestic violence on her children?
- Has she engaged in the *appropriate* protective behaviors in regard to her children?

The two questions are strongly linked because the main way that a survivor's insight is measured is by whether she engages in the correct, professionally sanctioned protective efforts. This almost always means leaving. Calling the police. Going to a refuge. Getting counseling for herself. This is what a "good" mother does. This is what a protective mother does. Acting in accordance with professionals' definition of "appropriate" protective behaviors demonstrates she has *insight*. Having insight equals leaving the relationship. Leaving a relationship is equated with being a good mother. It's very circular logic. For domestic violence survivors, leaving is the *sine qua non,* or the mandatory behavior, for being considered a good mother.

The problem with professionals defining *appropriate* protective behaviors is that it ignores many of the realities of adult and child survivors' lives. These realities take the form of diverse challenges and barriers. They also involve the survivor engaging a much wider spectrum of protective efforts. The culture of failure to protect ignores the wisdom contained in the oft-repeated mantra of the women's sector: *Domestic violence survivors are experts in their own experiences*. What does this phrase mean? It means that survivors' knowledge gives them unique insight into the pros and cons of different types of protective actions. One survivor may have learned that calling the police escalates her partner's violence and control. Another may have learned that calling the police is an effective intervention, stopping future assaults. Survivors actively test out different protective strategies and forms of resistance, informally analyzing the results to see what makes the situation better or worse and modifying their behavior based on their results. They've lived it. They've guided their children through all this. They may well still be living it. Failure-to-protect culture ignores all the ways that survivors are *already* protective of children—even when they aren't actively trying to leave the relationship. A comment by a Scottish survivor interviewed for this book illustrates this reality:

CHAPTER 6: THE MYTH OF FAILURE TO PROTECT

> **"***I was constantly pointing out to the social work department the things I'm doing right. They never brought up anything I was doing right. For them it was all about what I was doing wrong.***"**
>
> —Naomi, survivor, Scotland

Let's do a thought experiment. Imagine a survivor who believes that her partner will do everything in his power to take her children away from her if she ends the relationship. She believes this because he has proven his willingness and ability to really hurt her. She knows that this will also include not providing any child support and slandering her to professionals, her employer, her religious community, her family, and her friends. If she leaves, she knows her housing, financial, and childcare situation will become more precarious. She also knows that the children do not witness most of the physical abuse or the other forms of abuse. She also knows that their current situation has them attending a good school, living close to friends in a nice house in a nice neighborhood. All of this would be lost if she were to separate, with no guarantee of safety and stability for herself and her children. Now add in complications like she or the children having chronic health issues or the likelihood that she would experience racism while pursuing new housing or new employment. Add in that she comes from a culture that shuns or punishes women who leave or divorce their partners even when there is abuse. What if she were to lose her immigration status if she got divorced or what if she had to leave her community in order to fully escape the perpetrator?

It's pretty clear that, for this survivor, any attempt to leave the relationship (and the home) would come with a very high cost and lots of risk and uncertainty for herself and her children. So she decides to stay in the relationship. Now ask yourself these questions:

- Does this mean she is not actively trying to make the situation better for herself and her children?
- Does it mean that she is not engaging in protective efforts?

Someone who believes that leaving is the only true demonstration of protective efforts would answer: No, she's not being protective. But not leaving doesn't mean she is not engaging in protective efforts. Let's take a look at all the things this mother might be doing that are protective that might not fit the professional's limited definition of *appropriate*:

> Working extremely hard, in the context of chaos and disruptions caused by the perpetrator, to maintain the children's routines related to eating, sleeping, and going to school
>
> Using kinship networks to intervene with the perpetrator and help protect her children
>
> Creating safety plans with the children about how to remove themselves if their father's behaviors escalate
>
> Making regular attempts at setting boundaries with the perpetrator—"Don't talk to me that way in front of the children"—that are ignored and overridden by the perpetrator
>
> Keeping the children medically up-to-date and connected to a therapist despite the barriers placed in her way by the perpetrator's behaviors.

All these actions are protective and don't involve leaving or calling the police. Any balanced assessment of a survivor's protective capacities needs to consider these types of behaviors, which are often invisible due to failure-to-protect culture's high expectations of women as parents.

The focus on whether the survivor *appropriately* protects her children also ignores how the systems influence her decisions. The systems can contribute to continuing danger and teach survivors that the *appropriate* actions do not make her or her children safer. For example, how do professionals factor in the failure of systems to grant and endorse orders of protection? How often do courts grant orders that prevent the perpetrator from contacting her but ignore her request to prevent his contact with the children? How many survivors engage in *appropriate* behaviors to protect their children, only to see them endangered and harmed all over again when family court hands them over to the perpetrator? Failure-to-protect culture ignores the role that systems play in creating ongoing danger for children. Instead, it makes the survivor the sole person responsible. She's not only expected to overcome the perpetrator's actions but also the failures, limitations, and missteps of systems.

Mothers' protective efforts are regularly ignored, minimized, devalued, and even twisted around to be seen as deficits because mothers are perceived to be the primary caretakers. Higher standards for women make these efforts invisible, so they never show up in the "credit" side of the ledger as legitimate protective efforts when they are weighed and measured by professionals. Failure-to-protect culture thrives on this shared structural ignorance—the built-in, nonaccidental, persistent blindness to much of the hard parenting work, acts of resistance, and protective efforts of mothers who are domestic violence survivors.

Pillar 3—The Magic of Insight

Failure-to-protect culture and custom relies heavily on what I refer to as the "magic of insight." The thinking goes like this: "If she understands she's a victim and also how bad domestic violence is for her children, she can and will make the 'right' choice—to leave the relationship." When you believe in the magic of insight, all barriers to leaving safely melt away. Those inculcated into failure-to-protect culture think that education and awareness in the dynamics of domestic violence are the only steps necessary to move forward. And if the children remain in danger, it is the survivor's lack of insight that is the primary problem, not the perpetrator's continuous choice to harm her, the children, and the functioning of the family, and it's not due to the systems' failures either.

From the viewpoint of those with child protective services and many others, *insight* magically leads to *appropriate* action.

> Her insight and understanding that domestic violence is bad for her children = her leaving.
>
> Her not leaving the relationship = her strict liability for any harm that befalls the children.
>
> In the end, everything comes down to this: "Did she leave the relationship?"

This belief system is applied universally, with very little consideration of the context. It is very tempting to believe that insight is the golden key to safety. The problem is that insight does not provide the survivor with superpowers to overcome the reality of the perpetrator's pattern, the systems' failures, or economic barriers. Insight does not make risk factors any less dangerous, does not automatically create support and resources for safety, and does not change failed systems.

Here are just a few examples of how reality collides with the mistaken belief that insight automatically makes leaving the relationship possible, desirable, and safe. Insight or understanding by itself doesn't wipe away the dangers posed by these issues:

- the perpetrator's behavior pattern and the risk it poses to the survivor and children—for example, whether specific threats have been made to punish, harm, or kill the adult survivor, the children, himself, or extended family if the survivor leaves
- the perpetrator's court-ordered, postseparation access to the children, with its continued or escalated risk of harm—for example, whether the perpetrator may use unsupervised access time to physically, emotionally, and/or sexually abuse the children

- the perpetrator's false allegations made to child protective services or accusations of parental alienation made in family court
- cultural and economic consequences for leaving—for example, accusations of "dishonoring" the family and other forms of punishment and blame from extended family; loss of job; or loss of other supports, such as safe, accessible childcare when relocating

The "insight equals protective action" requires professionals to ignore everything about the situation that insight cannot automatically make vanish. In this way, failure-to-protect culture ignores the complexity of the reality of perpetrators' patterns and limitations of systems—substituting instead the magical thinking that "insight" equals safety and "appropriate" solutions.

Pillar 4—Seeing the Relationship or the Survivors' Choices, not the Perpetrator, as the Source of Harm to Children

"Appropriate protective behaviors" and "insight" are tightly linked with the misattribution of the source of the risk to children. The belief that the source of the harm and danger to children is the couple's relationship, not the perpetrator's behaviors, creates the following corollary: leaving or ending the relationship automatically equals child safety. It glibly—and dangerously—sets the expectations that if a mother ends the relationship, it will automatically end the risk and harm to the children.

When one sees the relationship dynamic as the wellspring of the danger to children, it is easy to see how ending the relationship is the logical and desirable answer. From there it is an easy leap to blame mothers for not taking the logical step of leaving. The kicker comes when people start reverse engineering an explanation for why she hasn't left—if she is not leaving, she must not have insight into how domestic violence is harmful to the children, or she's choosing him over her children. This explanation becomes the impetus for referring her to services so she can gain insight and then engage in the appropriate action—to leave! And when none of this happens—because the mother knows those steps don't address the person causing the harm—interventions with survivors escalate, often involving court cases and removal of children from her care.

But in reality, separation and the end of relationships offer zero guarantees that the violence and coercive control will stop or that the children will be better off. Because violence is often just one manifestation of coercive control, the perpetrator's influence and ability to hurt and control doesn't automatically go away with physical separation or the end of a relationship. In fact, certain dangers may escalate, and new threats, like the use of family court to harass and control, may appear. Children may have new types of risks, such as child abuse and neglect perpetrated during unsupervised visits or custody. Increased housing and financial instability could lead to greater child protection involvement. Perpetrators may start or escalate their campaign to manipulate systems against survivors, alleging bad parenting, mental health, or addiction issues. None of this means the danger of physical assault disappears. Postseparation, the risk of homicide may escalate and even encompass risk to the children. For those indoctrinated into failure-to-protect culture, rarely does their perspective widen to even consider that staying in the relationship may be part of the best safety plan possible.

Inefficient, Ineffective, Unethical, and Unsafe

While no one person is responsible for creating the four pillars of failure-to-protect culture, every individual practitioner who wants better outcomes for adult and child survivors has a responsibility to understand the negative effects of those pillars and to take steps to find a better way. In this section, I show how failure-to-protect culture practices are inefficient, ineffective, unsafe, and unethical. Overlapping and reinforcing in nature, these four outcomes demonstrate how costly failure-to-protect culture is to individuals, families, communities, organizations, and society at large. Let's look at each of these outcomes one at a time.

Inefficient

Talk to any frontline child protection worker and many other professionals, and you will quickly realize one of their most precious resources is time. Time pressure is enormous for anyone who works in systems that respond to a never-ending series of referrals with numerous time-sensitive mandates, like twenty-four- or seventy-two-hour deadlines for starting investigations. By promoting adversarial and suspicious attitudes toward domestic violence survivors, failure-to-protect culture creates unnecessary obstacles to constructive partnerships between practitioners and protective parents. I would argue that failure-to-protect culture wastes workers' time and other precious agency resources like goodwill with community partners and money that ends up getting spent on avoidable removals of children.

Trust and rapport, which are central to any helping relationship, are like a bridge between two people. When working with survivors, professionals have complete control over how they build their half of the bridge—how they approach their engagement with the survivor. It's up to the survivor to decide if it feels safe and beneficial to her and her children to step onto that bridge. For example, professionals can decide whether they talk to survivors in a way that clearly identifies perpetrators' behaviors as the source of the harm to the children. Or they can choose to use mutualizing or blaming language. They can use a narrow or wide definition of protective behaviors. Each of these choices impacts the quality of the bridge and whether it feels safe and strong to the survivor. The safety and strength of the bridge has an impact on the efficiency (and effectiveness) of the interaction with the survivor.

Every time a practitioner approaches a survivor with statements like "I'm here because you and your partner got into a fight last night in front of the children" instead of "I'm here because your partner assaulted you in front of the children last night," that survivor is less likely to open up about the situation. Negative practices create barriers to engagement that are avoidable and in complete control of the practitioner. Said plainly, mutualizing and blaming language costs the agency in terms of time, speed, and accuracy of assessments. It can lead to poorly developed, ill-suited, and dangerous case plans.

> ❝ *I say 'Here's twenty things that the survivor did to protect his or her children—do you still believe that the parent failed to protect?' I just love asking that question because it goes back to self-accountability and it's really helped child protection workers to think more about what they write. Do I really need to write this sentence? If I do, I better be damn sure that I know that this parent failed to protect. If I'm not, then I need to find out what this parent did to protect their child.* ❞
>
> —Eloise, independent consultant, child-adult survivor, US

When practitioners approach survivors with victim-blaming attitudes, questions, and statements, it usually means they will get more resistance. More resistance means less information about these issues:

- the perpetrators' pattern of behavior
- the impact of those behaviors on the children
- the survivors' protective efforts

Practice-generated resistance—that is, resistance created by the way the practitioners approach a case—has real costs. Agencies pay these costs in different ways. Cases take longer to resolve, so caseloads are higher than they might be. Workers spend more time on each case because they seem more complex and difficult than they might be if the practice was more domestic violence informed. These inefficiencies cost money, time, and worker morale.

But the biggest inefficiencies (and harms to the family) are related to preventable child removals.

It is difficult to quantify the social, emotional, and familial costs of preventable removals of children. Even in homes where there is abuse, separation from one's family can be a source of trauma. A child's connections with culture and family can become attenuated. Children may experience additional trauma and disruption if they are moved between foster homes. Data suggests that children in foster homes experience abuse at even higher rates than the general population. Add to this the impact on the parent(s) who lose their children. These effects can be profound and even deadly, including grief, depression, and suicidality. These are the costs that adult and child domestic violence survivors experience when child protective services engages in removals that could be prevented but for failure-to-protect culture.

Other social and financial costs of failure-to-protect culture include these consequences:

- continued contentious relationships between child protective services and domestic violence victims advocates
- decreased trust between child protective services and communities that have been overrepresented in the child protection system
- higher-than-necessary worker turnover rates because workers are expected to enforce unfair practices directed at domestic violence survivors

Failure-to-protect culture also creates broader inefficiencies because domestic violence survivors are less likely to reach out for help, including calling the police, because of the fear of being blamed and then losing their children. This is particularly powerful for First Nation, Black, and other marginalized women who have been losing children, due to racism and colonization, for generations. When domestic violence survivors come into contact with a child protection system that is poised to blame them for the behavior of their partner, they often withhold information about the domestic violence for fear of being judged, blamed, and eventually traumatized by having their children taken.

CHAPTER 6: THE MYTH OF FAILURE TO PROTECT

The potential financial costs of avoidable removals are tremendous because governments spend such large sums on child protective services, particularly when it comes to the placement of children in out-of-home care. As a thought experiment, let's try to figure out this cost by examining the potential cost savings if a certain percentage of child removals was prevented due to improved practice in domestic violence cases. In 2016/2017 in England, the average cost per child looked after by the state was £56,000 (US$67,000 as of February 2023). Overall, the total national budget for looked-after children in England was £4 billion (US$4.8 billion as of February 2023).[7]

Determining what percentage of these removals was related to domestic violence is challenging since data in this area is so poor. Yet we are not without ways to begin to piece the puzzle together. Using US data on domestic violence and foster care trauma treatment as a guide, we can get some idea of the percentage of children in foster care who come from homes impacted by domestic violence perpetrators. In one study, half the children in foster care who were receiving trauma treatment were there solely because of domestic violence. When that same study considered complex trauma (more than one type of trauma) the number jumps to over 70 percent.[8] I've been told more than once by child protection leaders in different parts of the world that 80 percent of their cases have domestic violence in them as a relevant factor. In jurisdictions such as Ohio, which has worked at identifying the impact of domestic violence on the child protection caseload, we have data that suggests that domestic violence in cases tops out above 40 percent.[9] A recent Ontario study confirmed that exposure to intimate partner violence was "the largest proportion of maltreatment investigations."[10]

So, for the purposes of this exercise, let's make a guesstimate based on the range of numbers above. Let's assume that the number of children in foster care where domestic violence is one of the factors leading to the removal is 50 percent.[11] Now let's add in *Safe & Together* data that associates the Model with a 50 percent decrease in out-of-home placements for domestic violence. Based on these parameters, meaningful implementation of domestic violence-informed child protection practices in England might lead to savings

139

of £1 billion annually. Even if we went more conservative in our numbers, decreasing domestic violence as a deciding factor in removal to 25 percent of cases and then reducing Safe & Together Model's impact to 25 percent, we would still have annual UK cost savings of £250 million (US$299 million as of February 2023). In Australia in 2013–2014, A$2.2 billion (US$1.5 billion) was spent on out-of-home care for children.[12] Using the same formulas, the range of savings would be between A$138 million (US$87 million at February 2023) to A$550 million (US$370 billion as of February 2023) annually.

Potential Children in Care Cost Savings from Safe & Together Model Implementation

Number of Children in Care	Annual National Cost	Annual Cost Savings if S&T is Applied (Range)
United Kingdom	£4 billion	£250 million–£1 billion
United States	US$6 billion	US$375 million–$1.5 billion
Australia	A$2.2 billion	A$138 million–$550 million

The potential financial savings from pivoting away from failure-to-protect culture to a perpetrator pattern-based approach are real and noteworthy. The human savings, in terms of children, families, and communities, are priceless.

Ineffective

How crazy would I appear if I told you I wanted to fix the problem of drivers running stop signs by educating car *passengers* about the dangers of failing to stop when legally required? How effective would this effort be in ending this dangerous behavior? Not effective at all. As you might have assumed already, the analogy refers to the amount of energy, time, and money focused on analyzing, educating, pressuring, and punishing domestic violence survivors as compared to the person who is actually choosing to engage in violence and coercive control. Ignoring the perpetrator of child abuse and neglect and instead focusing most of our energy on the nonoffending parent is an ineffective approach for any system that wants to keep children safe from domestic violence.

Failure-to-protect culture is fundamentally ineffective because it doesn't address the danger to children at its source.

The dangers and harms that children experience from domestic violence derive solely and exclusively from the behaviors of the perpetrator. Problem solving 101 teaches us that the definition of the problem determines the solutions. If we define the problem as "she keeps choosing him over the children," we focus our attention on educating the survivor or coercing her to leave. If we define the problem as "the father has engaged in a series of behaviors that have harmed the children," then a completely different set of solutions and strategies present themselves. Not only do we try to intervene with the perpetrator directly, but it completely reorients our relationship to the survivor, opening the door to collaboration instead of contention.

The widespread prevalence of postseparation violence and coercive control demonstrates one reason why failure-to-protect culture is ineffective. Many perpetrators turn to child protective services and family court to extend their abuse of adult and child survivors after the end of the couple's relationship. For example, a study from Canada shows that the majority of false allegations made to child protective services are coming from noncustodial parents, usually fathers, often in the context of custody battles.[13] It is easy to imagine that many of these false allegations are part of a wider pattern of coercive control by domestic violence perpetrators. Any approach that focuses on leaving as the answer to child safety will be dangerously ineffective at diagnosing continuing risk to adult and child survivors from perpetrators' manipulation of systems and from their postseparation violence, ongoing coercion, and child maltreatment.

To the detriment of adult and child survivors, failure-to-protect culture often allows the perpetrator to "disappear" from child protection radar and then "reappear" after the case is closed. I was often told a child protection investigation in a case of severe domestic violence was closed simply because there was a stay away order in place or the perpetrator was believed to no longer be in the home. This approach can have tragic consequences.

Case Example

A family was referred to child protective services after the father had severely assaulted the mother a few weeks earlier. Despite a warrant for the father's arrest, the police failed to search for him. The belief, with no evidence behind it, was that he had fled the area. Child protective services closed the case for the same reason and without significant involvement. Within a short period of time, he murdered the mother. This is what was true: He hadn't fled and was actually still having contact with at least one of his children during this period. While it's impossible to know if more active police and child protection involvement could have prevented this murder, it is important to acknowledge that the assumption that risk had disappeared was used to justify a less-than-robust response.

Nor is failure-to-protect culture effective in addressing children's needs in relationship to a parent who was and is a perpetrator. Ignoring the perpetrator of the violence and abuse, pretending that the person is no longer a factor in his children's lives, is hiding a dangerous reality. One study showed that 70 percent of children remain in contact with an abusive father postseparation.[14] A study by Katie Lamb, Cathy Humphreys, and Kelsey Hegarty [15] showed us that the children had very specific, understandable, and reasonable expectations for a father who abused their mother. The children and young people they interviewed wanted reparations in the form of acknowledgment of the harm caused by the abuse and in the form of positive behavior change, including positive parenting and better treatment of their mother. A failure-to-protect approach, which is heavily correlated with no or minimal interventions with abusive fathers, does very little to help children get their needs met.

> It's ineffective in other ways too. When domestic violence perpetrators are ignored as parents, this is often reflected in very tangible ways. They are less likely to be interviewed during a child protection case, which means their perceptions of their own behavior and its impact on their children will not be reflected in the case documentation. They are also less likely to have expectations or requirements placed on them by child protective services. And even when expectations are placed on them, their lack of compliance is less likely to trigger consequences for them. Without expectations or requirements being mandated to engage in services, perpetrators are less likely to take steps to change. Without clear expectations, the perpetrator's *failure to change* is not measured or documented. Each of these practices reduces the effectiveness of the intervention by ignoring the parent who has perpetrated the violence and abuse.

It would be better to be talking about perpetrators' "failure to change" instead of survivors' failure to protect.

And there are broader consequences —failure to intervene with the perpetrator increases the survivor's distrust and skepticism of professionals and the system. And the ineffectiveness may compound upon itself. When the nonabusive parent observes members of child protective services ignoring the perpetrator, it is easy for her to conclude that those professionals are also scared of him. It also may contribute to the survivor feeling abandoned to deal with the perpetrator herself. And perhaps most broadly, it fails to address the needs and desires of survivors, children, and communities that want their fathers to get help. It's help that is more than just his arrest; it's help that creates real, sustainable, meaningful change, particularly around his parenting.

Unethical

While the argument that failure-to-protect culture is unfair to survivors has not significantly moved the dial on systems change, the argument that it is unethical tackles the issue of fairness from a slightly different angle. Most professionals—whether they be social workers, counselors, or lawyers—have core values and ethics. These values and ethics act as a guide for decision-making and everyday professional conduct.

In Australia, social workers are bound by three core principles: respect for persons, social justice, and professional integrity. In the United States, social workers' core values are "service, social justice, dignity and worth of the person, importance of human relationships, integrity, and competence." In the United Kingdom, social workers' core values are human rights, social justice, and professional integrity. Gender inequality is a top issue when it comes to human rights, dignity, respect for persons, and social justice. So is the unnecessary removal of children and the overrepresentation of marginalized families in child protection systems.

If we consider the values and practices associated with failure-to-protect culture, it is easy to see where they rub against social work ethics. Take a look at this short chart:

Social Work Ethics and Domestic Violence-Informed Practice

	Which is more consistent with each social work ethics?	
Social Work Ethics	Failure-to-Protect Culture	Domestic Violence-Informed Practice
Social justice/ human rights	Removing children unnecessarily from protective parents	➤ Keeping children with protective parents
Professional integrity	Working with domestic violence as a factor without training or support for working with perpetrators	➤ Receiving training, support, and supervision to work with domestic violence perpetrators
Respect for persons	Not assessing for the full spectrum of survivors' protective efforts	➤ Giving survivors full credit for their efforts to promote child safety and well-being

Blaming mothers for the behavior of their male partners, ignoring fathers as important members of families, and the associated avoidable removal of children are some of the key ways that failure-to-protect culture flies in the face of social work values.

> **❝** *I used to work in child protection, so failure to protect was the language that I constantly used. I remember writing that in court reports and case notes. That was definitely my language, and I truly believed in it. We believed women were able to protect their children from family violence—if they weren't doing it, then they were failing to protect.* **❞**
>
> —Karen, child and young person practice lead, Australia

Unsafe

The fourth negative outcome from failure-to-protect culture is increased, avoidable danger for workers and survivors. When the survivor is more of the focal point of the case than the perpetrator and his behaviors, basic mistakes related to safety are more likely and even inevitable. The following are some examples of increased safety risks to adult and child survivors:

- Practitioners force a survivor to take "appropriate" actions, backed up by the threat of child removal, when it is already known, based on the perpetrator's pattern, that action is very likely to escalate risk. For example, a survivor might be expected to demonstrate protective capacity by calling the police even though the perpetrator has threatened to kill her and the children if the police are called again.
- Practitioners pressure a survivor to leave the relationship when the perpetrator has made a credible threat to hurt the children or take the children from her in family court if she leaves him.
- Practitioners expect a survivor to guarantee the children will not be exposed to violence or not have any contact with the perpetrator when she doesn't have ultimate control over either.

I refer to these expectations and actions as "domestic violence destructive" systems behaviors. "Domestic violence destructive" practices are ones that increase dangers and/or push survivors away from systemic support. Failure-to-protect culture epitomizes "domestic violence destructive" practice through its threats to take children from adult survivors who do not conform to its unrealistic expectations.

> Professionals are also endangered when they are expected to turn a blind eye to perpetrators' patterns. The following are some examples related to professional risk and safety:
> - **Expecting professionals to engage a domestic violence perpetrator without a thorough assessment of whether or not he has a pattern of targeting others outside the family, especially professionals**
> - **Offering little to no training around safe engagement of perpetrators**
> - **Providing little to no formal support for professional safety planning and risk management when there is identified danger for the professional**

When I started doing consultations with child protection workers around domestic violence and children, I was shocked and worried about how poorly prepared they were to assess the danger they themselves might be facing from the perpetrator. One of the ways I would try to connect workers to the importance of knowing the perpetrator's patterns of behaviors was to explore that pattern as it related to their own safety. I would ask them the following:

> Does he have a pattern of threatening or assaulting people outside the family?
>
> How has he treated other professionals intervening with the family, including law enforcement personnel or previous caseworkers?

They often had zero clue about these or other aspects of the perpetrator's pattern. Child protection workers, who regularly meet with families in the family's home, have much greater vulnerability to violence than professionals who meet clients in their offices. Yet I found they were ill-equipped to manage the potential threats from domestic violence perpetrators. Compare this to law enforcement agencies that openly identify domestic violence calls as one of the most dangerous situations for their own officers.

Failure-to-protect culture promotes blindness to practitioners' own potential danger from a perpetrator, making them more vulnerable to fear, manipulation, collusion, and victim-blaming. It is a common part of perpetrators' patterns to target professionals through manipulation, intimidation, or outright violence. When it comes to worker safety and failure to protect, it's a question of chicken or egg. Failure-to-protect culture focuses the worker on the survivor, not the perpetrator's behaviors. This lack of attention to the perpetrator's pattern can increase worker danger. On the other hand, the lack of training and supervision regarding the worker safety related to engaging perpetrators may contribute to failure-to-protect thinking as it leaves the worker feeling ill-prepared and lacking confidence in engaging this difficult population. Lacking skills, confidence, and a mandate to meet with violent fathers means practitioners take the path of least resistance to achieve child safety—focusing on survivors.

How the Safe & Together Model Innovates to Solve the Problem of Failure to Protect

If failure-to-protect culture is a failure, what is an alternative paradigm for approaching the very real danger that domestic violence perpetrators present to children? In this section, I outline how the Safe & Together Model's "pivot to the perpetrator as parent" offers a different, better way—a way that is more efficient, effective, ethical, and safe because it stops ignoring fathers and ends mother-blaming.

CHAPTER 6: THE MYTH OF FAILURE TO PROTECT

Because so much of the Model is about the "how" of practice, let's start with reimagining the mother-blaming conversations at the beginning of the chapter from a perpetrator pattern-based approach. This approach directs us to consider the perpetrators' choices and behaviors, not the survivors' choices or the relationship as the source of the danger to children.

Failure-to-protect culture promotes blindness to practitioners' own potential danger from a perpetrator, making them more vulnerable to fear, manipulation, collusion, and victim-blaming.

CHAPTER 6: THE MYTH OF FAILURE TO PROTECT

While these conversations start out similarly to the ones that kicked off the chapter, these transformed versions give you a taste of how the Safe & Together Model's *pivot to the perpetrator* can replace failure to protect as an approach that meets the needs of families and child protective services. Pivoting to the perpetrator as the source of the harm to children offers a different approach to each of the four pillars that hold up failure-to-protect culture.

Failure-to-protect culture v. Pivot to the perpetrator.

	Failure-to-protect culture	Pivot to the perpetrator
Gendered and racist expectations and responsibility for child safety and well-being	Mothers are more responsible than fathers for child safety and well being; Marginalized mothers are judged more quickly and severely	Equal responsibility for children's safety and well-being
Definitions of protective behaviors	Limited to leaving/going to refuge/ending relationship/calling police	Uses a wider definition of protective behaviors and considers the role of system failures, culture, and perpetrator actions undermining the efficacy of survivors' protective efforts
The role of survivors' "insight" into the domestic violence	Survivors' insight equals leaving the relationship, which equals child safety	Recognition that survivors' "insight" does not automatically create safety
Identified source of the harm to children from domestic violence	The relationship and the survivors' choices are the source of harm to children	Perpetrators' behaviors are the source of the harm to children

CHAPTER 6: THE MYTH OF FAILURE TO PROTECT

Pivoting to the perpetrator actively combats gendered expectations of parenting by explicitly saying this: "Domestic violence perpetrators, in their role as caregivers and parents, are responsible for the harm their behavior causes to children, partner, and family."

This is a declaration of equality of responsibility. Fathers and other male caregivers who engage in coercive control are acting in their capacity as parents. If that male is a biological or adoptive parent, he is legally an equal parent with the mother, and his negative behaviors are betrayals of his parental obligations. In many jurisdictions, even if the male is not a legal guardian or parent, an adult living with children in a caregiver capacity has legal responsibilities to those children.

To increase accountability for abusive men as parents, we need to stop ignoring how fathers' behaviors and choices impact child, partner, and family functioning. Raising expectations for all fathers as parents makes it easier to hold violent fathers responsible for their actions.

Establishing equality of parenting expectations between fathers and mothers makes it easier to shine a spotlight on the parenting of fathers who are domestic violence perpetrators. Higher standards for all fathers, most of whom are not violent, brings the negative behaviors of those fathers who are violent into stark relief. Imagine if psychosocial assessments of families included asking mothers this question: "How does your partner show your children through his behavior that he respects you?" Questions like this one would uncover both positive and negative behaviors. While it would be a useful question regardless of gender, it would yield particularly useful information about a male caregiver whose influence on the functioning of children, the family, and the other parent is often completely ignored. This means both the positive and negative contributions of men are being ignored. This is unfair to men, women, and children.

> *The myth of failure to protect is a common theme—one that goes to blaming and not acknowledging a mother's protective capacities. And it also doesn't acknowledge the gender bias that moms are responsible for so many things. And dad? If he goes to work, he gets a gold star, right?*
>
> —Carol, advocate, The Domestic Violence Project, US

When the perpetrator's choices, not the survivor's, are seen as the source of the harm to children, the professionals will place less pressure on the survivor to demonstrate *insight* and the "appropriate" protective actions. Under failure-to-protect culture, survivors must have *insight* into harm from domestic violence to their children in order to do what professionals wrongly believe is the only answer—leave the relationship. If the professional understands that the perpetrator's behavior is the source of the problem, the question is no longer why the mother stays but instead becomes "How could a father act this way to his children and their mother?" Now it's *his insight* (or lack thereof) into his own behavior that is the central point of focus. This allows the relationship between the professional and the survivor to shift, creating the possibility for a productive partnership with the survivor whether she leaves the relationship or not. A consistent focus on the perpetrators' choices, change, and accountability is what is needed, not judgments on whether the survivors have *insight* or not.

The Safe & Together Model widens the definition of appropriate, valued acts beyond the standard menu, to include the "full-spectrum of the nonoffending parent's efforts to promote the safety and well-being of the child." Mothers who are protective deserve full credit for *everything* they do to resist their partners' coercive control and protect their children. Giving them credit for leaving or calling the police is not enough. Shifting away from failure-to-protect culture involves clearing away the fog of unequal gender expectations in order to see more clearly the day-to-day protective actions of the mother. This might involve turning clothes inside out so a child on the autism spectrum doesn't become upset by irritating seams, particularly since the child's upset tends to trigger an abusive response from his father. Or it may involve sending children to live with relatives to reduce their exposure to the perpetrator or making sure those children engage in meals and bedtime routines before the perpetrator comes home. *The Model acknowledges that mothers' mundane and everyday caregiving actions are heroic when they are accomplished in the context of abuse and violence.* The mother doesn't need to jump from a metaphorical burning building. By seeing and valuing these everyday protective actions, which take more work and energy in the context of the perpetrator's pattern, we are making visible what sexism has made invisible. This is the corollary of higher standards for men as parents—giving mothers who are survivors full credit for parenting efforts that are normally expected of them culturally.

A tick box that indicates the children are "medically up-to-date" hides the often very gendered reality of *who did the work*. This means when you have children who are medically up-to-date in the context of chaos and disruptions created by a domestic violence perpetrator, it is important to see that required extra effort from the survivor. For example, a survivor may need to borrow a car from her sister to go to the pediatrician because the perpetrator takes the car every day in order to keep her trapped at home. The everyday invisibility of the actions taken by mothers to keep children on track and to maintain the household means that when mothers are parenting in the context of a father's coercive control, two things are happening: 1) her extra hard work to keep the children fed, housed, and medically up-to-date is ignored and kept invisible and 2) the father is not held accountable for how he's undermining her parenting and making it harder for the children's needs to be met.

> *When working as a domestic abuse advocate in multiagency settings where we were considering the risk to the nonabusing parent and the child, it was really difficult to portray the effort made by the nonabusing parent to create a childhood where the children could have good experiences despite the abuse they were experiencing. David's approach helped us by breaking the process down into small steps. We learned to go into detail and ask and document, 'Why is the child not getting to their music lesson?' or 'Why is the child always late for school?' Typically, the mother is usually blamed because the father is not living in the house. The social worker or child protection worker or the judge believes that if the abusive parent is not living in the house, then the abuse stops, and the mother should just get on with things. So, the social worker or the judge decides that it's the mother's fault that the child's not getting to school on time or that extracurricular activities are being missed—when*

> *in fact, she's had to contend with constant texts the perpetrator sent during the night or he's kept the car, so she has no transport to take her child wherever they're supposed to be. She's experiencing constant harassment, she's exhausted due to lack of sleep, she's trying to work out ways to resolve the lack of transport because she knows what he's doing and why he's doing it, but no one else sees the effort she's making or what's happening—that's the problem. David's approach gave us a way to articulate the depth of the undermining of her parenting, to express all the stuff that's invisible. How does she say all that? When she's asked why, she says 'Didn't get much sleep last night.' She can't say anything else because it sounds like excuses, and we as advocates would also get undermined in our efforts to explain, so a framework like Safe & Together that social workers or judges could understand relatively easily was incredibly useful, and we began to see a change almost immediately.* 99

—Mhairi, violence against women and girls consultant, Scotland

By focusing on the impact of fathers' behaviors on child, partner, and family functioning and giving mothers full credit for their protective efforts, the Safe & Together Model is offering a two-pronged approach to demolishing gender bias as a weapon against survivors. With perpetrators' behavior at the center of discussion of child harm, it becomes harder to ignore the father's role. The concept of "perpetration as a parenting choice" (act of commission) is now the root cause of the problem, not the alleged failure to protect (act of omission). On the second front, with the broadening of the definition of "willing and able" and "appropriate" acts of protection to encompass day-to-day care actions, mothers get more credit for parenting in a "war zone." Both fathers' hurtful actions and survivors' strengths are made more visible. The result is a more effective, efficient, ethical, and safe foundation for practice in domestic violence cases.

The Safe & Together Model's principles focus on partnering with survivors and intervening with perpetrators as parents. For practitioners to have effective, efficient, ethical, and safe relationships with survivors, they must concentrate on identifying their protective efforts. But it is impossible to fully understand the survivors' protective efforts until the perpetrator's pattern of behavior is clearly understood. If practitioners approach a survivor with the assumption that she was engaging in protective efforts and safety planning for herself and her children before they ever showed up, if they are curious about learning what her efforts have been, and if they seek out information about her partner's pattern of coercive control, then the likelihood of constructive partnership around the safety and well-being of the children increases.

The power of practitioners partnering with survivors is eloquently captured in this quote from a survivor interviewed for this book:

> *I could relax, I guess, and allow them to do their job. And not only could I feel safe that they were competent to do their job, but I didn't have to do the job for them. I could just relax and focus on my children's safety and my own well-being. It was such a relief that I wasn't having to manage them as well.*
>
> —Jane, victim survivor, Australia

CHAPTER 6: THE MYTH OF FAILURE TO PROTECT

The Safe & Together Model's six-step partnering process lays out the steps for practitioners who want to shift away from failure-to-protect culture. The following are the six steps, with a brief description following each step:

1. **Affirm:** Clearly state that the perpetrator, not the survivor, is responsible for the harm to the children resulting from his actions.
2. **Ask:** Invite the survivor to share specifics of the perpetrator's pattern and its impact on her, her children, and the functioning of the family.
3. **Assess:** Explore with the survivor the full spectrum of her efforts to promote the children's safety and well-being in the context of the abuse.
4. **Validate:** Explicitly validate those protective efforts and strengths.
5. **Collaboratively Plan:** Combine the mother's knowledge of the perpetrator and the wisdom she already gleaned from her own efforts with the professionals' skills, knowledge, and resources to develop a plan to improve the situation.
6. **Document:** Record the information about the perpetrator's actions, the impact of those actions, and the survivors' strengths so this critical information can inform future efforts and be shared with other systems when necessary (being mindful how sensitive information, which might compromise safety, is handled).

This is a behavioral, practical, concrete approach that is accessible to anyone regardless of that person's training, background, or theoretical orientation. The exploration of the perpetrator's pattern of behavior, its impact on child, partner, and family functioning, and the survivor's protective behaviors changes conversations. The behavioral nature of the approach interrupts the seduction of the failure-to-protect culture, replacing it with common sense, easy-to-see facts, and easy-to-follow steps for creating effective partnerships with survivors.

Final Thoughts on Dismantling the Culture of Failure to Protect

Failure-to-protect culture has no place in domestic violence-informed practice. Yes, this is a bold statement. Failure-to-protect culture represents the weaponization of motherhood against survivors. Harmful on the best of days, it's particularly unconscionable when there is a better way—a perpetrator pattern-based approach—to end the risk domestic violence creates for children. Harm to children from domestic violence can always be framed around the concerns related to the perpetrator's pattern and his ongoing access to the children.

This shift requires a deep commitment to be curious about the survivors' protective efforts and acts of resistance. Each survivor must be approached from the assumption that she is actively planning safety for herself and her children. The job of the professional is to be curious about those actions and to find evidence, when it's there, of those active efforts. It is upon this assessment of her willingness and ability to protect that effective partnerships are born.

> *I did the CORE training with some newly qualified social workers who'd been in practice for a year, and they said, 'Why would the mother be blamed?' That felt like the hope for the future.*
>
> —Debbie, practice development coordinator, Scotland

One case really solidified for me the correlation between professionals' determination that a survivor was active in protecting her children and the professionals partnering with survivors. In this instance, there was a high level of concern for the dangerousness of the father, who no longer lived in the home. Everyone was worried about his potential for serious, life-threatening violence. Despite this danger, the social workers were working in partnership with the mother to increase her safety and the safety of the children. Why were they partnering with her instead of just removing the children? The answer: The mother was building a concrete "panic room" in the house so they all could retreat there in the event of an attack by the father. Because they felt the mother was actively working to protect her children, the social work team members were bending over backward to keep the children with their mother. Despite the high level of danger, the mother's dramatic efforts to protect the children convinced the social workers that she was not failing to protect—even though the danger level was high.

While you may or may not agree with the decision to leave those children in that home, what I learned that day was that social workers will move heaven and earth to keep children with a survivor they believe in, even when the danger remains high. When protective efforts are measurable, social workers will fight hard to keep children safe and together with that protective parent. Not every parent can or should build a panic room to convince social workers that she is a worthy, protective parent. Everyday protective efforts deserve the same attention and value. When that happens, we will see the end to failure-to-protect culture and an explosion of perpetrator-focused child safety practice.

CHAPTER 7

The Myth of Perpetrator Accountability

For the first public speaking event of my career, around thirty years ago, I wanted to share my thoughts on the term "batterer accountability." What do we mean when we say we want to hold domestic violence perpetrators accountable? To what standards or expectations are we holding them accountable? What does it mean to hold them accountable for the harm they have caused?

Despite my first-time jitters, the talk went well. It was my first public effort at exploring the jargon of accountability—how that exploration helps us improve outcomes for survivors and promote meaningful, sustained behavior change and helps us see where the jargon creates blind spots or limits our efforts. Early in my career, I had a mainstream view of accountability—perpetrators needed to be arrested and held to account by the criminal justice system. Now, years later, my thinking has evolved. While the quest for perpetrator responsibility and change remains central to my work, I now see the limitations of carceral approaches, particularly how they unfairly impact marginalized communities and how they fail to hold perpetrators accountable as parents.

In the global public response to domestic violence, the word "accountability" is a central organizing concept when it comes to addressing domestic violence perpetrators. While references to perpetrator accountability are ubiquitous throughout policy and legislation, a clear definition is often absent. As a recent intensive review of Australian perpetrator accountability strategies pointed out, definitions of accountability are often missing, superficial, or contradictory with one another.[1] In my experience, this is also true in many other areas of the world.

In this chapter I explore the limits of and problems with accountability as it is currently defined (or not) and, more importantly, how it is currently practiced. Accountability starts with thoughts, concepts, and language. Our definition of the problem leads to our strategies for fixing that problem. We look closely at the myth of perpetrator accountability by highlighting the following:

> **The problematic dominance of the carceral approach to perpetrators over all other forms of interventions**
>
> **The fact that the concept of accountability has ignored perpetrators as parents**
>
> **The difference between intervention, engagement, and accountability strategies**

At the end of the chapter, I lay out how the Safe & Together Model's behavioral approach supports a more comprehensive, child-centered framework for approaching interventions with perpetrators as parents and how this approach is responsive to the hopes and fears of adult and child survivors. Along the way I will introduce new terms like "vectors of accountability" and "microaccountability" and also will explore established concepts such as reparations in order to help reorient practitioners and systems toward a wider menu of interventions with perpetrators.

The Myth of Perpetrator Accountability

Like other buzzwords or commonly used phrases, "accountability" comes with embedded biases and assumptions. The reference to "working with a family" is a great example of how phrases and terms contain hidden bias. In the human services field, the statement "we work with families" usually means "we work with the mother and the children, but not fathers." While the family encompasses every member, the colloquial use makes fathers invisible.

When it comes to the term "perpetrator accountability," I've developed my own analysis of its embedded biases. While the term could have broad implications and applications, it has been tightly tied to a narrow set of strategies:

> Arrest
>
> Issuance and enforcement of orders of protection (criminal and civil)
>
> Incarceration or probation
>
> Referral to men's behavior change programs (usually court mandated)

In most uses, the term usually leaves out any other form of accountability. In Western countries, perpetrator accountability has relied heavily on carceral, or criminal justice, approaches. The concept of perpetrator accountability does not show up with the same frequency or prominence in noncarceral settings like child protective services, family court, substance abuse programs, health or home visiting programs, and mental health treatment.

Pro-arrest, pro-charging, pro-prosecution policies are believed by some to have positive impact. Others feel like the benefits are inconclusive. In the United States, since 1994, the main federal legislation (the Violence Against Women Act) has pumped billions of dollars into law enforcement and criminal court responses to domestic violence. Despite this investment, domestic violence crimes saw a smaller decrease than the overall US violent crime rate.[2] Advocates for decriminalization and abolition go even further. They argue that communities of color and other oppressed groups, even domestic violence survivors, have been harmed by the criminalization of domestic violence. To them, carceral approaches need to be de-emphasized or completely dismantled and replaced by more community-oriented solutions.

Regardless of the data or the arguments pro and con for criminalized accountability, it is important to acknowledge that there is an inherent simplicity and power to the phrase "perpetrator accountability." Like failure to protect, it is a term whose use is very attractive because it captures the moral high ground and promises results.

Let's take a deeper dive into some of these limitations—or the myth of perpetrator accountability—as it has been practiced for the past decades.

Questioning the Dominance of Carceral Approaches to Accountability

Carceral approaches to domestic violence have fallen under heavy scrutiny from numerous perspectives, including from abolitionist, antiracism, and anticolonization activists. Survivors themselves often report having strong reservations and hesitations about engaging the criminal justice system. These fears and reservations are not unfounded. Lawrence Sherman, who conducted the groundbreaking late-1980s Milwaukee Domestic Violence Experiment, which showed the positive impacts of the pro-arrest approach to domestic violence, has since called into question the value of pro-arrest policing, especially for Black victims. In his 2013 follow-up study, he found a substantially higher mortality rate for all victims whose partners were arrested (versus warned), with employed Black victims experiencing the highest mortality rate. These deaths were mostly from heart disease, cancer, or other illnesses.[3]

High rates of officer-involved domestic violence, the prevalence of misogynistic and sexist attitudes among police, misidentification of survivors as perpetrators, and other failures and gaps in the criminal justice system support the legitimacy of survivors' reluctance to engage law enforcement. Survivors' reluctance to engage the criminal justice system is also the result of wider, specific barriers to effective justice. Those barriers to justice are indicated by statistics that reflect higher deaths in custody for Australian Black men and women and higher rates of police shootings of Black men in the United States. Yet investment in police and criminal court strategies overshadows all other accountability and intervention efforts.

Handcuffs Are Not the Only Vector of Accountability and Change

In the men's behavior change program I ran, about 10–15 percent of our clients were self-referred. This figure often surprises people who thought that you could only get men to attend a behavior change program if those men were forced to go by the court. A shared characteristic of many of these self-referred men was that they were recovering alcoholics. They had assumed that their violence toward partners would automatically subside when they got sober. This hadn't been true. As we know, violence and substance misuse are separate problems, and in their cases, being in recovery for alcoholism didn't resolve their issue with violence. So, without court intervention, these men committed themselves to addressing their violence the same way they had addressed their problems with alcohol—by regularly attending a group for the purpose of ending those behaviors. For them it was part of their overall commitment to recovery.

I share this story as an example of how some domestic violence perpetrators are not only responding to sitting handcuffed in a police cruiser or standing in front of a judge in the courtroom. They make decisions about their behaviors based on their values, experiences, and consequences. For the men in my group, continuing to be violent wasn't acceptable to them. They took action to make further changes based on their own hopes and fears. In another example of perpetrators making decisions based on their own assessment of their behaviors and their consequences, some immigrant men, coming from more openly patriarchal countries, choose to double down on that patriarchal control; others seek to change their attitudes and behaviors in order to better assimilate into their new culture. A third example is abusive men who voluntarily call helplines run

CHAPTER 7: THE MYTH OF PERPETRATOR ACCOUNTABILITY

by organizations like Respect in the United Kingdom and No To Violence in Australia. These men choose to call for help; again, it's usually because of a combination of fears and hopes—external and internal pressure. For example, he might say, "My partner will leave me if I don't change." Or he might say, "I don't like myself when I get violent." This is reinforced by Scotland's long-running Caledonian Men's Probation Project, a court-mandated men's behavior change program that was described by a Scottish social worker interviewed for this book:

> *In the past, there were so many men that came to the Caledonian Project who were ordered by the court to do the program but would never take responsibility for their behavior. The only reasons they were turning up was because they didn't want their partner to leave them, they wanted to see their kids, or they didn't want to get in any more trouble. But they weren't doing anything else to hold themselves accountable. Now that the project uses Safe & Together, they're more explicit with men, using questions like 'Why do you always have the car?' 'Why does she always take the kids to football practice?' Now they're drilling down into family functioning.*
>
> —Catriona, independent social worker, Scotland

Domestic violence perpetrators interact with multiple systems. And each of these interactions is a potential vector of accountability. A "vector of accountability" refers to any interaction a domestic violence perpetrator has with any system, professional, family, or friend where he can be held to account for his actions and statements and their impact on others. Here are a few examples:

> A friend who stops a perpetrator from going over to his ex-wife's house.
>
> An emergency department doctor who has a discussion with a patient who broke his hand punching a wall and asks who watched him do that and whether the viewer was scared by his display of violence.
>
> A substance misuse counselor who tells her client, who is violent and also has an alcohol problem, that he has two problems—drinking and abuse—and that he can't really get sober if he continues to be abusive.

Vectors of accountability are latent throughout our systems and our social interactions. Once we step away from the concept of accountability being wedded to carceral approaches, we begin to see the potential for accountability in different settings and interactions.

Domestic Violence Perpetrators Are Everywhere

Perpetrators' behavioral and mental health issues are being assessed in substance abuse programs and mental health clinics. They are answering health questions about sleep, drinking, and depression from their general practice medical practitioners. They visit emergency departments for broken hands after they've punched walls. They are being monitored by probation officers for drug offenses and are the parents of children involved with juvenile justice. They are the focus of child protection cases and parties in family court. They sit in pews listening to sermons, take part in religious fellowship activities, and attend premarital counseling sessions. They are exposed to advertisements and public service announcements like everyone else.

Domestic violence perpetrators are everywhere, yet the lion's share of accountability strategy and policy, with its focus on carceral approaches, ignores all the opportunities that exist in diverse settings to change the cultural conversation around men, engage individual men about their behavior, and promote change. Evidence of opportunities for intervention are available but are ignored. For example, one study by Kathleen Oriel[4] showed that men in a health-care setting will respond to questions about the perpetration of violence against a partner when asked. She found that almost 14 percent of men visiting a general medical practice, when asked, disclosed physical violence against their partner in the previous twelve months. Just under a third of those men admitted to severe violence. Other health-related studies have found men self-reporting levels of violence as high as almost 28 percent. While filling out a written survey or form does not automatically translate to answering screening questions by medical staff or having motivation to change, these numbers do suggest the potential value of perpetration screening in medical and other settings.

I remember reviewing a substance abuse evaluation where the client had reported to the practitioner that he had been violent with his partner in the last thirty days. The case summary and treatment recommendations ignored his admission of violence and solely addressed his drinking, housing, employment, and depression. A potential vector of accountability was missed. What might change if every substance abuse program extensively screened for coercive-control perpetration and tied ending those behaviors to treatment goals and recovery? What if being controlling toward a partner was monitored as a marker of a risk of relapse, and cessation of abuse was a marker of recovery?

These are just a few examples of potential vectors of accountability. Anywhere that men interact with professionals, family, and friends is a potential vector of accountability. Stepping away from the limiting perspective of carceral approaches to accountability allows us to map points of contact and related opportunities. In Australia, the Victorian Expert Advisory Committee on Perpetrator Interventions,[5] which I was part of, engaged in this type of mapping. It identified all the different organizations that might have opportunities to intervene with perpetrators, including childcare centers, schools, faith-based organizations, and more.

The idea was that mapping the potential points of contact between a domestic violence perpetrator and different systems creates potential to develop new vectors of accountability.

Seeing value in these potential vectors of accountability may be challenging to some, as it is dependent on seeing the perpetrator as a three-dimensional person—a person who is in relationship with family, friends, coworkers, and fellow congregants and who has a variety of needs and hopes. He can be seen as a person engaging with diverse systems to get different needs addressed. This more complex view of the perpetrator and his interactions is key to unlocking the potential of these other vectors of accountability.

> *Historically, accountability is calling 911, get them arrested, get them an order, get them thrown in jail. But when accountability is about asking the adult and child victim survivor what they want, very rarely do they say that's what they want. So, to be able to hold them accountable, that's not what people mean. They mean punished.*
>
> —Beth Ann, S&TI faculty, independent consultant, US

Police-Perpetrated Domestic Violence Is a Problem

Law enforcement is the cornerstone of the "myth of accountability." Much of what has been defined as accountability starts with a call to police and arrest. Yet survivors themselves have significant criticisms and concerns about the law enforcement response to domestic violence. A survey of callers to a US national domestic violence hotline (both women who had called the police and women who hadn't called the police) showed that women had a strong reluctance to turn to law enforcement for help.[6]

> One in four reported that she would not call the police in the future.
>
> More than half said calling the police would make things worse.
>
> Two-thirds or more said they were afraid the police would not believe them or do nothing.

The above statistics reflect numerous problems, including the following:

- How some perpetrators may escalate their abuse and violence in response to police involvement
- Survivors' fear about their mistreatment or their partner's mistreatment at the hands of the police
- Women's experience of not being believed when they report any abuse or harassment
- Law enforcement officers' macho culture (the majority of police in most countries are male, and plenty has been written about "cop culture" being macho)
- How that culture may create a response that is favorable to the male abuser
- Fear that an arrest might set off a chain reaction creating issues with finances, housing, childcare, employment, and family relationships

Digging a little deeper, it also may reflect that a significant number of police officers who are responding to domestic violence may be perpetrators themselves. While the problem of officer-involved domestic violence, also known as OIDV, has not gotten the full research attention it deserves, data that exists point to police officer-perpetrated domestic violence as a significant issue for police departments. In one study, conducted by trailblazing researcher Leanor Boulin Johnson, 40 percent of the police officers admitted to behaving violently toward a spouse or child in the prior six months.[7] In a separate study, Neidig, Russell, and Seng uncovered a perpetration rate of 28 percent (in the prior twelve months).[8] Another study found that 54 percent of police officers knew another officer who had been violent with a partner.[9] It is reasonable to question the ability of police officers to perform well while policing a crime that they themselves commit. High rates of officer-involved domestic violence suggest that the foundation of the carceral approach to accountability may not be as solid as it should be, with officers' personal attitudes and beliefs toward domestic violence carrying over into how they conduct themselves professionally. It's easy to imagine these police officers being more victim-blaming and more colluding with perpetrators than their nonabusive peers.

Uneven Justice

One of the most significant problems with carceral accountability strategies is that they rely on law enforcement mechanisms that are associated with colonization, slavery, Jim Crow, and racism. Feminist and antiracist, anticolonization academics and activists have been speaking out on this issue for years. In the United States, you can read the work of Beth Richie, Mimi Kim, or Leigh Goodmark, each of whom take a different angle on the critique of mainstream reliance on carceral approaches to domestic violence. Dorries and Harjo link the fight against violence against First Nation women with the fight against settler colonization.[10] Similar arguments are made by Aboriginal activists such as Ashlee Donohue in Australia. They argue for alternatives to state-based solutions since state-based solutions often lead to more incarceration and to surveillance of Black, First Nations, and other marginalized people. The researchers argue for more survivor- and community-led solutions like transformative justice.

CHAPTER 7: THE MYTH OF PERPETRATOR ACCOUNTABILITY

> *"The perpetrator-accountability piece is so important. For example, I have a colleague who's Aboriginal and she's always saying that Safe & Together is better for First Nations people because 'We don't write our men off. You white people do that, you know.'"*
>
> —Emma R, domestic and family violence principal project officer, Australia

Intersectional advocates who are opposed to men's violence against women recognize that minority men who are violent toward their partner have also been targeted by racist and colonizing systems. They have experienced systemic violence, limited economic opportunities, stereotyping, overpolicing, and incarceration. These realities and the related trauma must be addressed. Perpetration by minority men cannot be siloed from the reality of structural violence committed against these men. Accountability strategies that overly rely on carceral approaches will reinforce systemic racism and fall more heavily on minority men. A diversity of approaches, including noncarceral ones, are needed.

Accountability for Perpetrators as Parents

I really don't remember when I first had this thought: *How can we hold perpetrators accountable as parents when we have such low standards for men as fathers?* The evidence of culturally low expectations for men as parents is everywhere. For example, we start preparing girls for motherhood from an early age by giving them dolls, expecting them to babysit their siblings or other children, and just by talking to them about their futures as mothers. Boys get very little of this, and often their first introduction to the possibility of being a parent is a negative one—"Don't get anyone pregnant!" Those conversations rarely turn to the joys, challenges, and skills needed to be a good father, including treating your partner with respect. People often talk about fathers "babysitting" their own children, as if a man caring for his own children was only a placeholder for the "real" parent—the mother. In communities, our family support services networks mostly focused on women and children and rarely on men as parents. This is so common that I now think of "child and family" agencies as "child and mother" agencies since they provide so few services to fathers.

> ❝*I shifted from only working with the adult and child victim survivors to working with dads who had perpetrated domestic violence against their families. That changed everything for me as a professional. It changed most things as a person.*❞
>
> —Beth Ann, S&TI faculty, independent consultant, US

The Myth of Accountability Ignores Children as a Potential Vector of Accountability

When I look back at my early career as a men's behavior change facilitator, my self-assessment is that I did a poor job holding men accountable as parents. We talked about how perpetrators used children as weapons against their partner but didn't talk about child abuse or any of the other multiple pathways to harm that have become part of the Safe & Together Model.

The domestic violence field has struggled with the idea of perpetrators as parents. While some researchers and activists—such as Einat Peled, Katreena Scott, Juan Carlos Areán, Jeffrey Edleson, and Oliver Williams—have argued for the importance of engaging perpetrators as parents, others have felt that talking about perpetrators' role as parents draws attention away from the violence against women. Others worried that focusing on children would create a dynamic in which children would be perceived as the true innocent victims of domestic violence and mothers would be considered as culpable in the cocreation of the violence. Around twenty years ago, I was hired to write a curriculum to train perpetrator intervention facilitators. Excitedly, I had proposed the curriculum to include significant sections of material about how to engage perpetrators as parents. The oversight committee struck out all my proposed material about perpetrators as parents. The members of the committee wanted the perpetrator program facilitators to focus on holding men accountable for their violence against their partner but not engage with holding the perpetrator also accountable as a parent.

Evidence exists that engaging perpetrators as fathers is a viable pathway for engagement and accountability. For my master's thesis[11] I surveyed over 1,000 men from men's behavior change programs in Canada and the United States about their perceptions of the impact of their violence against their partner on their children. I wrote up the results of a subsample of 546 men involved with men's behavior change programs in multiple states in America for the thesis. My rationale for this survey was that the more information we could gather about how perpetrators thought about their actions as they related to children, the higher the likelihood we would discover better tools for encouraging behavior change. What I found out was illuminating, and my key results contain good and bad news, often mashed together. Here are some of the results:

- Around 91 percent of the men identified some negative emotional effect on their children of both their verbal and physical abuse of their partner. The top three feelings they identified in their children were scared, sad, and confused.
- Around 67 percent identified that their children's school performance was suffering to some degree.
- Around 78 percent identified some harm to their own relationship with their children.
- Around 74 percent were worried about long-term harm to their children.
- They were most upset about the following possible effects on their children:
  - Their children being accidentally harmed by their physical violence
  - Their children becoming involved with alcohol or drugs
  - Their children becoming abusive to their mother

One of the surprises in the data was the rate at which men reported violence to a partner when she was pregnant (about 16 percent). This percentage of men who admitted to ever being violent with a partner while she was pregnant was similar to women who reported lifetime prevalence rates of violence from a partner during pregnancy. While it is an appallingly high percentage, it offers a window into what perpetrators may be willing to report when they are asked. This may suggest another vector of accountability—engaging men around pregnancy and violence, especially first-time fathers.

The data also indicated that men were worried about the impact of emotional abuse on the children and the overall long-term effects of both physical and emotional abuse on their children. Again, this suggested new vectors of accountability—spending more time talking about how emotional abuse of partners affects children and what the long-term effects may be. Campaigns that emphasize the immediate harm of physical violence may not be the only way to reach perpetrators or to engage in prevention work with men.

Not surprisingly, one of the areas that men seemed to struggle with most was understanding the impact of their behavior on their partner's parenting. While the data did not offer an answer to why that was true, we might speculate that it was part of their overall lack of regard for their partner or a lack of appreciation of their partner's work around parenting.

My research isn't the only work that has focused on perpetrators as parents. In 2002, Western Australia used market research to test out different messages that might influence perpetrators to voluntarily seek out help for their behavior. The message that tested best, including with men who were violent, was that your violence to your partner will harm your children. This message won out over messages like "you'll go to jail," or "your mates won't like you." This messaging became the foundation of the Freedom from Fear campaign, which generated thousands of calls to a helpline by men who were seeking help for their violence.[12]

Join me in a thought experiment: Let's imagine a world where the primary prevention efforts against domestic violence are universally directed at men. In that scenario, everyone (perinatal health workers, pediatricians, health or home visitors, etc.) who had contact with any new father or father-to-be would educate the father about the harm that might result from abuse toward the father's partner and children. Imagine if every time the father went to a doctor for an annual physical, the father would be asked questions about his behavior toward family members as part of any health screening, along with questions about sleep, drinking, stress, and smoking. What if schools held regular education programs for parents that highlighted the impact of partner abuse and other forms of abuse on academic performance, social development, and mental health? What if substance abuse programs, mental health programs, and other services included screening and education around the impact of domestic violence perpetration on children? What if barbershops and men's hair salons had educational material about the effects of domestic violence perpetration on children?

Now let's expand this thought experiment to known perpetrators. What if police officers, every time they made a domestic violence arrest, took the opportunity to educate the alleged perpetrator about the harm his behavior might have for his children? What if judges lectured perpetrators about their responsibility to their children in every case that came before the court? What if probation officers regularly reinforced messages about harm to children as part of their supervision? What would be the result?

Some will dismiss this vision out of hand as it doesn't emphasize punishment and formal consequences. This vision isn't meant to replace those efforts; it's meant to augment them. The intent of this thought exercise was not to dismiss the value of formal forms of accountability, but to envision the way we change culture and create new, additional vectors of accountability. By using the knowledge we have about perpetrators as parents, we can embed accountability and education strategies into a wide range of daily interactions and diverse sectors.

Engagement and Intervention Barriers: Is It Us or Them?

Working with child protection workers, I would often hear statements like this: "I can't find him, but even if I could find him, he wouldn't change." Initially I took these statements at face value. From my days running men's behavior change groups, I knew that perpetrators could be resistant and noncompliant. Practitioners were just reporting back on the challenges of working with a difficult population. Over time my understanding of these statements evolved. I realized that the practitioners making those declarations of despair had little to no experience working directly with violent men; nor did they have the necessary training, support, and supervision regarding working with perpetrators.

Pulling the view back a little further, I realized that practitioners' worries about the potential efficacy of working with male domestic violence perpetrators was heavily influenced by their lack of training and experience and support working with any father, violent or not. I had been working with practitioners who were ill-prepared for working with any fathers, which handicapped them when it came to working with violent fathers. They lacked the confidence, skills, experience, and knowledge they needed to work with men as parents. Most of them had no formal education related to working with fathers. Few had practical training in working with men in general. And they weren't under the same pressure to work with men as to work with women. The "low expectation of fathers" culture of child protective services (and other sectors) was and is this: "You can get your job done (child safety) in domestic violence cases without ever working with the (perpetrating) fathers." Finally, these workers also had legitimate, unaddressed worker safety issues—physical and emotional—related to engaging perpetrators.

Slowly it dawned on me that statements like "I can't find him" were more damning of professional systems and culture than they were reflective of the very real challenges of working with perpetrators. This epiphany has been reinforced through observation, experience, and, conversely, the successes of workers who actually receive training and support around working with violent fathers. In one research project, a team of workers was able to develop a plan to work with a resistant, violent father after receiving supervision and support around the team's own safety. As a result, the members created a plan for engaging the father that accounted for their own safety needs. The result: They were able to successfully overcome a violent father's initial resistance, help him acknowledge that his behavior was a problem, and start a plan for change. Because the workers felt safe to persist in their engagement, he eventually acknowledged that his violence was a problem and agreed to take steps to address it.

Without that supervision around their safety, it is much more likely that this father would've continued to be labeled "resistant."

> ❝*Safe & Together certainly made a difference. We have more respectful communication. Things have improved as a result of our involvement with an agency that's used Safe & Together to hold him to account.*❞
>
> —Jane, survivor, Australia

In another jurisdiction, I was involved in a study in which child protection investigators in an urban area found and met with 73 percent of the domestic violence perpetrators on their caseloads within one to two months. They achieved this because they were trained, supported, and *expected* to meet with each perpetrator.[13]

Blaming perpetrators for being difficult to find, engage, and change is an excuse for the failures of systems to prepare practitioners for working with perpetrators in ways consistent with their roles. When systems don't support workers, the lack of support reinforces the convenient narrative that perpetrators are too difficult to work with. This narrative justifies the lack of investment in training the workforce and expecting practitioners to address perpetrators—another chicken-and-egg situation.

In many ways it is convenient for systems to ignore fathers' roles in families and to see perpetrators as too difficult to work with. It allows practitioners to remain in their comfort zone—working with women and children. It creates the illusion of reduced workloads because they don't need to spend energy trying to meet with a father who may work during the day or may live at another location. (I say the illusion of reduced workload because, as we know, ignoring fathers means practitioners are not engaging or intervening with fathers whose behaviors may be having a significant negative impact on the functioning of the family.) It may also work well with narratives that certain men—for example, men with criminal histories or men from marginalized groups—are more disposable. Because we are treating perpetrators as being an inaccessible, unworkable population, we have systems that are failing to intervene with perpetrators to improve outcomes for adult and child survivors. These failures interfere with the exploration of new vectors of accountability.

Engagement with perpetrators, when it's done right, can pay huge dividends even when the perpetrator denies the violence or is resistant to meaningful engagement. A constructive engagement could increase motivation to change and support the development of meaningful behavior change goals. A negative engagement, in which the perpetrator doesn't engage, blames others, and denies the impact of his behavior on his partner and his children, can also increase accountability because at that point his attitudes and statements of denial are memorialized in documentation. This can make it more difficult for the perpetrator to manipulate systems. It also makes visible his lack of commitment to his children's safety and well-being. Documentation of this lack of regard for his children can play a key role in future court decisions.

How the Safe & Together Model Innovates to Challenge the Myth of Perpetrator Accountability

When I first started in the domestic violence field, I was guilty of many of the things that I'm critiquing in this chapter. I led a men's behavior change group for men, most of whom were court-ordered to participate. Most of my training and consulting focused on criminal court and corrections. I believed in the importance of pro-arrest policy and was caught in the dominant racist paradigm of being blind, or at least insensitive, to how the emphasis on carceral approaches reinforced racial inequality. I mostly ignored men as parents and didn't really focus on other potential vectors of accountability.

But eventually I started changing my thinking and practice. I became more aware of the limitations of the criminal justice system with regard to domestic violence and in general. And I was drawn slowly into work with noncarceral systems such as child protective services, health visitors, mental health, and substance misuse. As a result of the findings from a child death review of a toddler at the hands of her mother's boyfriend, who was also abusing the mother, I was asked to join a team of domestic violence specialists training child protection workers. My role was to teach perpetrator engagement. This was the beginning of my exploration of perpetrator accountability and change outside the context of the criminal court and men's behavior change framework. In this setting there were different types of interactions, most of them voluntary and all of them focused on child safety and well-being. There was more potential to address a wider range of harms caused by domestic violence perpetrators—harms that were very important to adult and child survivors and were often not addressed by carceral strategies that focused primarily on physical violence. Also, believing that children are likely to be one of the major motivators of change, potentially a more potent motivator than the fear of arrest and incarceration, child protection felt like a fertile area to explore how to create other opportunities for engagement, accountability, and change.

> **My work with child protective services enabled my development of the Safe & Together Model's perpetrator pattern-based approach.**

CHAPTER 7: THE MYTH OF PERPETRATOR ACCOUNTABILITY

"What drew me to the Safe & Together Model was definitely working with the person using family violence—and how important that work was in order to keep children safe and to work with the adult survivor. I think there was an understanding within the sector that in order to create change, you work with children, women, and mothers. But you can't create change unless you work with the perpetrator. The Model gives you the confidence and the skills and the framework to do that work."

—Karen, child and young person practice lead, Australia

My work with child protective services enabled my development of the Safe & Together Model's perpetrator pattern-based approach. It inspired me to start talking about domestic violence perpetration as a parenting choice, bringing together the concept of accountability with the idea of perpetrators as parents. It also helped me focus on the mechanics of "microaccountability" in the form of the language used by practitioners in their conversations with one another and with families as well as in their documentation and case plans. Instead of focusing on "macroaccountability" strategies involving legislation, service delivery, and large system initiatives, I began to focus on creating shifts from the bottom up, starting with the very language used to describe the problem and therefore the very definition of the problem itself.

What Adult and Child Survivors Say They Want

Research with adult and child survivors highlights their desire for interventions with perpetrators as parents. Liz Kelly and Nicole Westmarland's Mirabal study highlighted survivors' strong focus on the well-being of their children and perpetrators' improved parenting.[14] In another study, Katie Lamb and others interviewed children and young people about the change they wanted to see in their abusive fathers.[15] The children spoke clearly and eloquently about their desire for reparations, including acknowledgment of the harm caused, behavior change, more involved parenting, and better treatment of their mother. It was reported that participants in an Aboriginal men's behavior change group were positively impacted by listening to the recordings of these young people. This adds to the evidence that if it is done right, educating fathers about how their behaviors harm children may be an important vector of accountability—one that is very in line with adult and child survivors' wishes and hopes that the perpetrator be held accountable as a parent.

CHAPTER 7: THE MYTH OF PERPETRATOR ACCOUNTABILITY

> ❝*I'd be called into meetings with child protection, and my own social worker, who was advocating for me, would ask why we were at the meeting. The answer was usually because of something my ex had done. My social worker would point out to everybody in the meeting that actually he wasn't there and ask why we were having all these meetings. It was constant—every time anything would happen, we were all pulled in for it—except my ex. He just didn't have any accountability whatsoever. My social worker would listen to the list of issues, and say, "Actually, that wasn't her, that wasn't her, and neither was that." It was all the time, and it constantly felt like I was having to defend myself.* ❞
>
> —Naomi, survivor, Scotland

In order to approach perpetrator accountability in a way that results in meaningful change, here are a few things we need to consider:

> How is accountability defined or operationalized?
>
> Who is defining accountability—survivors or systems?
>
> How do accountability strategies address the perpetrator as parent?
>
> How do accountability strategies lead to improvements in adult and child lives, including safety, improved well-being, improved financial well-being, and healing?

> How do we fairly administer in systems where Black, First Nation, and other marginalized people are wrongly stereotyped as more violent and are overrepresented in our criminal justice and child protection systems?
>
> How do we provide professionals with the skills, knowledge, and confidence to implement diverse accountability strategies on a day-to-day level?
>
> How does our language, including how we describe our worries associated with domestic violence and children, help or hinder accountability?
>
> Finally, how do we develop strategies that are inclusive of the concepts of accountability, engagement, intervention, and reparations?

Expanding the Language of Accountability to the Language of Interventions

In the language of the Safe & Together Model, the focus is on "intervening with perpetrators to reduce risk and harm to the child." Accountability is mentioned in the Model but as only one strategy among many. The elevation of the concept "intervene" above the concept of "accountability" is very deliberate. The purpose of the language is to communicate that interventions can take many forms, not just the carceral approaches. This is especially important if we are going to try to become less dependent on systems that unfairly target marginalized groups. The explicit reference to the risk that perpetrators' behaviors pose to children is critical. This is meant as a counterbalance to how children have been absent from the traditional accountability conversations.

Interventions are defined very widely. They can range from a social worker's perpetrator pattern-based engagement strategies to family court screening and evaluation processes. A social worker's conversation with a perpetrator is an intervention. How the social worker talks to the perpetrator about his behavior and its impact on his children creates a potential vector of (micro) accountability. By focusing the conversation on the perpetrator's responsibility for his behavior, the social worker is potentially a force for change. A family court process that uses a perpetrator pattern assessment lens can help identify dynamics of coercive control and harm to child, partner, and family caused by the perpetrator. This analysis can set the stage for effective court orders, such as one granting sole legal custody to the protective parent. An order that gives a survivor complete legal authority over decisions related to a child can reduce the perpetrator's ability to interfere with the survivor's parenting, can enhance the probability of the child's needs being met, and can reduce the possibility of the child being used as a weapon against the survivor. These are all interventions that fall outside the usual carceral definition of accountability.

Engagement is another intervention strategy included in the Safe & Together Model approach to perpetrators. It refers to the way we engage perpetrators about their behavior, including attempts to motivate and encourage voluntary change. This type of intervention is possible in multiple settings and sectors. I've taught perpetrator engagement strategies in medical and early childhood intervention settings. Child protection workers have reported back to me, pleasantly surprised, that with coaching and support, they have been able engage perpetrators about their behaviors. One of my staff members reported back to me about a conversation she had while accompanying a social worker on a home visit. After watching the social worker skirt around the issue of the father's violence to his partner, she stepped in and asked the father if he thought his behavior toward his wife was harmful to his child. After a brief pause, the father simply said, yes, he thought his behavior was harmful to his child. Without skilled, knowledgeable, supported, and confident workers, engagement becomes harder or impossible. That's why the Safe & Together Institute is supporting domestic violence-informed practice in community health centers, child and family agencies, and substance abuse programs.

CHAPTER 7: THE MYTH OF PERPETRATOR ACCOUNTABILITY

Lastly, the Model recognizes that courts still have a role to play in interventions with perpetrators. And "courts," in this instance, refers to all the courts, not just criminal courts, that might interact with perpetrators. We need to be thinking about family court and child protection courts, not just criminal court when it comes to effective interventions with perpetrators. Child protection courts, if they can switch from a compliance model (where they monitor completion of services such as men's behavior change programming) to a behavior change model (where behavioral change expectations are set and measured), could be more of a force for perpetrator accountability. Instead of just expecting a perpetrator to attend and complete a behavior change program (a worthy goal), a child protection court could set down simple, clear behavioral expectations. These might include the perpetrator needing to demonstrate a willingness and ability to admit to the harmful behaviors, demonstrate insight into the harm he has caused, and actively show evidence of meaningful and consistent behavior change, including participating in the repair of past damage. These same interventions could also occur in family court.

Inspired by voices of children and young people captured in the work of Katie Lamb, Cathy Humphreys, and Kelsey Hegarty, I've begun to highlight the concept of repair or reparations in my work. Expectations of perpetrator change cannot stop at the cessation of control and violence. They need to include the expectation that the perpetrator will do whatever is safe, reasonable, and possible to help his children heal from the harm that he himself has caused. Parents have a responsibility to care for their children when they have physically or emotionally wounded them. This responsibility is no less when they themselves have caused the harm. Reparations can take many forms, from admitting to being wrong for acting abusively to supporting a child in counseling. This is not theoretical. I have numerous stories of perpetrators who acknowledge to their children the wrongness of their behaviors, and in doing so, created some healing in their relationship with their children. Expecting abusive fathers to make reparations to their children should be a common element in a child-centered intervention provided through family court or child protective services. This can come in the form of taking responsibility for the behavior and changing sufficiently so that the child can safely talk about the experience of the abuse, including difficult feelings such as anger and fear. It can also come in the form of the father's admitting and acknowledging the harm he has caused and supporting the child's receiving professional help when necessary.

Stop Bad Practices and Start Better Ones

When I was training domestic violence consultants to use the Safe & Together Model with child protective services, I would tell them it wasn't enough to identify bad practices. It was important to replace them with good practices. Not only does this help make things better for the family, but it also makes for more confident and effective practitioners. If you take away problematic practices but fail to offer alternatives, practitioners are likely to become frustrated and return to their bad habits. Below is a chart with three paired examples of changes in language that are central to "microaccountability" in interviewing, documentation, supervision, and other basic practitioner activities.

Microaccountability practices

STOP	START
Stop referring to domestic violence harming children	**Start referring to domestic violence perpetrators' behaviors harming children.** By making the person who is choosing the behaviors that harm the children visible, we are setting the stage for addressing that person and those behaviors. Any deviation from this opens the door up for victim-blaming, whether in the form of failure-to-protect allegations or trumped-up charges of parental alienation.
Stop talking about domestic violence as something that occurs just between adults.	**Start referring to domestic violence perpetration as a parenting choice.** Over the years, this is one of the messages of the Safe & Together Model that both professionals and survivors have resonated with most strongly. This statement is compelling and important because in one sentence it ties together domestic violence perpetration against a partner with the responsibility perpetrators have as parents. It is also meant as a corrective to the low standard for men as parents.
Stop talking about children witnessing domestic violence	**Start talking about how perpetrators' patterns impact child, partner, and family functioning.** This wider understanding of harm creates a stronger foundation for perpetrator responsibility and behavior change, including reparations. Start by asking, "What is the perpetrator's pattern of coercive control and actions taken to harm the children?" And then ask, "What are the impacts of those behaviors on child, partner, and family functioning?"

Language changes like these may seem small, but they are the foundation of a true paradigm shift—especially if they are used throughout an agency or across sectors. The more this language is used by more practitioners in different disciplines, the more vectors of accountability will start to open up, reinforcing one another.

Accountability for Perpetrators as Parents (in Action)

Because I wanted to explore new vectors of accountability and microaccountability, the development of the Safe & Together Model was very focused on the "how" of domestic violence assessments. Let's look at two ways the Model guides micropractice for the purposes of increasing accountability for perpetrators.

Mapping Perpetrators' Patterns

I developed the Safe & Together Model Perpetrator Pattern Mapping Tool and process over ten years. The purpose of the tool was to formalize, in writing, the process I had been using to facilitate domestic violence cases consultation. The tool asks practitioners to complete a series of questions about the perpetrator's pattern and its impact on children, partner, family functioning, intersections, intersectionalities, worker safety, and more. It was designed to help individual workers with their cases, improve documentation, aid in supervision, and offer managers and quality assurance teams a way to check fidelity to the Model. (Originally a "paper and pen" process, it has recently become web based.) The tool (and domestic violence consultation) starts out with some version of this question:

> *"What do you know, from whatever sources you have available to you—interviews, record reviews, arrest reports, and collateral contacts—about the perpetrator's pattern of coercive control and actions taken to harm children?"*

It asks the user to consider the behaviors across relationships, including past partners, other children, and violence and abuse toward other family members and toward nonfamily contacts such as police and neighbors.

Let's look at how this step in the mapping process helps promote microaccountability:

- **Accessing multiple sources of information** increases the quality of the information and reduces likelihood that perpetrators can manipulate professionals.
- **Using a pattern approach** versus an incident approach helps create a fuller, more accurate assessment of the perpetrator's behavior—making it less likely to fall into mutualizing language or misidentifying a survivor who is engaging in defensive violence and erroneously characterizing the survivor as a perpetrator.
- **Focusing on behavior** directed at adult partners and children together increases the power of the assessment—siloed or limited assessments do not match the experience of the family.
- **Getting a fuller picture** of the perpetrator's pattern of behavior makes it easier to contextualize the survivor's decision-making. Seen in context, the rationale behind a survivor's decisions becomes clearer, reducing the chances of victim-blaming or pathologizing and increasing the chance of keeping the focus on the perpetrator's behaviors and holding him accountable as a parent.
- **Including past partners and other children** in an assessment can provide vital information about dangerousness and persistence of behaviors over time. This helps keep **focus on the perpetrator, not the relationship**.
- **Including behavior toward extended family and nonfamily** can help with understanding dangerousness and entrapment since violent behaviors toward others can increase

entrapment. This also relates to danger to professionals as revealed in violence, threats, and manipulation, and it adds to our assessment of the danger to the adult and child survivors.
- **Knowing behaviors** of the perpetrator helps the professional develop individualized behavior-change goals for the perpetrator, increasing the ability to hold him accountable.
- **Sharing the past behaviors of the perpetrator** with organizations he has been referred to, such as men's behavior change and substance abuse programs, increases the chances of treatment success and reduces the chances that the perpetrator will be able to manipulate the professionals involved.
- **Setting behavior change goals** based on the perpetrator's pattern helps professionals focus on real change versus just program compliance or completion.
- **Validating a survivor** by focusing on her partner's behaviors and identifying those behaviors as the source of the danger and harm helps with partnering.
- **Focusing on all behaviors associated with coercive control**, not just arrestable behaviors, brings the system in more alignment with the lived experience of survivors, and it increases accountability.
- **Focusing on all behaviors associated with coercion control and actions taken to harm children as a starting point**—versus a focus on criminal behaviors—opens the door to more systems intervening with the perpetrator.

These are all the benefits that can derive from this approach even before we start talking about the impact of the perpetrator's behaviors on child partners and family functioning.

A practitioner recently told me how she used the Perpetrator Pattern Mapping Tool with a survivor who had been targeted for years by her ex-partner, who was perpetrating postseparation coercive control. The practitioner told me that not only did the survivor feel validated by the process but also that the results of the mapping produced the information needed to keep her children with her. Family court and child protection found the information critical in identifying the perpetrator's ongoing abuse, including his attempts to manipulate systems and other practitioners through threats and misinformation. It was the microaccountability practices of the mapping process that made effective intervention by the court and child protection possible.

Multiple Pathways to Harm

The Model's Multiple Pathways to Harm framework, which I introduced in chapter 5, is another example of a tool that improves accountability and sets the stage for behaviorally focused interventions with the perpetrator. It focuses on the connection between perpetrators' behaviors and harm to children. If professionals recognize seeing and hearing incidents of violence as the only pathway to harm for children, then they are limiting what perpetrators are responsible for and de facto blaming survivors for everything else that goes wrong with children as a result of the domestic violence perpetrator's behaviors.

> *One practitioner said to me, 'Well I can't unhear or unsee any of this. It's going to change me as a person and as a social worker to know about Multiple Pathways to Harm and the devastating impact of living with coercive control every day for children and how it will impact on their development, social skills, and basically everything else. Even if there's only one incident recorded on the case file, it's not just that incident. It's the constant dripping tap of harms caused by the perpetrator, never going away, never stopping.*
>
> —Debbie, practice development coordinator, Scotland

I also saw this framework as essential to combating low expectations for men as parents when they were the ones perpetrating domestic violence. The MPH framework explicitly connects the perpetrator's behaviors to issues such as housing, school, financial status, the survivors' mental health, and parenting. Without these explicit connections, it is nearly impossible for the paradigm to shift away from ignoring fathers and blaming mothers. I wanted to combat gender bias through practice changes, not just education about domestic violence being harmful to children. The idea was to show, not tell.

The rationale is that if survivors, family violence researchers, activists, and advocates are right, we don't need to lecture social workers on how bad domestic violence perpetrators are for children. We need to give them the tools to assess those behaviors and their harm to the child, partner, and family functioning.

The MPH framework lays out the following pathways to harm:

> **Children's safety and trauma**—Domestic violence perpetrators' behaviors are harmful to children's emotional and physical safety. Violence toward a parent, a sibling, or the children themselves can lead to physical harm and to psychological trauma.
>
> **Effects on family ecology**—This captures the avalanche of effects on families from patterns of coercive control. Perpetrators' behaviors may negatively impact family income, housing, schooling, and relationships with kin. When we think about domestic violence only in terms of what is added—violence and danger—instead of what is taken away, we fail at naming some of the most profound effects of domestic violence perpetrators' behaviors on adult and child survivors—the loss of self-determination, satisfaction, connection, and safety. Often these effects are interrelated. Being forced to move to be physically safer may mean a loss of a favorite teacher, a familiar corner store, a meaningful job, and a best friend.

> **Effects on partner's parenting**—Accountability for perpetrators as parents needs to include the effects of his behaviors on her ability to parent. Otherwise, mothers who are survivors will be seen through a *parenting deficit lens instead of a domestic violence-informed lens.*

Both the Perpetrator Pattern Mapping Tool and the Multiple Pathways to Harm framework offer concepts and tools to operationalize perpetrator (micro) accountability. When we use this language, documentation becomes clearer, more powerful, and more focused on the perpetrator's behaviors. This documentation is the foundation of interventions and vectors of accountability.

Final Thoughts on the Myth of Perpetrator Accountability

As you can see, years after my first talk on accountability, I'm still deeply invested in how we collectively create more and stronger vectors of accountability. At the end of the day, all actions related to accountability need to be guided by what survivors say will make their situation better. Policies and practices need to be in alignment with the wishes and desires of adult and child survivors.

For so long, our efforts at perpetrator accountability have been centered on the criminal justice system while survivors have been fighting lonely battles on the other planets—battles that often have lifelong implications for themselves and their children. Custody is won or lost. Parenting time is decided. Children are unnecessarily removed by child protective services. We can no longer continue to relegate accountability for perpetrators as parents to second-class status in our discussion around systems change.

We need to use all the tools we have, like the mapping tool, to open new vectors of accountability, and that starts with our naming the perpetrators' behavior patterns and their impact on the family.

"I think there's an underlying assumption that you can't change these men, that they're irredeemable. I think we've absorbed that attitude over many, many decades of working with victims. And we concluded that she's the most malleable, the most changeable. She's the one most likely to change because she's more pleasant to deal with. But, you know, a lot of these guys are written off as being irredeemable and that's just not true. They can change, and they should be held to account so that they are inspired and motivated to change."

—Jane, survivor, Australia

CHAPTER 7: THE MYTH OF PERPETRATOR ACCOUNTABILITY

> *In our practice, we asked ourselves how we could make the person using family violence accountable? We wanted to write a letter of support for a victim survivor going to court. We changed our way of doing the support letter by outlining the following:*
>
> - *Mary is attending a particular program and what the program is about.*
> - *The reason she is attending this program is in relation to her ex-partner's abusive behaviors.*
> - *The perpetrator has these specified behaviors and they have this impact on Mary.*
> - *The perpetrator's behavior has these specific impacts on each of her children.*
> - *Follow-up questions are encouraged as part of the process.*
>
> *We write support letters all the time, and what was great about this is that we could articulate the behaviors and make the perpetrator accountable in that letter. The victim survivor was able to take that letter to court. We also did the Perpetrator Pattern Mapping Tool. When the case went to court for the intervention order, the lawyer for the perpetrator said, 'You need to settle. We can't put this forward now.'*

—Karen, child and young person practice lead, Australia

CHAPTER 8

The Myth of Parental Alienation

Through my work and personal life, I've had a front row seat to how threats of parental alienation can loom large over the parenting of domestic violence survivors. I've watched fear, insecurity, and anger blossom in survivors with phrases from the perpetrator such as "stop interfering with my relationship with my children," or "you are turning the kids against me," or "I'll take you back to court, tell them you are alienating them from me, and take the children from you." Whether spoken or texted by someone who has engaged in coercive control, such statements are crazy making, chilling, and ominous to a parent who has legitimate reasons to be worried about the safety and well-being of her children. Few things are scarier to a parent who is trying to protect herself and her children from a domestic violence perpetrator.

Unfortunately, these kinds of threats are not rare. And domestic violence survivors have good reasons to be afraid. Approximately one-third of mothers alleging a father's abuse lose custody; when the father files a cross-complaint alleging alienation, that increases to one-half.[1] When it comes to discussion of domestic violence in individual custody cases or family law policy debates, parental alienation is a topic that often dominates. Even when a survivor doesn't experience a direct accusation of parental alienation, it may loom large in her mind, powerfully lurking in the shadows—never directly spoken but still a powerful, fear-inducing force.

CHAPTER 8: THE MYTH OF PARENTAL ALIENATION

In this chapter, you won't find an examination of all legal and courtroom nuances related to parental alienation. The subject has been the focus of much research and discussion elsewhere. Instead, I look at the factors that facilitate parental alienation being wrongly applied in domestic violence cases—how it has become a "myth" that blames mothers, ignores fathers, and hinders the safety of children. I follow this with a detailed look at how the Safe & Together Model can help family courts and other systems make themselves less vulnerable to perpetrators' attempts to use accusations of parental alienation to harm adult and child survivors.

Parental alienation is the idea that a parent can, through a series of behaviors, turn a child against the other parent. Richard Gardner coined the term "parental alienation syndrome,"[2] and the concept has been resoundingly debunked as pseudoscience. Nevertheless, the concept of parental alienation, like a zombie, refuses to die. It continues to be a highly influential and contested concept, especially in family courts across the globe. It has achieved continued life in the concepts of child resistance, child refusal, and child estrangement. It is the animating force behind terms like "malicious parent syndrome."

"Clean cases" of parental alienation, in which the alienating parent's actions are the singular reason a child rejects the other parent, are extremely rare. Most situations are much more complex, and many, especially those situations involving allegations of domestic violence and child abuse, do not come close to fitting the most thoughtful and thorough definitions of parental alienation. Even advocates for the legitimacy of the concept of parental alienation acknowledge that a child's rejection of a parent needs to be "unjustified" or "unreasonable." Fears about contact, resistance to seeing a parent, and estrangement are all in the realm of "reasonable" and "justifiable" responses to a domestic violence perpetrator. **In order for the diagnosis of parental alienation to be meaningfully considered, there needs to have been a prior positive, abuse-free relationship between the child and that parent.** This is almost never the case in domestic violence situations. Therefore, parental alienation is not a relevant or applicable diagnosis when a child has experienced no or little prior relationship with that parent, or the existing relationship contains other significant negative elements such as abuse, violence, or coercion. Johnston and Kelly and others highlight domestic violence and even inept parenting as legitimate reasons for a child rejecting a parent.[3] Some researchers have even gone as far as developing the concept of self-estrangement, in which a parent who engages in abusive behaviors undermines his own relationship with his child.[4] All these scenarios need to be ruled out before "true" parental alienation can even be considered as an option.

On one of my trips to Australia, I was sharing the keynote slot with a national expert in parental alienation who said something that stood out to me: *parental alienation is not an option as a diagnosis when there is even a suspicion of abuse*. In light of this assertion, any discussion of parental alienation directed at a survivor mother when there is a history of domestic violence is a victory for abusers. When the goal is improving outcomes for survivors, arguments that center on parental alienation are defensive battles for survivors and their advocates, and they are playing on the home field of perpetrators. While effective defense is sometimes necessary, the dominance of the parental alienation discussion in the family court environment means that survivors and their advocates are regularly being backed into the position of refuting allegations, making it even harder to turn the conversation back to the perpetrators' behaviors and their harm to children.

Once again for those in the back: Parental alienation is not a relevant concept when children's (and adults') resistance to contact and custody are (or are suspected to be) the product of *reasonable* and *justified* fears about physical and emotional safety. In order to determine reasonableness or justification for fears related to contact, accurate context and history is critical. This context and history needs to include domestic violence and child maltreatment. Based on this, it is reasonable to define the myth of parental alienation as this: the inappropriate application of the concept of parental alienation to cases involving concerns about domestic violence and/or child abuse. This application in those cases is not consistent with the very definitions of parental alienation. Nor is that application consistent with systems' stated desires to prioritize child safety and well-being in family court matters or trauma-informed approaches.

Yet in the family court arena, the accusation of parental alienation is such a powerful force that it regularly overwhelms documented histories of domestic violence, child sexual and physical abuse, and other forms of maltreatments to become the central issue for courts. Joan Meier, an attorney and international expert on family court and domestic violence, found "that mothers' claims of abuse, especially child physical or sexual abuse, increase their risk of losing custody, and that fathers' cross-claims of alienation virtually double that risk."[5] Inside and outside of court, domestic violence perpetrators have been able to successfully wield accusations of parental alienation against survivors, often twisting protective behaviors into false evidence of malicious attacks on the perpetrators' rights to a relationship with their child.

While family courts are mandated to consider children's best interest, in their decisions, contact, even with parents with known histories of abuse toward the child and the other parent, is often prioritized over safety and well-being. This "pro-contact" culture empowers domestic violence perpetrators to wield parental alienation as an effective threat and weapon at the expense of the safety and well-being of both adult and child survivors.

The Myth of Parental Alienation

In this section I analyze various problems with the myth of parental alienation. I will examine the underlying gaps in thinking associated with postseparation coercive control and the implications of a limited definition of domestic violence. Together we will consider how risk assessment frameworks fail to help develop the evidence needed to understand the damage already done to children by the perpetrator and how gender does matter in the application of parental alienation as an allegation. Finally, we'll consider how the concept of collaborative co-parenting is used as a weapon against survivors.

The Lack of Understanding of Postseparation Coercive Control Creates Fertile Ground for Mother-Blaming

While domestic violence survivors can be threatened with allegations of parental alienation before a couple separates, it usually comes to the forefront after a couple is apart. One of the reasons these allegations can gain so much traction in the postseparation environment is the commonly held assumption that once the relationship ends, domestic violence stops being an issue, particularly as it relates to children. This is far from true. In many instances, behaviors morph and change, but the pattern of coercive control continues. Not only may the survivor be contending with new behaviors, but her decision-making is still being shaped by the perpetrator's past behavior.

> *Systems like child protective services and family court offer perpetrators the ability to punish and harm survivors by proxy.*

Systems like child protective services and family court offer perpetrators the ability to punish and harm survivors by proxy. Domestic violence perpetrators target family court decision-makers and other professionals for grooming and manipulation. This might involve false reports of child abuse or neglect; harassment via malicious requests for "wellness checks"; vexatious litigation; interfering with an ex-partner's ability to retain counsel by creating conflicts of interest; false allegations in family court against the survivor; charming self-presentation; and other forms of manipulation.

Practitioners need to recognize when coercive control is a factor in survivors' calculations about the family court process. Even when there have been no recent incidents of physical violence, fears about future violence or other forms of retaliation may make a survivor reluctant to file motions in court for the levels of financial support or custody she may be entitled to. For example, a survivor may be afraid to ask for financial support for fear that it will trigger a perpetrators' punitive demand for full custody or physical violence and threats.

Demonstrated capacity to cause harm, especially at the expense of the children, and explicit threats about what would happen to her and the children if she left all shape how a survivor approaches the postseparation period. Survivors would be foolish to assume that the perpetrator has "changed his spots" just because the relationship has ended. Domestic violence perpetrators may (or may not) stop physical assaults, but in many instances they escalate their harassment, stalking, and attempts to control their estranged partner. The children are often central to these efforts. When practitioners fail to understand this continuing dynamic, survivors' acts of protection and resistance are ripe for misinterpretation.

Here is one example of how a failure to understand a perpetrator's pattern of postseparation coercive control translated into mother-blaming by practitioners:

CHAPTER 8: THE MYTH OF PARENTAL ALIENATION

When I could finally get the social worker to pivot to the father's behavior pattern, what I learned in addition to the general statement of a history of violence toward the mother was:

> The father was telling his son that the mother had stolen the father's money and keys. Why? So, the child would steal her money and her keys for the father.
>
> When the son saw the new keys to the apartment, after his mother had changed the locks for safety reasons, he wouldn't believe her or the female social worker when they said the keys were not his father's keys. Not believing either woman, he tested the keys in the lock himself.
>
> The mother, who was forced to change her mobile phone number to prevent harassment from the father, was afraid to share her new phone number with her own son. She was fearful that if the son had the new number, he would give it to his father, who then could use it harass her.

Not only were the father's continued efforts at control being ignored, but his instrumental use of his son was also not being considered to be a form of abuse and neglect (which it was). Nor did they identify his efforts to actively drive a wedge between the mother and her own child as a problem. The practice of the professionals in this case is an example of the two main themes in this book: mother-blaming and ignoring fathers. Their anger and frustration with the mother overrode any focus on the perpetrator's pattern, including postseparation coercive control in the form of a perpetrator's use of his own child as a spy and a tool of his control. The perpetrator's abusive parenting and continuing risk for physical violence to the mother was being ignored. It is especially important to note that their knowledge of his history of violence failed to deter them from mother-blaming. They even knew about his weaponization of his own son against his son's mother. But habit, shaped by culture and institutional forces and driven by underlying gender bias, was the overriding force. In this case, it led them to ignore the serious risk to the child from the father. And let's not forget that any of the mother's feelings of frustration, anger, and resistance might very well have arisen as a reaction to the system blaming her and failing to hold her ex-partner accountable as a parent.

The lack of attention to postseparation coercive control is a cause and effect of mother-blaming and father-ignoring. Whether it results in labels such as "difficult to deal with" or "alienating," the outcomes are the same: the spotlight is put on the survivors' behaviors, not on the perpetrators' actions. More attention needs to be paid to postseparation coercive control if we are going to challenge the myth of parental alienation.

Limited Definitions of Domestic Violence Perpetrators' Patterns of Behavior

Limited definitions of domestic violence make it harder to establish a context for adult and child survivors' worries about contact with an abusive parent. Unfortunately, instead of a comprehensive, objective, behavioral pattern-based approach that encompasses coercive control and other actions to harm children, in most settings, including family courts, the definitions of domestic violence are frequently tied to criminal code definitions of domestic violence, which, in turn, are very focused on incidents of physical violence instead of patterns of coercive control.

These definitions, like most domestic violence definitions, heavily focus on the perpetrator's behaviors toward the adult survivor and offer limited perspectives on the harm or involvement of children, which is the central issue before family court. For example, in the state of Michigan in the US, the definition of domestic violence in the investigation guidebook for friends of the court, who evaluate parents and make recommendations for parenting time, are tied back to legal definitions heavily focused on physical and sexual violence.[6] This is part of the reason why there has been a movement in the last few years to embed the concept of coercive control into the family court environment.

Incomplete, partial, or limited definitions of domestic violence are not consistent with the reality of adult and child survivors or with the mission of courts to promote child safety and well-being. And they make it harder for courts to understand and supportively respond to the survivors' legitimate fears and worries and resistance to contact between her children and the perpetrator.

The fullest view into the perpetrator's pattern of threats, intimidation, and forms of control such as financial control is necessary for an accurate understanding of the harm to children and survivors' protective efforts. Anything less than this opens the door to effective manipulation of systems using allegations of parental alienation.

> *In a family court situation, the allegations of what is often referred to as parental alienation can be quite hard to cut through. We come back to using the perpetrator pattern approach to talk about family violence, which really allows us to navigate some of those entrenched ideas that lawyers or other professionals can come into the proceedings with. It allows us to address those allegations that are before the court in an active way and speak to it more confidently.*
>
> —Melody, court child expert, Australia

CHAPTER 8: THE MYTH OF PARENTAL ALIENATION

A Focus on Risk of Future Severe Violence to the Adult Survivor, Little to No Focus on Harm to Children

Risk assessments are a standard process in the toolkit of systems' responses to domestic violence. Whether in the criminal court or family court environment, practitioners are often expected to complete a risk assessment to help determine what steps need to be taken in a case to manage potential danger. Domestic violence risk assessment frameworks are designed primarily to predict future harm to the adult survivor. These risk assessments, with their tight focus on the potential for future severe physical violence and lethality, are not quite fit-for-purpose for settings where children are part of the equation. They often do not touch on direct risk of physical harm, including sexual abuse, of children. And they almost never assess for the risk that the perpetrator will try to take children through the manipulation of family court and/or child protection processes.

Risk assessments usually do not tease out the impact of the perpetrator's pattern on child, partner, and family functioning. Risk assessments consider multiple factors, including past behaviors of the perpetrator—for example, violence to the survivor during pregnancy, strangulation attempts, severity of injury from physical violence, or direct threats of homicide. While these are important as factors to consider in triaging resources, listing or scaling these factors is not the same as describing the impact of these behaviors on child, partner, and family functioning. In cases involving children, it is not enough to know the history of violence and the risk for future violence to the adult survivor. The perpetrator's risk to the child needs to be explored, and this really depends on a clear picture of the harm already perpetrated against the child. Strangulation cannot only be looked at as a risk marker for future lethal violence. It needs to be understood as an act of control that is likely to have a profound impact on the functioning of the survivor, the children, and the family.

Consider the scenario in which the survivor's boyfriend, jealous and worried she is having an affair with another student at night school, stalks her on campus. He hides in the bathrooms, waits for her, and assaults her while she is on a break from class. For sure, his stalking and extreme jealousy is a risk factor for postseparation violence. But that's not enough if we want to evaluate the perpetrator as a parent. Let's say he left their six-year-old child alone at home to pursue his obsessive quest to control her mother. This would be child neglect. What if his stalking and assault created anxiety and fear related to going to school, so the survivor drops out of school, losing her chance to advance in her career and perhaps gain the financial independence needed to leave her abusive partner? What would happen to the child if the survivor lied to her to protect her from painful information about her father being the cause of the survivor's injuries? Would this child grow up with her own anxieties about the world? Now multiply this over and over again beyond a single incident to a pattern of coercive control and actions taken to harm children. Traditional risk frameworks usually do not prioritize the development of this information to guide legal and administrative assessments and decisions.

To illustrate the importance of these missing elements, I want you to imagine you are responsible for making decisions related to parenting time and custody for a family where the father has a history of domestic violence. I would imagine it would feel important and useful to know the following:

> The exact nature of harm caused by the father's violent and controlling behavior to child, partner, and family functioning
>
> The full range of potential future harms to the children that might result if the perpetrator continues his behaviors
>
> How past coercive control is shaping current family court dynamics to the detriment of the adult and child survivors, with, for example, a survivor not pressing for full custody or half the assets in family court when that is what she really wants

CHAPTER 8: THE MYTH OF PARENTAL ALIENATION

> Whether the domestic violence perpetrator is targeting professionals and trying to influence their input through manipulation or threats

I've come to believe that these are critical areas that need to be explored, alongside any risk assessment for future violence toward the adult survivor. When courts do not consider evidence of the connection between a perpetrator's behaviors and their impact on child, partner, and family functioning, it becomes exponentially easier for a perpetrator to claim that the other parent is alienating when in actuality she is protecting. This, combined with a lack of focus on postseparation coercive control and a perpetrator's patterns of manipulating systems, leaves courts vulnerable to being targeted by the perpetrator who wants to use those systems via accusations of alienation or other means.

Gender and Parental Alienation

The same Australian parental alienation expert—the one who insisted that it was not appropriate to explore parental alienation if there was a suspicion of abuse—also told me she had *never* seen parental alienation alleged against a father. Like "failure to protect" in theory, parental alienation on its face is gender neutral. And also, like failure to protect in practice, parental alienation in practice is highly gendered. This gendered application helps explain why parental alienation is successful in swamping histories of domestic violence and child abuse. Gender bias was present from the inception of the concept of parental alienation as evidenced by Gardner's dismissive attitudes toward the veracity of child sexual abuse allegations and his apologies for pedophilia, his misogynistic views of women, and his belief that mothers fabricate allegations of abuse because they are angry and punishing.[7]

Low expectations for men as parents, a corollary to misogynistic attitudes toward mothers, operate as both a sword and shield for men who are perpetrators. Low expectations shield men's parenting from close scrutiny and, more broadly, the same applies to implications of their life choices for their children. While women's choices, from her meal preparation to employment and relationship choices, are part of the cultural scorecard of her parenting, men's value to their children is often primarily viewed through the lens of his role as a breadwinner. This means that the rest of his behaviors—which can have a profound influence on the day-to-day functioning of his partner, his children, and his family—often fall outside the sphere of meaningful professional scrutiny. And even when his behaviors are examined, they are given different weight and meaning. They are considered less central to the children's emotional and physical needs and less central to their healthy development.

The minimization of men's parenting and life choices is cumulative over the life of a case and challenging to identify because it is about what is absent or missing, not what is present. The information about his parenting and its impact is often not developed in the first place. Professionals ask fewer questions about his role in the family, and therefore this information is never fully documented or factored into reports or other sources of information presented to a court.

For example, I regularly asked professionals working with children who were on some form of psychotropic medications if they knew whether the fathers (any fathers, not just violent fathers) were in favor of or against the medication regimen. The majority had no idea if the father was supportive of, opposed to, or neutral about his child taking this medication. How could his role in the therapeutic success or his role in the failure of his child even be assessed if the question was never even considered? Whether a father is actively involved with his child's mental health treatment or not is not the point. **The point is that professionals don't even consider the question of his involvement to be relevant.** Even his lack of involvement in his own child's treatment should be considered relevant, important information for any discussion regarding parenting time and custody.

Therefore, we can assume that assessments of families are often skewed, leaving blank the spaces that belong to the descriptions of fathers' behaviors and their impact. Instead, reports are lopsided, with mothers' behaviors, not fathers', under the microscope of professional scrutiny. Fathers are ignored and their influence over the functioning of the family is minimized in favor of a model of family functioning that makes mothers responsible for *everything*, good or bad, that happens with children.

(Another friendly reminder: I'm not talking about what *actually happens* in families but the approach that professionals and systems take to working with families. My point is that fathers' real-life involvement in the development of their children is complex, varied, and rich, but that professionals often ignore it in the way they assess families.)

Low standards for men as parents also mean that even when the behaviors of a domestic violence perpetrator are presented to a court, their relevance to children's safety and well-being is ignored or minimized. One way it shows up is in statements like these:

> "Yes, he was violent, but because it happened between him and his partner, it isn't relevant to his parenting."
>
> "Yes, he was violent, but the children didn't see it or were too young to understand it."
>
> "Yes, he was violent, but he says he really loves his kids."

Not only is he benefitting from implicit gender bias around men, women, and parenting but he is also benefiting from the myth of the domestic violence incident and the myth of the child witness. So, in this way, low expectations for men as parents also shield them from the consequences of their behavior, even when it is laid out in detail by a survivor or through evidence provided by other systems.

Domestic violence perpetrators regularly argue for their rights to have contact with their children. Used as a sword, low standards for men as parents help perpetrators manipulate the court into focusing more on survivors' behaviors than their own. Low expectations for a man as a parent means that even his insistence that he is worried about her parenting can be perceived as a sign of his dedication to his children. The effective use of parental alienation against a protective parent is the quintessential example of how domestic violence perpetrators can use the sword of low expectations of men as parents.

Co-Parenting and Pro-Contact Frameworks Overpower the Abuse Concerns

In the family law sector, cooperative or collaborative co-parenting is the North Star for postseparation parenting. "Good" parents need to put aside the differences with their partner that led to their divorce or separation and work together, focusing on the needs of their children. This is not an unreasonable expectation. Co-parenting practitioners place a strong emphasis on behaviors such as empathy and flexibility, promoting the relationship between the child and the other parent, respecting the other parent, setting aside feelings of hurt and anger, and owning mistakes. Data suggest that if parents, postseparation, can co-parent well, then their children are likely to have similar outcomes to children with parents who stay together and parent well together.[8]

Unfortunately, in instances where there has been domestic violence, the survivor may not feel safe enough, physically and emotionally, to work collaboratively with the person who has hurt and controlled her. This same person may also have shown disregard for the children's needs, ignored the damage caused by his behavior, and/or engaged in direct forms of child abuse. In many of these cases that person has not acknowledged his hurtful behaviors, nor has he stopped them. In fact, in many instances, the perpetrator is continuing to actively work against the ideals of collaborative co-parenting.

In many family law settings, there is implicit and explicit expectation that parents will engage in collaborative co-parenting. The basic definition of collaborative co-parenting is "being able to work well with the other parent, keeping the focus on the children's needs, and not complaining about the other parent." The dominance of this ideal often places tremendous pressure on survivor parents to work with the perpetrating parent regardless of destroyed trust and respect, honorably earned anger, fear of future violence, or current manipulation and control. This expectation is often present regardless of the perpetrator's creation of an environment of distrust and continuing postseparation attacks, actions that are all inconsistent with the spirit of collaborative co-parenting. Pressure and scrutiny of the survivor often escalates when she expresses reasonable and justifiable concerns about the other parent. This can be seen as evidence of poor co-parenting, instead of protection, and at the extreme the expressed concerns become twisted into unfair accusations of parental alienation.

The collaborative co-parenting lens is rarely applied with any real rigor to the behavior of perpetrators whose coercive control and lack of responsibility for their own behavior is the antithesis of collaborative co-parenting. Courts often do not require perpetrators to acknowledge their behaviors, especially the damage it has done to the trust of the other parent. Nor are the perpetrators expected to repair the damage they have caused their children or the co-parenting relationship with their ex-partner.

Consider how a domestic violence perpetrator you are familiar with would score on the following scales. On a scale of one to ten with one being "awful" and ten being "amazing," how would this person score in each of the following areas:

> Shows ability to put aside differences with the other parent
>
> Shows ability to focus on the needs of his children and not on his conflict with his ex-partner
>
> Works to empathize with the other parent's struggles
>
> Shows flexibility around negotiations with the other parent

> Demonstrates a consistent pattern of respect for the other parent
>
> Demonstrates support for the other parent's relationship with the children
>
> Owns his own mistakes
>
> Handles responsibly his own feelings of hurt and anger

More attention needs to be put on how perpetrators score on scales such as this before we turn attention to the survivor's co-parenting.

These failures to examine a perpetrator's history of collaborative co-parenting (or lack thereof) before and after separation makes systems more vulnerable to manipulation and collusion with perpetrators. And it also makes it easier to "flip the script" and start alleging that the survivor is "alienating" or trying to prevent contact when, in reality, it is his behavior that has blown up the co-parenting relationship.

How the Safe & Together Model Innovates to Challenge the Myth of Parental Alienation

The Safe & Together Model's perpetrator pattern-based approach offers a way to combat perpetrators' use of the myth of parental alienation as their sword and shield. It does this by offering an objective, behavioral-focused assessment framework that can be applied, without prejudice or prejudgment, to any domestic violence-related scenario. At the same time, this behavioral approach inoculates assessments, and therefore the decisions that arise from them, from the gender double standards of low expectations of fathers and high expectations of mothers that can facilitate the weaponization of parental alienation allegations against adult and child survivors.

> **❝The Model explains really well how the perpetrator's behavior and pattern is impacting on parenting. That was the missing piece for me in terms of recognizing that survivors aren't to blame and are not responsible for the perpetrator's behavior.❞**
>
> —Melody, court child expert, Australia

Correcting for Gender Bias

Quantum physics teaches us that light is both a wave and a particle. Similarly, the Safe & Together Model's perpetrator pattern-based approach is both objective, eschewing prejudgment based on gender, and at the same time acts to unravel and rectify low expectations of men as parents. The objective, comprehensive framework that can identify when a woman is a primary aggressor in a heterosexual relationship is the same framework that helps articulate a level playing field of expectations of men and women as parents. Instead of defaulting to an unfair, gendered expectation of parenting where day-to-day care of children is seen primarily as the domains of mothers, a behavioral framework helps explain how the behaviors of any perpetrator, male or female, are harming child, partner, and family functioning.

When applied in the context of systems that historically have had low standards for men as parents, an objective and comprehensive behavioral assessment lens applied to all parents automatically corrects for the importance of fathers' behaviors to child, partner, and family functioning. By simply asking more regularly how the father's violence and abuse impacted his relationship with the children, we can get a sense of how those behaviors may have played into the estrangement and distance between that father and his children—again offering an antidote to the myth of parental alienation. When we are more holistic and comprehensive in our assessment of the quality of fathers' parenting, we can neutralize the use of the concept of parental alienation as a weapon against survivors by perpetrators and practitioners. By pivoting to the perpetrator as parent, which involves raising expectations of fathers who are abusive, we recontextualize the survivors' decision-making. Just as a perpetrator pattern-based approach helps create an alternative to failure to protect as the focal point in child protection, it helps shift the focal point of attention in family court onto the perpetrator as parent.

The following chart lays out the Model's "both/and" approach that rests on an objective behavioral approach and addresses gender double standards in parenting expectations.

Safe & Together Model's "both/and" approach to gender in domestic violence cases.

Problem		Solution	
The myth of parental alienation	Domestic violence-informed practice	Objective and gender-neutral	Equalizes gendered parenting expectations
Provides a limited definition of abuse—heavily focused on physical violence, not coercive control or child maltreatment, as part of patterns; focus on risk not harm	Uses perpetrator pattern-based lens	Provides a wider behavioral approach that can be applied equally to diverse situations, including women's use of violence and control against men, men's use of violence and control against women, and same-sex and trans relationships	Provides an equally applied, wider behavioral lens and a more comprehensive assessment of how those behaviors impact child, partner, and family functioning and corrects for low expectations of fathers as parents
Provides a limited understanding of protective behaviors	Provides a fuller spectrum of understanding of survivors' efforts to promote the safety and well-being of children	Provides a comprehensive behavioral approach to assessing protective efforts, which is used in the context of a perpetrator pattern-based approach and offers the most accurate assessment of survivors' parenting	Provides a full-spectrum approach that gives more accurate credit to protective mothers for their efforts, which are often overlooked due to gender bias

CHAPTER 8: THE MYTH OF PARENTAL ALIENATION

Problem	Solution		
Confuses alignment with protective parenting as "failing to be neutral between the parties"	Partners with protective parents	Yields child-safety-driven decisions by family court, which will naturally be more aligned with and supportive of a protective parents' efforts—this is not bias but judicial decision-making in alignment with statutory mandates around child safety and best interests	Removes the argument that courts are biased based on gender if they rule in favor of protective mothers. Decisions that support the efforts of protective mothers are decisions that support child safety
Fails to identify postseparation coercive control as a relevant issue	Highlights post-separation coercive control and perpetrator manipulation of systems	Gives attention to post-separation behavior patterns and decreases the likelihood that courts and professionals will be recruited or bullied into colluding with perpetrators	Stresses post-separation coercive control, which has often been ignored in family court settings, thus allowing fathers who have histories of coercive control to manipulate systems; attention to this dynamic reduces the likelihood of successful use of courts and other systems to extend coercive control
Decontextualizes survivors' mental health and addiction from perpetrators' coercive control	Recontextualizes mental health and substance misuse to include the perpetrators' patterns	Pays attention to connections between perpetrators' behaviors and survivors' mental health and addiction issues, including interference with recovery and treatment, fabricated allegations, and overall weaponization of mental health and substance use issues against survivors	Combats cultural stereotyping of women being "unstable" and "crazy" by identifying the role of perpetrating fathers in the mental health and addiction issues of the survivor
Uses collaborative parenting and pro-contact culture to judge survivor parents, not perpetrators	Focuses on the collaborative co-parenting (or lack thereof) of the perpetrator	Applies collaborative co-parenting standards usefully to improve the assessment of perpetrators as parents	Provides consistent application of the collaborative co-parenting standards to fathers who are perpetrators in order to improve outcomes for children. This helps since low standards for fathers have meant less accountability for behaviors that have interfered with the needs of the children being met.

While potentially seeming paradoxical to some, this equality-based approach corrects for gender bias by equally applying an objective behavioral framework that works regardless of sex, gender, or sexual orientation.

The Value of Applying an Objective, Comprehensive Behavioral Lens

The Safe & Together Model assessment framework was designed from its inception to be comprehensive and objective. Its behavioral, pattern-based approach was crafted to work regardless of sex, gender, sexual orientation, race, or other demographic factors. Objectivity and neutrality in government, especially court processes, are essential to fairness, equality, impartiality, and due process. A behavioral assessment framework approaches all individuals equally and dispassionately. More comprehensive, and therefore more accurate, assessments require a broader lens than one that just focuses on adult-to-adult physical violence. Instead, the lens needs to embrace wider dynamics of coercive control, including the social dynamics of power, privilege, and institutional responses that contribute to entrapment.

Using a wider, pattern-based lens makes it easier to contextualize the reactions and fears of both adult and child survivors. One of the core advantages of this approach is it helps practitioners better understand how a perpetrator's control does not disappear just because there have not been any recent incidents of physical violence. When the issue of domestic violence is understood to be shaped by the control by one person over the functioning of other family members, then it becomes easier to see the continuing impact of past behaviors, to make sense of shifting tactics, and to appreciate how a lack of trust in the perpetrator is reasonable and justified. The more accurately we understand the pattern of abuse, the more sense we can make of survivors' fears and worries. This helps systems to achieve one of the hallmarks of being domestic violence-informed: respecting and honoring survivors' assessments of their situation based on their knowledge of the perpetrators' patterns.

CHAPTER 8: THE MYTH OF PARENTAL ALIENATION

When an objective, comprehensive, impartial assessment process leads the court to identify that one parent has been shaping the children's environment through patterns of coercive control and the other parent has been engaging in patterns of protection and resistance for the children, then it becomes the obligation of the court to recognize this difference and build its decisions on the foundation of those facts. This should not be understood as unfairly taking the side of one parent over the other. **When a court enters orders that align with and support the protective efforts of a parent, this is the logical fulfillment of the court's obligation to child safety and to meaningful relationships with the parents.**

Post-separation coercive control deserves its own special place in the discussion of a wider assessment lens because of the commonly held but mistaken belief that the end of a relationship signals the end of the abuse. Domestic violence perpetrators are varied in how they handle the end of a relationship. Many move on. Others escalate their abuse, frequently modifying behaviors to the new circumstance. This often means an escalation in threats, continued or intensified physical violence, increased focus on children as tools of coercion, stalking, and the use of systems to threaten, punish, and harm.

Mapping harm and identifying ongoing dynamics of coercive control that are actively impacting the court process are necessary to give context to any resistance or refusal around contact or custody. An understanding of patterns of coercive control and their ongoing impact is required in order to be able to identify when an adult or a child survivor's acts of resistance or refusal around contact are justified and reasonable—a necessary step in disarming the weaponization of the myth of parental alienation. Without this framework, practitioners can inadvertently—but easily—collude with perpetrators.

In each case, practitioners should be asking:

> What postseparation coercive control behaviors is the perpetrator engaging in?

> How is past perpetrator behavior—for example, threats to take children—impacting the mother's approach to family court?
>
> How are professionals involved with the court process being targeted for manipulation, intimidation, or threats?
>
> How is the perpetrator presenting himself and/or representing the mother in identifiably false ways—for instance, lying about past arrests?

When ongoing, postseparation coercive control dynamics are identified, here are a few questions about the systems' response:

a. What is the court doing to address the unequal, unsafe playing field?
b. How is the court factoring in the ongoing manipulation of professionals and systems into any assessment of parenting?
c. How are professionals' safety (emotional and physical) being protected?
d. How are obvious falsehoods and manipulations being addressed by the court?

To successfully address domestic violence in postseparation situations, perpetrators' patterns of behavior must be addressed, and tailored interventions regarding those patterns are necessary.

Behavior Change Standards and Collaborative Co-parenting

Increased accountability for perpetrators as parents cannot stop with a clearer identification of patterns of behavior and their impact. Clear expectations of behavior change are required. There are two ways to approach this. The first way is a focus on what real change looks like in general. In a white paper on perpetrators and change, I defined a set of expectations related to assessing change.[9] Instead of demanding just compliance with a program, we want to see meaningful, consistent change in line with the following standards:

> The perpetrator needs to be able to admit to the abusive behaviors ("name it").
>
> The perpetrator needs to be able to acknowledge that his behaviors have created harm to others and to describe the nature of the harms he has caused ("claim it").
>
> The perpetrator needs to change his behavior patterns, stopping the abuse and supporting the healing and recovery of others, particularly children ("change it").

Having high, clearly articulated behavior-change standards for perpetrators can help keep the courts and practitioners focused on the perpetrator and his change (or lack thereof). In a wonderful example of how this might translate into judicial decision-making, a senior judge, after receiving Safe & Together Model training, said that he was going to expect perpetrators to take these steps or pay the consequences in terms of the court's decision related to custody and parenting time. There have been some promising changes in Scotland:

> *"I spoke about Safe & Together to a clinical psychologist, who at the time was one of the foremost experts in court cases around child contact. After that, she framed every report she made to court around Safe & Together—and she championed it as well. So, it's not just about changing the language and practices of social workers—it's across the system."*

—Mhairi, violence against women and girls consultant, Scotland

Secondly, these standards need to extend specifically to perpetrators as parents. Behavior-change expectations cannot just reflect how the perpetrator has acted toward his partner. When we are considering the reasonable expectations of a perpetrator as a parent, we cannot stop at the cessation of violence. For example, professionals need to articulate that a perpetrator is also responsible for repairing the harm he has created for his children.

We can also increase accountability for perpetrators as parents by applying the gold standard expectation of collaborative co-parenting to the behavior of the perpetrator. Healthy and collaborative co-parenting after divorce, and even while married, have some commonly understood ideas associated with it. Here is a smattering of statements from websites about co-parenting after divorce. All of them speak to the benefits to children of this type of parenting relationship.

> **Successful co-parenting means that your own emotions—any anger, resentment, or hurt—must take a back seat to the needs of your children.**
>
> **Don't put your children in the middle.**
>
> **Show empathy and be flexible. Ask your ex's opinion. Apologize.**
>
> **Do not let your feelings be in control.**
>
> **Understand you can't control your co-parent.**
>
> **Look for common ground as you make decisions.**

It is easy to see that most domestic violence perpetrators who are unrepentant in their patterns of coercive control will fail to meet these basic criteria. For others, the articulation of these expectations may be able to encourage positive change or, at a minimum, help measure failure of the father to focus on his children's needs.

Final Thoughts on the Myth of Parental Alienation

Accusations of parental alienation against protective parents is one of the most harmful myths in this book because it is used to turn family court proceedings, which lead to decisions that can have far-reaching effects on the lives of children, on their head. Situations where the facts of the abuse should lead to slam-dunk decisions related to children remaining in the custody of the survivor become twisted into scenarios in which children are being placed unsupervised in dangerous custody and parenting situations. The Model offers a chance to reset the playing field to one that is more objective and behaviorally focused, helping courts remain true to their mandate to focus on child safety in their decision-making.

CHAPTER 9

The Myth of Trauma-Informed Practice

I hate (yes, I think that is the right word) the phrase "noncompliant." Notes and reports, by diverse professionals ranging from child protection workers to attorneys, are littered with references to the "noncompliance" of a parent with the court or social worker expectations of participation in some counseling or educational program. It is a catchall phrase that emphasizes the failure of the parent to attend or complete the program. It's often thrown around without context, curiosity, or compassion.

I especially hate the term when it is applied to domestic violence survivors' involvement with services such as specialists in family violence, mental health programs, and substance abuse programs. I hate that term because it is part of a professional paradigm that regularly ignores the forces that may make it hard or impossible or inappropriate for a survivor to comply with expectations placed on her by often-well-meaning practitioners. For example, a survivor whose partner sabotages her ability to attend a treatment program through harassment, accusations, and control over transportation might be labeled as "noncompliant." No distinction is usually made between a person who fails on her own and a person whose participation is sabotaged by another. The term also is a fig leaf for other forms of systemic issues such as culturally unsafe services or gaps in childcare that prevent attendance in programs.

CHAPTER 9: THE MYTH OF TRAUMA-INFORMED PRACTICE

...a survivor whose partner sabotages her ability to attend a treatment program through harassment, accusations, and control over transportation might be labeled as "noncompliant." No distinction is usually made between a person who fails on her own and a person whose participation is sabotaged by another.

Systems that are heavily invested in the mental health and/or substance misuse treatment of survivors as central intervention with families impacted by perpetrators can easily become part of the systemic blaming of mothers and ignoring of fathers. In domestic violence cases, it is much more likely that discussions will focus on a mother's "noncompliance" with (domestic violence, mental health, or substance misuse) treatment than it will be about how the perpetrator sabotaged the mother's access to services, interfered with her ability to attend counseling, or caused the mother's depression through abuse.

The use of the term "noncompliance" deflects attention from the perpetrators' role in sabotaging survivors' access to and success in mental health and substance misuse treatment. It is just one of the many ways that practitioners blame mothers and ignore fathers when it comes to the intersection of mental health, substance misuse, and domestic violence. The following dialogues offer other examples of how practitioners can ignore fathers and blame mothers. **Each example, which is a composite of real conversations, also includes my efforts redirecting practitioners' inappropriate focus on survivors back on the perpetrator and his behaviors.**

CHAPTER 9: THE MYTH OF TRAUMA-INFORMED PRACTICE

CHAPTER 9: THE MYTH OF TRAUMA-INFORMED PRACTICE

Worker: He needs to heal his trauma history. That will help him stop his violence. He needs to heal first.

Me: How long will it take for him to heal? Healing from trauma is a lifelong process. Acting violently does not assist his healing, in fact it may make it harder.

Worker: There is something wrong with this mom. She said to me that she liked it better when he was drinking and drugging. I think she may be codependent.

Me: Did she say why?

Worker: Yes. She said his control has gotten worse. He's criticizing her parenting. He's controlling all the money. He's taking the car to go to his meetings. He tells her that his counselor says that his sobriety is more important than anything else, so she's being selfish when she wants to use the car to go grocery shopping for the family because it interferes with his meetings. She says before, he was so wrapped up in drinking and drugging, he left her alone a lot of the time to parent and run the household the way she wanted. And she's worried he'll get violent.

Me: So stopping drinking didn't stop his abuse and control. I'm not sure she's codependent. Sounds like she's having an understandable response to his continuing pattern of abuse.

Conversations like these can be understood through a number of different lenses. Some would label these attitudes as victim-blaming. Others might see the failure of systems to hold perpetrators accountable for their behaviors or the influence of sexism on professional practice (regardless of whether the practitioner is male or female or nonbinary). None of these is an unreasonable assessment, yet none of these perspectives offers an analysis into the underlying dynamics, challenges, and solutions specific to the situations in which domestic violence intersects with mental health and substance misuse.

Practitioners across the globe refer to the prevalence of the combination of these three issues—domestic violence, mental health, and substance misuse—with clever shorthand phrases such as "toxic trio" (United Kingdom),[1] "triple play" (United States), or "trifecta" (Australia). A 2018 report from the UK Office of the Children's Commissioner estimated that the prevalence rate of children aged zero through seventeen who lived in households in England with an adult where there is domestic violence plus substance misuse or mental health issues was 15.9 percent, or 1.88 million children.[2] A 2016 needs assessment of families involved with the Ohio Department of Job and Family Services found that domestic violence, mental health, and substance misuse were the top three issues facing families. The Ohio study further found that among the permutations of these issues, domestic violence was the most common of three issues once they were broken out into a series of case profiles.[3]

Much has been written about the co-occurrence of domestic violence, substance misuse, and mental health issues. Researchers, advocates, and professionals have probed the relationship between these problems for years, but there is still a long way to go in understanding the complex interactions. Early theories about domestic violence show the influence of psychology on the understanding of the problem. Ideas have included awful misogynistic pop psychology concepts such as the theory that domestic violence survivors are "masochists" who enjoy being hurt and more nuanced theories such as "learned helplessness." More recent explorations of the intersection of mental health and domestic violence reflect the dominance of trauma theory. The trauma framework is sprawling enough that it includes the misuse of substances, which is often seen as a symptom or a correlate of trauma histories. In many ways, the trauma lens dominates conversations about the intersection of mental health, substance misuse, and domestic violence.

> ❝ *You can't be trauma-informed unless you are domestic violence-informed, and because you're using Safe & Together in regard to looking at intersections, you are aware of where perpetrators (and their workers) are trying to open the door to weaponization of a survivor's mental health and addiction.* ❞
>
> —Emma S., specialist family violence advisor, Australia

A Groundbreaking Approach

Trauma approaches have been groundbreaking in terms of creating understanding and support for survivors. Developed out of work with war veterans, the concept of trauma has grown and expanded to cover a wide variety of experiences, including domestic violence. The Australian Institute of Health and Welfare has this to say about what can be potentially traumatic: "Any event that involves exposure to actual or threatened death, serious injury, or sexual violence has the potential to be traumatic."[4] The UK Trauma Council says trauma can come about because of "the way that some distressing events are so extreme or intense that they overwhelm a person's ability to cope, resulting in lasting negative impact."[5] The US-based National Child Traumatic Stress Network defines a traumatic event as a "frightening, dangerous, or violent event that poses a threat to a child's life or bodily integrity."[6] The mainstream understanding of trauma is tightly tied to extreme events, whether they be violence by people, natural disasters, accidents, war, or other similar circumstances.

Often the conversation about trauma ignores the diversity and complexity of the different sources of trauma and focuses primarily on the symptoms and the treatment of the symptoms that arise from these "distressing events." The concept of trauma, therefore, is closely associated with a wide range of mental health disorders, such as anxiety, post-traumatic stress disorder, depression, suicidality, and disassociation. Research has also supported a strong connection between trauma and substance misuse. Driven by research such as Felitti's and others' "Adverse Childhood Experiences" study,[7] these diagnoses have legitimized the effects of the violence, sexual abuse, and other potentially traumatic events and led to the development of a treatment industry that utilizes a mixture of pharmaceutical, medical, and counseling treatment interventions. In this way, trauma and the associated diagnoses have become a primary lens for understanding survivors' experience of domestic violence.

The ubiquity and related far-reaching influence of the concept of trauma cannot be overestimated. What started as a framework for psychological diagnosis and treatment has spiraled out to become a touchstone for public health efforts and wide-ranging educational efforts with professionals ranging from teachers to doctors to lawyers. The concept of being "trauma-informed" means that even those who are not providing direct mental health treatment have a role to play in understanding trauma and adapting their practice to prevent further harm and to support healing. Treating trauma survivors with compassion, offering emotional safety, and being nonjudgmental all help that individual and also benefit the professional's efficacy with the client, the operational success of organizations and businesses, and the health and well-being of the wider community. Trauma-informed practices, at their best, offer domestic violence survivors compassion and support instead of judgment and blame.

How the Current Trauma-Informed Lens Is Not Enough and Fails Victims

Take this scenario as an example. The line in the mental health program

CHAPTER 9: THE MYTH OF TRAUMA-INFORMED PRACTICE

discharge summary read: "Maria needs further treatment for post-traumatic stress disorder and participation in a program for family members with addiction." On the surface this sounds like a straightforward, sound mental health discharge recommendation for an adolescent girl who has a history of depression, anxiety, and suicidality. The recommendations' massive gaps only come into shape when you put them into the context of domestic violence-informed practice:

> The recommendations don't specifically say that the person who caused her trauma was her father.
>
> They don't specifically say that it was her father who had the drug problem.
>
> They don't say that abuse wasn't just "historic" but also current and ongoing. She was not in a situation of "post" abuse because the abuse was ongoing.
>
> They don't say anything about safety planning around the potential for further violence.
>
> They don't say anything of the father's pattern of controlling Maria's therapy or of his bullying counselors.
>
> They don't say anything of the ongoing family court order for Maria to be in therapy with her father, the very person who was abusing her.
>
> They don't document any assessment for sexual abuse.

Maria's high-status, wealthy-business-owner father had been abusing her mom, her, and her siblings for years, and the abuse and coercive control continued postseparation. The mental health system's intervention, which was heavily focused on Maria's symptoms and their treatment, failed to identify the ongoing dynamics of coercive control and their implications for Maria's safety and well-being. Unfortunately, these are not uncommon holes in the mental health response to domestic violence and adult and child survivors.

Despite efforts of advocates, survivors, and researchers, mainstream mental health and substance use programs are not domestic violence informed. Assessment and service delivery is siloed. Assessments do not capture the way that patterns of coercive control change (or don't) with mental health treatment or substance use. They do not capture how perpetrators' behaviors cause or exacerbate a survivors' mental health or substance use issues. And they almost never assess for issues of false allegations, weaponization of these issues against survivors, or wider issues of entrapment and deprivation of liberties.

Despite its tremendous benefits, the trauma lens does have significant flaws and limitations that allow us to talk about the myth of "trauma-informed practice." In this dense chapter, I explore the myth of "trauma-informed" practice and how the dominance of the trauma framework crowds out other important perspectives on the intersection of domestic violence, mental health, and addiction. I explore the multiple permutations of how these three issues interact and how coercive control is often missing from the conversations about mental health and substance misuse issues. I explore how the orientation toward pathology overshadows any assessment of protective efforts and how trauma frameworks' backward-looking nature doesn't promote a focus on current dynamics of coercive control. Together we'll dive into how perpetrators' behaviors intersect with their own substance abuse and trauma. The middle section of this chapter ends with an examination of the challenges associated with perpetrators' threats of suicide, how perpetrators' false allegations of substance misuse and mental health issues fall outside the purview of the mainstream mental health and substance misuse frameworks, and how survivors' trauma histories become disconnected from the person who caused them. Finally, the chapter finishes with a look at how the Safe & Together Model's conceptualization of the relationship between these three issues as a series of intersections, instead of co-occurring issues, can help bring practice into better alignment with the experience of adult and child survivors.

The Myth of Trauma-Informed Practice

While academics have struggled to sort out the different relationships between these three issues, time-strapped, service-driven practitioners have often boiled down the complexity to a laundry list of "co-occurring problems." This "laundry list" of problems is then translated into the jargon of risk factors or into reasons for referral to specialized and often-siloed services. Substance misuse issues equal a referral to substance misuse treatment. Depression and anxiety result in referral to a mental health professional. Domestic violence issues result in referral to men's behavior change services or victim services. In almost every case, each problem is assessed separately, and each problem is treated by a separate, specialized service. The "laundry list" approach simplifies and silos the complex relationship between all three issues. It glosses over the importance of identifying the differences in each combination of these three issues, how they interact with one another, and what that means for intervention and support.

Complexity takes many forms. When I was running a men's behavior change program, there was a substantial minority of men who identified as recovering alcoholics and addicts who self-referred because they continued abusing intimate partners even after years of sobriety. In another permutation of the intersection of mental health, substance misuse, and domestic violence, I worked with other men who were trauma survivors of violence in their childhood home. These men were both survivors with mental health issues and adult perpetrators who inflicted trauma on others. In another variation on complexity, domestic violence survivors who were identified as having mental health and/or substance use issues were having those problems used against them in family court and in child protection cases. Perpetrators may make false allegations about a partner's mental health problems in order to isolate the partner and gain allies in controlling her. In another example, perpetrators often use diagnoses of mental health and/or substance abuse issues to deflect attention and accountability away from their choice to be violent.

Each of these situations, which are a tiny fraction of the possible examples, has widely different dynamics. For example, when men are perpetrators of adult abuse and also survivors of childhood violence, an approach is needed that helps them recover from their childhood trauma without allowing it to become an excuse for their adult violence toward others. When a survivor has mental health issues in the context of being coercively controlled, she needs support for her mental health and interventions directed to her partner's control. Many situations require attention to multiple issues, including the role of the perpetrator in causing the survivors' issues and the potential for perpetrator interference with treatment.

> *Substance misuse issues equal a referral to substance misuse treatment. Depression and anxiety result in referral to a mental health professional. Domestic violence issues result in referral to men's behavior change services or victim services. In almost every case, each problem is assessed separately, and each problem is treated by a separate, specialized service. The "laundry list" approach simplifies and silos the complex relationship between all three issues.*

Multiple Permutations

Here is a chart with examples of the major possible combinations of these three issues related to adults. If we included other combinations of adult substance use and mental health diagnoses or children's mental health or substance use, the picture would become even more complex!

CHAPTER 9: THE MYTH OF TRAUMA-INFORMED PRACTICE

Multiple combinations of domestic violence, mental health, and substance use

	SURVIVOR MENTAL HEALTH (MH)	SURVIVOR SUBSTANCE USE	SURVIVOR MH AND SUBSTANCE USE	SURVIVOR NEITHER
PERPETRATOR SUBSTANCE USE	**Perpetrator:** alcoholic **Survivor:** depressed	**Perpetrator:** alcoholic **Survivor:** alcoholic	**Perpetrator:** alcoholic **Survivor:** PTSD and opioid addicted	**Perpetrator:** alcoholic **Survivor:** No issues (except being abused)
PERPETRATOR MENTAL HEALTH (MH)	**Perpetrator:** OCD **Survivor:** anxiety disorder	**Perpetrator:** OCD **Survivor:** meth addicted	**Perpetrator:** OCD **Survivor:** meth addicted and anxiety disorder	**Perpetrator:** OCD **Survivor:** No issues (except being abused)
Perpetrator MH and substance use	**Perpetrator:** depression, alcoholism **Survivor:** anxiety	**Perpetrator:** depression, alcoholism **Survivor:** alcoholism	**Perpetrator:** depression, alcoholism **Survivor:** anxiety; meth	**Perpetrator:** depression, alcoholism **Survivor:** No issues (except being abused)
Perpetrator neither	**Survivor:** anxiety	**Survivor:** meth addiction	**Survivor:** meth and anxiety	**Perpetrator & Survivor:** Neither

This chart shows the potential for sixteen permutations of these three issues. Each of one of these scenarios can involve different patterns of coercive control and vulnerabilities. This doesn't even take into account the major differences that are glossed over with the broad terms of "mental health" and "substance misuse." Different substances may have different effects on functioning or associated patterns of behavior. For example, alcohol and methamphetamines differ in their effects on the body and may intersect differently with coercive control. Different mental health issues, similarly, have differences in how they manifest and how they impact a person's functioning. Major mental health issues, such as schizophrenia, may severely impair functioning over long periods of time. Other mental health issues can be more situational and temporary.

Contextual differences also matter. Individual childhood trauma may be associated with a different constellation of dynamics than, say, cultural and societal trauma inflicted by racism or colonization. Someone may be treated or untreated for issues. Different problems may offer different vulnerabilities for the survivor. For example, substance misuse that involves illegal substances may make the survivor vulnerable to control by the perpetrator through threats to report her to the police. The importance of understanding the complex interactions between domestic violence, substance misuse, and mental health issues cannot be ignored, underestimated, or dumbed down.

Coercive Control Is Missing from the Trauma Lens

> Setting up "nanny cams" in the house to monitor the activities of all family members and visitors to the home
>
> Illegally turning off power to the house, through personal connections at the power company so that she and the children have no lights and heat
>
> Taking possession of the lone family car after being ordered out of the house on a court order
>
> Making completely fabricated allegations of the mother's mental health problems to child protection
>
> Filing hundreds of motions in family court against the other parent in one year

What do these items have in common? They are examples of significant and serious controlling behaviors of domestic violence perpetrators that do not fall on the spectrum of "potentially traumatic events" (formal lingo about situations that might cause trauma). They are examples of behaviors that are part of perpetrators' patterns of entrapment and deprivation of liberties, but they do not fit into the common conception of events or actions that can cause traumatic symptoms. While trauma theory, as it is currently understood and practiced, aligns with the aspects of domestic violence that include severe violence, life-endangering threats, and sexual assault, it doesn't include many other aspects of coercive control. In fact, it could be argued it doesn't capture the majority of behaviors and dynamics associated with coercive control.

In some situations of even extreme coercive control, there is no or minimal physical violence. Physical violence does not have to be severe in order to cause humiliation, violate autonomy, and demonstrate control. It's unlikely for professionals to identify throwing food onto a survivor in front of her children as fitting the formal definition of a "potentially traumatic event," a definition that hinges on the victim being worried about her physical integrity or very survival. Yet the survivor may experience significant feelings of humiliation, embarrassment, and shame—feelings that are likely to change her functioning and generate strategies of resistance and protection in order to avoid future attacks.

The trauma model doesn't easily encompass or capture dynamics associated with low-level violence that demonstrate the perpetrator's ability to cross boundaries with impunity, as these types of demonstrations of power, by themselves, do not meet the criteria of a "potentially traumatic event." Similarly, rule setting, monitoring, and other behaviors that do not involve any forms of physical violence—such as placing cameras in the house to observe family members or placing a tracker on a car—are not part of the traditional trauma concept. In these ways, trauma approaches do not fully align with or respond to all the dynamics associated with coercive control and lived experiences of survivors.

Missing Acts of Resistance and Protection

The trauma lens and the substance abuse diagnosis and treatment lens offer primarily deficit-based approaches to survivors. The focus is on assessing harm, understanding symptoms, and healing the impact of the perpetrators' behaviors. Similar to the medical model, which is organized around the diagnosis of pathologies and their treatment, the trauma framework does not emphasize or prioritize the assessment of survivors' strengths, including acts of resistance and protection that survivors engage in for themselves and their children.

This absence of a focus on the strengths of survivors by mental health and other professionals is deeply problematic. Mental health and addiction counselors, through their approaches, shape survivors' understanding of their situation and themselves. Practices that only mirror back to survivors their psychological injuries, but not their strengths, may reinforce a negative sense of self. Beyond the mental health implications, there are practical implications of the absence of attention to strengths, acts of resistance, and acts of protection. Mental health and substance use professionals often provide reports and testimony to child protective services and family court. Reports that focus narrowly on symptoms and diagnosis and treatment goals will not reference how a survivor has worked to keep herself and her children safe or how she has worked to keep them on track and engaged in basic activities like going to school. Such reports are not likely to outline how she is maintaining the children's daily schedule, despite the chaos, disruptions, and challenges thrown up by the perpetrator's behaviors.

When professionals do not include acts of protection and resistance in their reports, survivors are at greater risk of being revictimized by systems, particularly as it relates to children. Deficit-focused reports, even when well-intentioned, can fuel destructive responses by systems. Children can pay the price of the failure to focus on the survivors' parenting strengths. When therapist reports lack information about active efforts to protect children, child protective services may make avoidable removals and family court is more likely to make decisions that harm children.

Backward Looking

The word "post" in the term "post-traumatic stress disorder" tells us a lot

CHAPTER 9: THE MYTH OF TRAUMA-INFORMED PRACTICE

about a key orientation of the trauma field. While trauma professionals are focused on healing for improved futures, they are very past-focused in their understanding of the source of the problem. "Post" traumatic stress disorder and other trauma-related diagnoses assume the event(s) or circumstances that cause the trauma are no longer actively occurring. The work is focused on past sexual assaults, past car accidents, past natural disasters, etc. In fact, literature on trauma treatment suggests it cannot start until the person is no longer experiencing those circumstances, such as torture or sexual assault.

Trauma frameworks were not designed to diagnose the current dynamics of coercion control or current active physical safety concerns. They are designed only to understand the link between past violence and current symptoms. The use of the term "safety" in trauma practice can be misleading. In this context it usually relates to a survivor's current emotional safety associated with the fears, anxieties, and broken trust created by past assaults and events. It does not refer to current physical and emotional safety concerns generated by active threats of violence or control.

Here's a metaphor that was used with me in my therapeutic training: It's normal to be afraid when a bear attacks you. It's normal to be traumatized after that assault and, as a result, to not feel safe walking in the woods, even woods that are not home to bears. Smells, sounds, and sights might trigger memories and overwhelming feelings associated with the assault. This is "normal" in the sense of being common, but it's not useful to be reacting to situations as if the bear were there attacking you when there is no bear. In fact, it is draining and limiting to react to threats that are no longer present. Trauma treatment helps the person assaulted by the bear live a more normal, functional life after the assault has passed.

The trauma paradigm fails to recognize that when it comes to domestic violence, the bear may not live off in the woods far away, but instead the bear may still live with us. We may share children with the bear, and the bear doesn't just assault us. The bear may influence or control our finances, lie to others about us, and may not even look dangerous to others. To ignore these bear dynamics might lead to professionals blaming the survivor for "overreacting," or more insidiously, labeling the survivor as having a "trauma reaction" and allowing the bear's threatening and controlling behavior to continue unchecked.

In general, mental health and substance use practitioners are not trained to or expected to assess current dynamics of coercive control and related safety issues. The dominant concept of safety in the trauma-informed lens is the emotional safety that is needed to heal and is the product of healing. While physical safety is considered a prerequisite to healing, assessing physical safety and creating safety plans around immediate physical safety or even coercive control is usually not integrated into trauma treatment. Instead, it is seen as the purview of other systems and professionals, such as law enforcement or domestic violence advocates. Trauma treatment usually doesn't involve mapping any of the following:

> the current danger of physical violence
>
> the dynamics of coercive control
>
> the risks of future violence or control
>
> the gaslighting of the survivor regarding her mental health
>
> the interference by the perpetrator with the survivor's access to treatment
>
> the use of a mental health diagnosis in creating new vulnerabilities to control and manipulate systems to the detriment of the survivor

The "looking backward" model of mental health and the assumption of personal autonomy that underlies both mental health and substance abuse treatment fail to capture key dynamics of the lived experience of many domestic violence survivors.

Trauma Lens and Domestic Violence Perpetrators

The conversation about trauma and domestic violence continues to grow and now encompasses the trauma histories of domestic violence perpetrators. In a contested discussion, some argue that perpetrators' own trauma histories, whether of childhood abuse or the intergenerational trauma of colonization and racism, need to be addressed as part of any response to domestic violence. Others see a focus on perpetrators' trauma histories serving as an excuse for violence and deflection from accountability. No matter where you stand, perpetrators' trauma histories are now part of the broader discussion around domestic violence and trauma. The stakes of this conversation are high. If a trauma is successfully used as an excuse for a pattern of coercive control, accountability and safety suffer. If trauma histories of perpetrators are ignored, the opportunity to help the perpetrator heal and end his abuse at the same time may be missed.

> *I do believe there is a time and place for real trauma-informed work for perpetrating parents who were victimized by domestic violence in their homes when they were younger. I'm not someone who believes that that's irrelevant. However, I take the approach of 'I am not going to allow you to utilize your childhood trauma to excuse what you're doing today.'*
>
> —Beth Ann, S&TI faculty, independent consultant, US

If the complexity of perpetrators who also have their own history of victimization is ignored, certain types of violence and abuse, familial or cultural, are invisible and effectively condoned. Unfortunately, discussions about trauma are often silent about how to handle someone with trauma who is also hurting and controlling others. When it is discussed, it is often through a simplistic lens—if we treat the past trauma, the current abusive behavior will automatically stop. This is a dangerous assumption to make. In a conversation about domestic violence perpetrators with histories of intergenerational trauma, a therapist made this statement: "He needs to heal his trauma history before he addresses his violence." This plan demonstrates the dominance of the trauma framework and the dangers of a simplistic, one-to-one interpretation of the relationship between past trauma and current violence. Built into the statement are numerous assumptions, including that healing would have an endpoint, that it would be acceptable to allow this person to hurt others while he was going through his own healing process, and that there was some insurmountable barrier to tackling both at the same time. These were all dangerous and misguided assumptions. Trauma histories are not an excuse for harming others—and creating new victims with new trauma histories. In fact, I could argue that when someone who has a trauma history hurts others, it's a lose-lose. The victim gets hurt and the perpetrator is adding in new problems to his own life that may impede his healing because of, for example, increased shame and destroyed support networks.

The trauma field and the domestic violence field need to more directly tackle the intersection of trauma and perpetrators. Domestic violence and trauma-informed practice need to work together to support real behavior change and healing.

Substance misuse and Domestic Violence Perpetrators

As part of my work with abusers, I would regularly make contact with their partners. While much of my work was with men in heterosexual relationships, occasionally I would work with same-sex couples. In a particular instance, Jake, a domestic violence survivor, described how he often gave Brandon, his abusive partner, alcohol. It would have been easy for me to misinterpret Jake's behavior as dangerous, codependent, or naive. Assuming that his behavior might actually be protective, I further probed the intersection of Brandon's substance misuse and violence. Jake revealed that if he and Brandon drank on the couch at home watching television, Brandon would often fall peacefully asleep. If Brandon went out to a bar to drink, then he would often turn to other drugs and come home and assault him. Jake couldn't control whether Brandon used substances or not, but he could take steps, which involved drinking with him, to reduce the likelihood and severity of violence.

This is one of many scenarios of the intersection of substance misuse and violence that I encountered over the years. It was a significant theme in my men's behavior change groups and in the systems-change work I have done. Researchers have been examining the intersection of substance misuse and domestic violence perpetration for decades. Many questions remain. The literature is filled with conflicting statistics around the intersection of domestic violence perpetration and substance misuse. Depending on definitions of substance misuse and domestic violence, the population, and the theorized relationship between perpetration and substance misuse, the numbers can vary widely.

Regardless of the prevalence rates, there is broad agreement that the substance misuse of a domestic violence perpetrator is relevant to risk assessment, treatment, and interventions. What is actually less broadly agreed upon is the relevance of domestic violence perpetration to the assessment and treatment of substance users. Here is where we find another aspect of the myth of trauma-informed practice—we can see the connection between substance abuse and trauma. For example, trauma increases the risk for substance misuse. But we ignore or simplify the relationship between domestic violence perpetrators' behavior and substance misuse. It is much less common to find substance use programs that thoroughly assess the perpetration of domestic violence and highlight the need to address those behaviors as part of a recovery plan. In many ways, the substance use treatment field treats violence perpetration as an afterthought, and in many instances, as a symptom of the substance use. The latter can lead to interventions that naively assume that if the substance misuse is resolved, the domestic violence is automatically resolved as well.

Suicidal Gestures as Manipulation

They had been arguing for hours. John had made it clear that he felt like Anna didn't love him or care about him. He stopped talking, got up from the couch, and in full view of Anna, grabbed a knife from the kitchen, walked into the bathroom, locked the door, and turned on the water. Earlier he had said that if she didn't love him, he didn't have anything to live for. Images of him killing himself flashed through her mind. But instead of rushing to the door, yelling for him to stop, proclaiming her love for him, and telling him that she wouldn't leave him, she called emergency services. Because of his manipulative behavior in the past, she had worked with her domestic violence counselor to prepare for moments like this. So when emergency services came, ready to break down the door to save him, what they found was John, in his towel stepping out of the shower. He later admitted in his men's behavior change group that his actions were pure manipulation. There was no intent to hurt himself. Only a desire to guilt her into staying with him.

Suicidal ideation, gestures, and attempts need to be treated seriously. And when there is an intersection of suicidal threats, gestures, attempts, and patterns of coercive control, the assessment lens needs to be wider than just self-harm. When someone who is a domestic violence perpetrator threatens to hurt himself, it needs to be evaluated in three ways: the person's potential to harm himself, his danger to others, and the potential that the statements and gestures are attempts to manipulate and control others. Each of these three areas deserves attention. Suicidal statements or gestures need to be taken seriously as a risk factor for actual suicide and also as a marker for depression, trauma, and other emotional states. We also know that when someone who has a history of violence becomes depressed and suicidal, the danger to others increases. Suicidal gestures or thinking, in the context of perpetrators' patterns, represent an elevated risk for murder or murder-suicide. Suicidal gestures and threats, as a form of manipulation and coercion, receive the least attention when it comes to assessment process. Yet threats such as "if you leave me, I'll kill myself" or "if you leave me, I'll drink myself to death" are a very potent form of coercive control, deserving of serious attention.

One way to think about the gap between the mental health and substance use fields and the domestic violence field is to think about their orientation to extreme harm: homicide and suicide. The substance abuse and mental health fields are much better at and more focused on the harm a person might inflict on himself. Suicide hotlines, depression checklists, concerns about suicidal ideation, the dangers of self-induced physical harm from "drinking oneself to death," or accidental or purposeful overdose are very much a part of those fields. The domestic violence field is very much organized around the danger of lethal violence by one person against another. Each field is weaker in the area where the other field is stronger. While this may be a bit of an oversimplification, it's a useful lens to help identify the gap between the two approaches. Domestic violence-informed mental health and substance misuse approaches need to consider all three areas: threat to self, threat to others, and the potential for manipulation when confronted with clients with self-harming behaviors. Failure to consider all three, especially when someone has an identified history of coercive control and violence, makes it easier for perpetrators to harm and control survivors.

Substance Use and Domestic Violence Survivors

There is strong agreement that domestic violence survivors are likely to have higher rates of substance use than non-domestic violence survivors. One of the main explanations is that trauma survivors are more likely to self-medicate their symptoms with substances, such as dealing with their anxiety by drinking. The intersection of survivor substance use and domestic violence is likely more complicated. When we expand our vision beyond the trauma paradigm, we see other pathways. For example, some survivors are coerced or tricked into drug use. Others use medications, like opioids, to address physical pain and injury caused by the perpetrators. This may open the door to addiction. In other instances, perpetrators actively interfere with a survivor's recovery efforts. In many ways, we are failing survivors when we only see one pathway between the perpetrators' behaviors and their substance use.

Not only do we need to be worried about the pathways from domestic violence to substance use by survivors, but we also need to expand our view further to include how perpetrators often weaponize, or threaten to weaponize, substance use (and mental health issues) against the survivor. The following chart details how sophisticated and multilayered the weaponization of substance use can be. Perpetrators target different people with different messages for different effects. (The following are examples of how a domestic violence perpetrator can manipulate a survivor's substance use to gain increased control and entrapment. The examples are not referring to scenarios where a person had genuine concern for his substance-using partner. The examples also do not attempt to speak to any real risk that a person's substance use may represent to herself or others. Statements such as "my children are not safe with their substance-abusing mother" may be genuine in one situation, an attack in another, or even both in some circumstances.

> *We also need to expand our view further to include how perpetrators often weaponize, or threaten to weaponize, substance use, and mental health issues.*

CHAPTER 9: THE MYTH OF TRAUMA-INFORMED PRACTICE

How domestic violence perpetrators can manipulate survivors' substance use

Domestic violence perpetrator statement	Nature of attack	Primary target for the attack	Effects on target	Wider effects on survivor, child, and family functioning
"You're nothing but a piece-of-shit drug addict. Nobody will believe you if you call the police."	Attack on survivor's sense of self and ability to reach out for help	Survivor	Shame; anger; fear related to reaching out for help; feelings of hopelessness and entrapment	Increased danger; increased addiction; further isolation from others; depression; loss of job, housing, and children
"Your mother cares more about getting high than she does about you."	Attack on mother, child, and their relationship	Their children	Anger at mother; shame about mother's addiction; damage to the mother-child relationship; not listening to mother; gravitating toward the perpetrator	Greater overall problems in family functioning; involvement of child protective services; loss of children into care; mother may experience increased use and depression
"Your daughter (friend, parishioner) has a problem. I'm just trying to make things better."	Attack on survivor-support network relationship	Family; friends; support network;	Allying with the perpetrator; distancing from the survivor	Support network for survivor is neutralized through manipulation of perception; at extremes becomes allied with perpetrator; survivor's functioning may drop; danger increases
"I'm so glad you're involved. She needs help."	Manipulation of helping systems	Counselors; therapists	Survivor feels crazy; counselor focuses on the substance use, not the violence	Service support for survivor around violence is neutralized through manipulation of perception; at extremes professionals become allied with perpetrator; survivor's functioning may drop; danger increases; may lead to loss of children; increased pressure to attend and comply with court orders; counselors' reports may negatively influence child protection and family court outcomes
"She's so messed up on drugs that her children are not safe with her."	Manipulation of systems with the power of the state: arrest, removal of children, custody and access orders	Child safety; family court; police	Survivor feels crazy and unsafe accessing systems that could help keep her safe and connected to her children	Children are removed from survivor; placed with dangerous parent; undermining of survivor-child relationship

This chart is not meant to be a substitute for comprehensive assessments of a situation.

While the content statement is similar, the weaponization of allegations of drug use, the exact audience, and the context of statements make them each different forms of abuse. It's not enough to say, "He uses her substance use against her." It is important to understand all these different forms of attacks and the different forms of damage each causes. This is particularly important for anyone who is trying to hold perpetrators accountable as parents. (This same chart can be created for mental health!)

The Invisible Hand of the Perpetrator: Mental Health and Substance Misuse Get Decontextualized

A domestic violence advocate recently related the following story to me:

A survivor told the advocate that she felt "crazy" and thought she needed a diagnosis. In the past the worker would have made a referral for the survivor to go to see a mental health practitioner. But this time, because of her training in the Safe & Together Model, she started to ask the survivor questions about her partner's pattern of behavior. At the end of the discussion, the survivor better understood how she wasn't "crazy" but was having understandable feelings and reactions to her partner's coercive control. The survivor and the worker agreed that no mental health referral was needed. The advocate's "pivot to the perpetrator" helped validate the survivor's experience, helping her understand her experiences as being the result of her partner's behavior, not the result of a mental health condition. She didn't need mental health services. She needed safety and support and freedom from her partner's gaslighting, manipulation, and control.

This is an example of how survivors' experiences run the risk of being pathologized by a mental health framework and how that risk can be lowered when a perpetrator pattern-based approach helps recontextualize survivors' thoughts and feelings as "normal."

CHAPTER 9: THE MYTH OF TRAUMA-INFORMED PRACTICE

The myth of the trauma-informed practice shines a spotlight on some things and leaves other things in the shadows. Symptoms, diagnoses, and treatment plans get tons of attention. Conversely, the perpetrator's choices and behaviors remain in the shadows because even though they are present and influential, they are often invisible. In this way, the mental health and substance use disciplines decontextualize the effects of abuse from the person who is doing the abuse. Sometimes the abuse is the cause of the mental health or substance use issues. Other times it is an important context. Sometimes it is both. The mental health and substance use paradigms often sever those symptoms from the cause and context—the perpetrators' coercive control. The result is a focus on survivors' deficits and pathologies decontextualized from the perpetrators' behaviors. This is what can result from this:

> Survivor treatment resulting in failures and setbacks because of lack of planning around how the perpetrator may sabotage access to treatment or sabotage its success in different ways
>
> Mental health and substance use problems being weaponized against survivors in family court and child protection settings
>
> Reports being provided to child protective services and family court that identify mental health issues but failing to name the perpetrators' behaviors as context and/or cause
>
> Survivors internalizing the sense that something is broken or wrong in themselves instead of being validated in the wrongness of their partners' behavior toward them
>
> Survivors not receiving validation from treating professionals for their protective efforts, acts of resistance, and strengths

The mental health and substance use fields often make the perpetrator invisible at the expense of the health and safety of adult and child survivors. Mental health or substance use treatment providers cannot approach the treatment of domestic violence survivors the same as the treatment of non-domestic violence survivors. Important dynamics are likely to be missed.

When coercive control dynamics are not factored into treatment with survivors, problems are likely to ensue. Let's consider the situation in which a survivor genuinely needs substance use treatment. And let's raise the stakes by imagining that she needs to be successful in her recovery to get her children back from child protective services. Finally, let's assume she has a partner who doesn't want her to get her children back (because they are children from her last partner). And let's assume that he has a history of promoting her drug habit and interfering with her recovery. In this situation, any plan around her substance use treatment that fails to strategize around his likely efforts to sabotage her recovery will be incomplete—leaving the door open for his continuing efforts to hinder her recovery, setting her up to be labeled "noncompliant," and increasing the chances she will never get her children back.

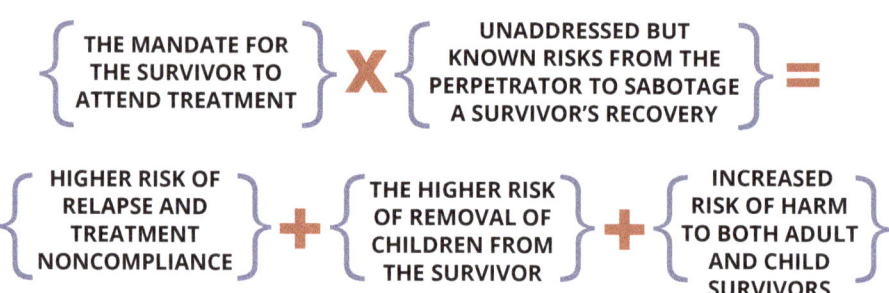

Failing to factor in the potential for the perpetrator to sabotage the survivor's treatment can be seen as a form of professional negligence or malpractice.

CHAPTER 9: THE MYTH OF TRAUMA-INFORMED PRACTICE

Fabricated allegations: Another Way Perpetrators Weaponize Mental Health and Substance Use

After Giancarlo physically assaulted Dana in front of the children, the responding police officers made a referral to child protective services. Since Giancarlo was not able to obtain immediate release for himself, the social worker interviewed him in jail. During the interview, he admitted to pushing Dana but nothing else. He said he pushed her because she was trying to leave with the children while under the influence of substances. He was afraid she was going to drive with the children in the car. He told the worker that she drank and did meth. After the interview with Giancarlo, the worker called Dana and told her she would need her to take a drug test. Dana, who never took drugs and only drank occasionally and without problem, was scared and angry. During her initial visit with the social worker, Dana had been open about the violence, hoping that child protective services would intervene with Giancarlo, who was the children's father. Now, angry that the social worker was allowing herself to be manipulated by Giancarlo, she told the social worker to "fuck off." The social worker documented that Dana was "resistant" to taking a drug test and may have "an issue she is trying to avoid." At the next visit, Dana was quiet, nonresponsive, and agitated. The social worker documented that "Dana's presentation may be another sign of drug use, perhaps withdrawal from substances." The social worker mandated Dana to get a full substance use assessment.

The social worker stopped meeting with Giancarlo, who was at that point released from jail and living with his parents. He saw the children whenever he wanted since there were no court orders stopping him. The social worker focused all her attention on Dana, who the children were living with, expecting her to attend a domestic violence program and substance use program. Giancarlo filed for full custody in family court, alleging that Dana's involvement with child protective services, her substance use, and her mental health issues made her a poor parent.

What did Giancarlo accomplish through his behavior, and how was the system his unwitting accomplice?

- He successfully deflected attention off his violence, which was the reason for child protective services' involvement, and onto Dana's parenting through completely fabricated allegations.
- He sowed distrust and suspicion between the social worker and Dana. Instead of the social worker being a source of support for Dana and the children, which Dana had hoped for during the initial contact, Dana became fearful of the social worker. The social worker started to view all of Dana's actions through the lens of denial of potential substance use issues.
- Giancarlo was leveraging the system through his actions:
  - His false allegations gained so much traction because systems such as child protective services often have personnel who feel compelled to assess all allegations—even when the source is a person with a history of violence and abuse.
  - Gender double standards worked in his favor. As the custodial parent and mother, Dana was facing more scrutiny than Giancarlo, who was the father and not living in the home.
  - He was able to leverage the child protection focus on Dana into a potential advantage in family court. His allegations of substance misuse, made to child protective services, followed her into the family court setting.

While the child protection worker's attempt to assess Dana for substance misuse may have seemed benign to some—for example, if Dana had just complied, it would have proven that she was clean—it missed the point that the damage was already done. Giancarlo had demonstrated to Dana that he was willing to lie and manipulate professionals with very serious allegations that could have severe consequences for her and her

CHAPTER 9: THE MYTH OF TRAUMA-INFORMED PRACTICE

children. What Dana also learned was that professionals cannot be trusted to see through Giancarlo's lies. She also experienced the catch-22 that many survivors experience—the more she talked about the abuse or tried to deny false allegations against her, the more she was going to be perceived as "crazy," "noncompliant," or "vindictive." (Many or all of these impacts could have been avoided if the social worker had started with the idea that Giancarlo's allegations of Dana's substance misuse were likely part of his pattern of coercive control since there was no other evidence of Dana's substance misuse. Instead of demanding a drug test, the social worker could have taken a more observational approach, remaining open-minded but not rushing in to become an agent of Giancarlo's control.)

The point of this example is that the complexity around survivors, mental health, and substance misuse means that professionals should not focus only on real problems, but they should also include the dynamics associated with the patently false allegations of perpetrators. It is not enough to approach survivors from a simplistic, A-equals-B, substance use-equals-substance treatment model. This is not domestic-violence informed. Our approach to the intersections of domestic violence, mental health, and substance misuse must also account for completely fabricated allegations.

Domestic violence perpetrators can be relentless in repeating fabricated allegations, often using mental health and substance use terminology to their advantage. Through repetition and the naive engagement by professionals with these allegations—which could include allegations of bipolar disorder, borderline personality disorders, depression, drug use, and other issues—the allegations start seeping into the narrative about a situation. Over time, the allegations take on a life of their own, disconnected from their original source, the perpetrator, and simply start appearing in the record as "mother has been alleged to have depression and borderline personality disorder." This lays the groundwork for professionals to either see both parents as being "dysfunctional" or even further swinging away from the perpetrator's behavior to focus exclusively on the parenting of the survivor (gender double standards at play again here!).

Fabricated allegations fall outside the traditional understanding of trauma and substance misuse clinical work. Clinicians are not trained to screen for false allegations or to contextualize those allegations back to broader patterns of coercive control. In order to unwind the myth of trauma-informed practice, this needs to change.

> *A practitioner cannot truly be trauma-informed without being domestic violence-informed and vice versa.*

How the Safe & Together Model Innovates to Challenge the Myth of Trauma-Informed Practice

The Safe & Together Model's perpetrator pattern-based approach offers the power and structure to weave together trauma and domestic violence-informed practice. Whether we are considering how the perpetrator's abusive behavior relates back to his own trauma history or a survivor's substance use, the perpetrator's pattern-based approach offers a road map for good practice.

The following is a chart of how domestic violence-informed practice fills in important gaps in the trauma practice framework.

Domestic violence-informed response to the myth of trauma-informed practice

	Myth of trauma-informed	Domestic violence-informed
Coercive control	Ignores or minimizes coercive control dynamics; focuses heavily on diagnosis and treatment of symptoms related to physical and sexual violence	Assesses dynamics of coercive control, actions taken to harm children, and their relevance to current safety, functioning, diagnosis, and treatment interactions with professionals and institutions such as family court. Is inclusive of different forms of violence
Source of harm	Focuses more on symptoms and treatment than contextualizing trauma back to the source of the harm	Names the person or persons and their actions to help increase accountability for perpetrators as parents and reduce victim-blaming
Gender	Primarily approaches trauma from a gender-neutral, universal perspective	Recognizes the role of gender in the shaping of narratives of accountability, the dynamics of entrapment, and the differential response of systems to men and women as parents
Directionality	Considers source of the trauma to be "historic"	Considers past abuse, current dynamics of coercion, and future danger—connecting the dots between all these and different impacts on the survivor
Approach to perpetrators	Trauma history needs to be addressed first to prevent abusive behavior	Trauma history cannot be used as an excuse for abusive behavior; there needs to be a clear focus on behavior change, not just trauma healing; true trauma healing is important but cannot happen without the cessation of perpetration of violence and control
Systems approach	Systems need to be trauma-informed	Understand that perpetrators target systems and practitioners as part of their coercive control; believe systems need to change to prevent this
Intersectionalities	Trauma is an individual problem with the focus of the solution primarily at the individual level	Dynamics of oppression need to be factored in to understanding dynamics of coercive control, including compounded trauma resulting from domestic violence scaffolded onto trauma of other societal forms of violence, such as colonization, racism, transphobia, homophobia, and gender-based societal violence

So how do we change our practice when it is at the intersection of mental health, substance misuse, and domestic violence? We make sure that we are applying a perpetrator pattern-based approach. Let's start by examining some of the questions that will help us make better domestic violence-informed assessments related to perpetrators' mental health and/or substance use issues:

Q: What is the relationship between the perpetrator's pattern of coercive control and actions taken to harm the children and the perpetrator's own substance use and/or mental health issues?

- Is he more or less abusive, violent, or controlling when he is actively drinking or using substances? Is he getting mental health treatment? Is he taking prescribed psychotropic medication?

- Does his pattern of abuse include coercing or pressuring his partner to use substances with them?

- How do his substance use and/or mental health issues fit into his overall pattern of behavior and its impact? How do those issues affect the functioning of his partner, the children, and the overall family functioning?

  - Does spending money on drugs deprive the children of critical needs being met; for instance, are there housing issues due to his spending money on substances?

  - How do treated or untreated mental health conditions such as depression correlate with parenting and co-parenting?

CHAPTER 9: THE MYTH OF TRAUMA-INFORMED PRACTICE

➔ What changes in those patterns when he abstains from substances? When he is actively engaged in treatment?

- Does his abusive behavior stop?
- Does he acknowledge the harm his behavior has caused?
- Is he willing to make reparations for the harm?

These are just a few questions that need to be explored when it comes to the issue of substance use, mental health, and domestic violence perpetration.

But just as importantly, the perpetrator's pattern needs to remain central to conversations about the survivor's mental health and/or substance misuse. Now let's look at some questions that will help us make better domestic violence-informed assessments related to survivors' mental health and/or substance use issues:

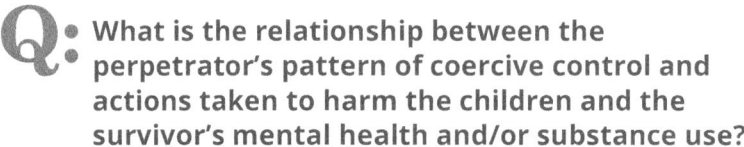

Q: What is the relationship between the perpetrator's pattern of coercive control and actions taken to harm the children and the survivor's mental health and/or substance use?

➔ Is his behavior the cause of those issues for the survivor?

➔ Does his abuse exacerbate any preexisting issues?

➔ Does he pressure or coerce her into using substances with him?

➔ Does he interfere with her ability to access and complete treatment?

➔ Is he trying to use any issues to gain an advantage in family court or use other systems such as child protective services to hurt or punish her?

263

- Does he have a history of making false allegations about her substance use?
- Does he degrade, threaten, or otherwise emotionally abuse the survivor with information about her mental health and substances?

Substance use and mental health issues have been central to the Safe & Together Model since its inception. They are woven throughout each critical component but have their main home in the fifth critical component, which identifies issues, dynamics, or contexts that are not causal to domestic violence but are yet important to understanding entrapment, complexity, and harm.

> *Decontextualizing survivors' mental health and substance use issues from the context of the perpetrators' behaviors is dangerous and inaccurate, and it increases the likelihood of victim-blaming.*

Holding Perpetrators Accountable When There Is Complexity

To become domestic violence-informed, we need to be able to describe how the perpetrator's behavior intersects with the experience of the survivors—recontextualizing what is often siloed or individualized. We can break down into five categories how the perpetrator impacts his partner with respect to her mental health and substance abuse.

CHAPTER 9: THE MYTH OF TRAUMA-INFORMED PRACTICE

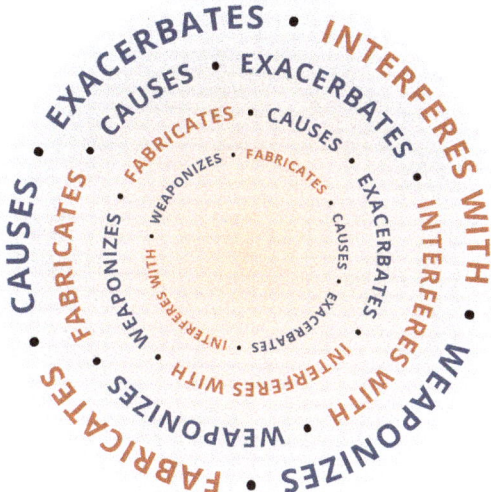

- **Causes:** This is when the perpetrator's behavior is the only context for the survivor's issues. For example, he forces her into substance use when she had no prior history. This includes normal, common, expected responses to coercive control and violence such as anxiety or depression symptoms. Just like any illness, we can point to the etiology, or cause: the perpetrator's behavior.

- **Exacerbates:** This acknowledges that some survivors who become entrapped in abusive relationships have preexisting histories of mental health and/or substance use issues. Some of these will have arisen from other abusive situations in adulthood or childhood. Some will have arisen from other circumstances, such as colonization and intergenerational cultural trauma. Regardless, the current domestic violence perpetrator's behavior exacerbates that problem. One of the clearest examples occurs when a domestic violence perpetrator's behavior precipitates a substance use relapse. This can happen through coercion, disruption of support networks, or renewed need to self-medicate for physical or emotional pain. In the same way, the perpetrator's behaviors can cause a reemergence of other trauma-related problems, such as depression, anxiety, sleep troubles, or other symptoms associated with trauma.

- **Interferes with:** Another major bucket is how the domestic violence perpetrator interferes with the treatment or access to support for the survivor. This can include controlling access to transport to and from treatment, accusations of affairs with other participants in a program or a therapist, coercing the use of substances, or interfering with medication. Such interference can have a major impact on the survivor and is rarely identified as the cause of a survivor dropping out of a treatment program.

- **Weaponizes:** This occurs when a perpetrator starts using a survivor's mental health and/or substance use issues as ways to hurt, punish, or undermine the survivor. This weaponization can involve making malicious reports to child protective services or other systems, using a survivor's issues to attack her relationships, or using her own issues as the foundation of emotional abuse. It usually happens in the context of the perpetrator not taking responsibility for his own behavior.

- **Fabricates:** This involves the perpetrator completely making up allegations of mental health and/or substance issues. This can take the form of gaslighting—for example, telling the survivor she "has a mental illness"—and spreading disinformation about the survivor to loved ones and professionals. It would be considered a form of "weaponization" except for the fact that there is nothing to weaponize. The concerns are made up.

The use of these categories can help practitioners partner with survivors and intervene with perpetrators when there are complex intersections of multiple issues. The Safe & Together Model offers language and a framework to make perpetrators' behaviors visible. An inferior assessment might be that "the mother is noncompliant with treatment recommendations." A superior one might be that "the father has interfered with the mother's access to treatment by denying her access to the car and by taking away her phone so she couldn't receive calls from the program." Those offer two completely different explanations for a parent's inability to complete a program. The former implicitly lays the blame on the survivor. The latter explicitly identifies the perpetrator as the actor and stipulates his mechanism of interference.

Changing language allows for different interventions and support by professionals. The latter formulation totally changes the paradigm. It names the behavior of someone who is often in a parenting role. When it is a father sabotaging the other person's recovery, this needs to be seen as a choice that willfully interferes with the improvement of the other parent's ability to function, with potential implications for children's safety, health, and well-being. Accountability starts with this language. Without it, there is no chance to create accurate documentation, no chance to craft a new plan with the survivor that accounts for potential interference, and no chance to intervene with this father.

This change offers a stable base for intervening with perpetrators as parents. Here are some ways that perpetrators might be approached:

> "If you are getting violent with your partner when you are drinking (or depressed), you have two problems: your violence and your substance use (or mental health)."
>
> "You cannot use your or your partner's substance use as an excuse for your violence."
>
> "Healing your own trauma history is important, but it can't come at the expense of the safety and well-being of your loved ones."

By keeping an eye on a perpetrator's patterns of behaviors, accountability is increased, and interventions stay focused on behavior change and improvements in the safety, stability, and satisfaction of adult and child survivors. It changes everything.

Partnering with Survivors in Complexity

Partnering with a domestic violence survivor who also has a substance use or mental health issue is much easier and effective when using a perpetrator pattern-based approach. When a practitioner is clear about the fact that the perpetrator is 100 percent responsible for his own behaviors, regardless of the survivor's issues, then complexity can be handled more effectively and efficiently.

Here are examples of domestic violence-informed statements that can be made to a survivor who has mental health and/or addiction issues:

> "Your substance abuse does not cause him to be violent to you."
>
> "He has no right to be abusive to you even when you are using."
>
> "We want to learn more about his pattern of coercive control so we can understand how it influences your substance use and so we can plan for any attempts he may make to sabotage your recovery."
>
> "Let's talk about any fear or worries you have about him using your substance use or mental health issues against you."

Statements like these interrupt mother-blaming, creating a clear pathway for addressing survivors' substance use and mental health issues without blaming her for the perpetrator's behaviors and choices.

Partnering with survivors in complexity also can involve identifying the things she has been doing to be protective even amid her substance use and/or mental health struggles. Struggling with an addiction doesn't preclude acting in protective ways. Nor does depression or anxiety. Partnering practice guides us to be curious about protective acts that survivors may have taken despite her struggles with these other issues. These should be treated as "both/and" situations. A survivor may be drinking too much at times but still making sure her mother—not her boyfriend—is watching the children because the children are not safe with him alone. A mother may be struggling with her depression but still taking her children to see their own counselor.

Professionals can still collaboratively plan with survivors in complexity as well. Depending on the severity of their issues, and how those issues impact the survivors' functioning, survivors' mental health or substance use should not automatically rule out the exploration of safety planning. This can involve collaboratively planning with her for her safety even as she continues to use or when a perpetrator tries to undermine her recovery efforts. It also might involve how she can best get out of the house safely to attend counseling or how to hide her medication from the perpetrator, who has thrown it away in the past. Survivors with mental health and/or substance use issues deserve safety and freedom from control as much as any other survivor.

Final Thoughts on the Myth of Trauma-Informed Practice

When I think about helping mental health and substance use professionals become domestic violence informed, I get very excited. Specialized domestic violence services are a critical part of any response system, and yet they only touch a fraction of survivors and perpetrators who need assistance. A domestic violence-informed behavioral health system could reach so many more people, improve mental health and substance misuse outcomes, change how child protection and family court systems interact with families, and strike a decisive blow against blaming mothers and ignoring fathers.

CHAPTER 10

Critical Components and Principles: A Common Language

If you walk away from this book with an understanding of how the Safe & Together Model helps unwind each of the individual myths outlined in the previous chapters, that would be a good outcome. A great outcome would be understanding how the Safe & Together Model offers a unified framework for transforming the paradigm of domestic violence practice across all the myths and across diverse sectors. As Radford and Hester[1] suggested, if we want to change the way multiple systems respond to domestic violence survivors, we need to challenge the gender double standards that operate across sectors—adding new services and improved coordination is not enough.

Unfortunately, the transformation of gender double standards in domestic violence practice across systems isn't as simple as saying, "Treat men and women equally as parents." It requires a common language and approach consistent with the mission and activities of each of these systems—a set of tools and practices foundational enough that each system can utilize it. The Safe & Together Model's behavioral focus does just that. In child protection services, it improves processes that help keep children safe. In family court, it helps develop the evidence that improves decisions related to custody and parenting time. In high-risk teams, it improves accountability and interventions with perpetrators. Regardless of sector and mission, the Safe & Together Model's Critical Components

CHAPTER 10: CRITICAL COMPONENTS AND PRINCIPLES: A COMMON LANGUAGE

help practitioners stop blaming mothers and ignoring fathers. It does it in a way that can be applied objectively, without prejudgment, and in a way that accelerates systems transformation the more it is adopted by diverse sectors.

In this chapter, I offer more insight into how the Safe & Together Model promotes a practice revolution by creating a common language and approach that cut across different sectors. Ignoring fathers and blaming mothers is not a problem of one sector or service. It is a problem that cuts across sectors. To create lasting change, there needs to be a new paradigm that not only works in each sector but offers a unifying approach that accelerates transformation as more sectors and more professionals adopt it.

> *"I don't even think I'd be alive if I didn't get to keep my children. I cannot tell you; (the Safe & Together Model) is literally the difference between life and death for me. I would never have been able to cope if my children had been taken from me. Because I would not have any reason left to live or to continue."*
>
> —Naomi, survivor, Scotland

Roots in Child Protection

The Safe & Together Model's focus on the foundations of practice resulted from my worry about how child protection operated. When I first started working with child protective services, as a perpetrator intervention specialist, I was afraid that my involvement would lead to child protective services only adding men's behavior change programming to the menu of services they offered to families. I was worried about this being considered the "solution" to perpetrators as parents even though most men's behavior change programs at that time (and now) barely addressed the idea of perpetrators as parents. I was concerned that as long as survivors' relationship choices were seen as more of the problem than perpetrators' behaviors, that mother-blaming would continue. I was worried that adding in a new service would not build up child protection workers' capacity to intervene with perpetrators, especially when they were so focused on mothers and knew so little about fathers who were abusive.

In numerous conversations with child protection workers, I observed their struggle to articulate the most basic information about the perpetrator's pattern. I watched how time and time again they formulated the problem through the lens of the survivor's poor choices. I also watched how, when successfully guided to focus more on the perpetrator's behaviors, far-reaching shifts occurred in their thinking, practice, and decision-making. For example, one supervisor, who was a participant in a research project on the response by child protective services to perpetrators, told me that since becoming more skilled in focusing her workers on perpetrators, she had completely stopped mandating mothers into refuge. In multiple cases, workers were better able to understand survivors' decision-making after being asked to explore the perpetrators' influence over their choices or the failures of systems to effectively intervene with those perpetrators. Each of these interactions confirmed for me that not only did workers need more skills and confidence to work with perpetrators, but they also needed to increase their capacity to focus on perpetrators, and by doing so, they had the potential for shifting their relationship to survivors—making that relationship less adversarial and ripe for improved partnership.

I came to believe that a pivot to the perpetrators' pattern of behaviors might be a powerful enough change in practice to create the desired ripple effect throughout the practice, with the ripple starting with individual workers and spreading beyond them to their entire agency. If assessments were focused on the perpetrators' (not the survivors') behaviors as the source of the domestic violence danger to children, we could change how the problem of domestic violence and children was understood, and therefore we could change everything that flowed from the foundational understanding of what the problem was. It could change the way professionals worked with perpetrators—and survivors and their children.

The Safe & Together Model always differed from a perpetrator engagement approach. It was designed to use the focus on the perpetrators' behaviors as the source of the harm to child, partner, and family functioning as a way to improve the work with the whole family regardless of their point of contact with systems. While perpetrator engagement is one of the tools in the domestic violence-informed tool kit, a perpetrator pattern-based approach is intended to impact every aspect of the work with families, rebuilding domestic violence practice from the ground up.

Once the perpetrators' choices and behaviors—not the survivors' choices—were defined as the source of the harm to children, then all interviewing, assessment, documentation, and case management would change. The goal was not the provision of better service. It was the wholesale rethinking of the practice around domestic violence and children. Instead of inventing a new program, policy, or initiative to "fix" families, the Model focused on "fixing" the thinking and practices of practitioners.

I came to believe that a pivot to the perpetrators' pattern of behaviors might be a powerful enough change in practice to create the desired ripple effect throughout the practice, with the ripple starting with individual workers and spreading beyond them to their entire agency.

CHAPTER 10: CRITICAL COMPONENTS AND PRINCIPLES: A COMMON LANGUAGE

At the inception of the Model, I was also aware of the historic tensions between domestic violence advocates and child protective services. Finger pointing and conflict over approaches dominated any conversation about domestic violence and children. Child protective services accused victim advocates in the field of ignoring the safety of children. Victim advocates blamed child protective services for revictimizing mothers. Long-standing battle lines had been drawn over issues such as confidentiality and information sharing. Despite their shared interests in safety for the family, both sectors, with their focus on mothers, were unwittingly colluding to keep domestic violence perpetrators invisible as parents. I hoped that a perpetrator pattern-based approach could not only help child protective services in its day-to-day work but also improve collaboration between the sectors because the pattern-based approach aligned with the mission and values of both sides.

The Safe & Together Model's Critical Components developed directly out of case consultations with child protection workers. In my conversations with child protection workers, I found myself asking the same questions over and over again:

> What patterns of behaviors did the perpetrator engage in?
>
> What did the survivor do to protect herself and the children?
>
> What was the specific impact of this perpetrator's behavior on his children?
>
> What was the role of substances and mental health?
>
> How did culture, privilege, and vulnerability impact the situation?

In these conversations, I encountered two different answer scenarios. In the first scenario, the worker didn't have the information to answer the questions. The worker might only have the most superficial level of understanding—"There is history of domestic violence in this family"—and nothing else. This was especially true when the case had been transferred to the worker or the child was already in foster care. In the second scenario, which taught me something very important, the worker actually had loads of information about each question but had not documented most of it. The worker knew it but had not written it down, which meant that it was often not known to anyone else involved with the case. And if the worker had documented important aspects of the domestic violence, it was spread out across the case file in separate contact-based case notes. Even when written down in the case file, this spread-out information had little impact on case practice because it was never synthesized into a single, coherent, organized description of the most salient aspects of the case.

It became clear that both the absence of basic behavioral information or its poor organization hampered good practice and good decisions. This was not a problem of a single worker's poor practice. This was a direct product of a system that allowed cases to progress, to even be presented in court, with only one line about domestic violence: The family has a history of domestic violence. For service-driven systems, this was enough information to justify referrals to domestic violence services. But it wasn't enough to accurately assess the harm that the perpetrator was creating for the family, it wasn't enough to fully understand the survivor's protective efforts, and it wasn't enough to gain insight into so much more that was critical to working well with the family. And for sure it didn't guarantee the end of mother-blaming or real attention being paid to perpetrators as the source of the harm to child, partner, and family functioning.

The information that workers had about the domestic violence was mostly administrative or high-level information but rarely included specific information about behaviors. They might know how many times the perpetrator had been arrested but not the specific nature of his violence. They knew how many child protection reports they had received on the mother but not the full spectrum of her protective efforts. They knew how many days of school or doctor's appointments were missed but not how the perpetrator's behaviors had caused or contributed to the child's neglect. They knew that the family faced multiple intersecting issues such as substance use, mental illness, and domestic violence, but they couldn't describe whether the perpetrator was still controlling and abusive when he wasn't drinking. They could describe families' demographics but not how the perpetrator was manipulating culture or status to maintain his control over his family.

The question became how to respond to the structural issues that led to this lack of insight. We needed an organized framework that closed these gaps in a way that was *neutral and objective*, that didn't judge the family, presume who the abuser was, or assume the nature of the harm to the children. As members of an agency that was tasked with investigating or assessing specific allegations related to specific families, the workers (and the families) needed a describable methodology that helped identify what was happening in *this* family. The commitment to close multiple practice gaps in a way that could be applied objectively to any family led to an approach that not only had application in child protective services but also across multiple sectors.

The first piece in the response was the Model's Critical Components. The Model's Critical Components were envisioned as categories of information that needed to be filled in with information absolutely essential to good decision-making in cases involving children. But I didn't just see them as static receptacles for information or tick boxes to be checked off. I envisioned them as a way to drive transformative, paradigm-busting practice change leading to better outcomes for families. For example, if child protection workers were required to become knowledgeable about perpetrators' patterns of coercive control and actions taken to harm their children, they would need to ask different questions and review collateral information from a different perspective. Since the majority, but not all, of the domestic violence perpetrators were fathers, it would become harder for child protective services to keep ignoring the fathers who were causing the harm.

Safe & Together Critical Components

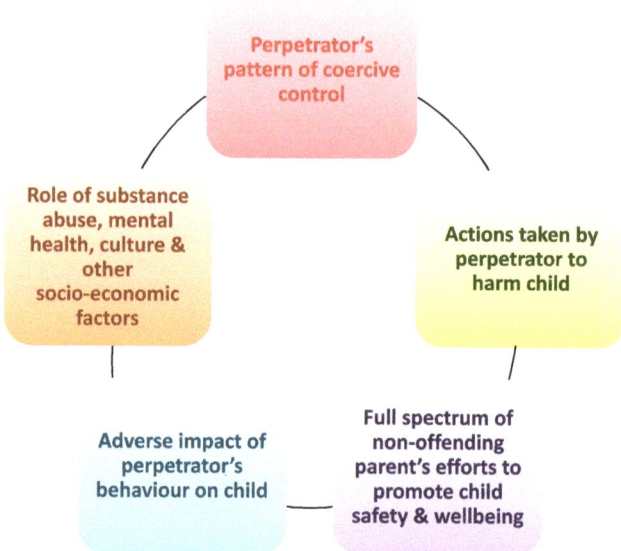

Over time it became clearer that the Model's Critical Components and other aspects of the Model were applicable beyond child protective services and across diverse sectors. Because they are focused on foundational behavioral information about the perpetrator and the survivor, because they explore the connection between those behaviors and child safety and well-being, and because they consider key issues such as intersectionalities and intersections, the Model Critical Components provide raw data that could be plugged into any system's decision-making process. Regardless of the context or sector, an assessment of behavior patterns related to coercive control offers a more accurate and more comprehensive method for identifying harm to children than focusing on histories of arrest. Assessing the full spectrum of a survivor's protective efforts is a better path to assessing her strengths than just expecting her to escape to a refuge or call the police. Over time, it has become clearer that the

Model's behavioral focus could help improve practice in diverse arenas, such as family court, multiagency teams, mental health, and substance misuse. By improving the quality of information, it could also improve existing tools and procedures in those different systems—sidestepping the perpetual issue of conflicting models.

The Critical Role of Case Documentation

Before I dive deeper into each of the Critical Components, I think it would be useful to talk about the importance of written case documentation as a focal point for creating and evaluating systems transformation. In many bureaucracies, practitioners are familiar with the phrase "if it's not written down, it didn't happen." I learned that what was written was the "reality" of the case, often perceived as more real than the family's own experience and understanding of its situation. What was written was taken as the "truth" of the situation that became the foundation for and justification of decisions made by professionals. Conversations with judges reinforced this understanding since the professionals explained that their job was to read briefs and make decisions. The judges' job was to interrogate the evidence presented to them; it was not for them to act as investigators. To influence administrative and legal decision-making, documentation needed to be better at reflecting the realities of families and not the myths that had been dominating practice.

> *"My favorite part of the Model is the documentation. When delivering the four-day CORE Training, my favorite day is "documentation day." I'm so passionate about it because of how it influences trainees in their current practice and causes them to reflect on previous practice."*
>
> —Beth Ann, S&TI faculty, independent consultant, US

Documentation practices can also be understood as a reflection of the organization's priorities, procedures, culture, and values. In a hectic workplace, workers quickly learn to document what has been deemed most important by their supervisors and managers. Certain actions need to occur in every case. For example, in each case, child protection workers are required to check a child's medical status. Certain forms have to be completed. Organizational expectations and values are transmitted to new workers through supervision and through interactions with managers and the legal system. If your supervisor or your attorney never asks you questions about fathers, you quickly realize that you don't need to spend your precious time learning about the father or trying to meet with him. What is required and what is prioritized by your chain of command teaches you what to pay attention to what is important and what needs to be documented.

So the idea was this: **change the documentation, change the practice**. This was a bottom-up practice approach instead of a top-down policy approach. If there was one place all this information needed to be compiled, it would change the way workers gathered and synthesized information. Instead of reciting numbers of arrests and reports, this new approach would force the workers to gather information about patterns of behavior. Interviews with family members would change. The way workers reviewed prior case involvements would change. How they wrote about the family would change. How they presented the case in meetings and to their supervisor would change. Most importantly, the way they worked with the family and made child protection decisions would change.

The theory was that a focus on improved documentation of "critical" aspects of the domestic violence case using a perpetrator pattern-based approach would ripple backward to the information collection and forward to case decision-making and outward to the work with the family and interactions with other professionals.

Documenting the "Critical Components" eventually became one of the key pillars of the Model's implementation in child protection and beyond. By leveraging the theory that bureaucratic documentation expectations are a consistent driver of practice across sectors, domestic violence practice can become measurable and enforceable. For example, I expected the first group of domestic violence consultants who used the Model to document their cases using the Critical Components. This requirement was enforceable. For example, the consultants were required to produce reports using this framework. And the requirement was measurable. How close the consultants came to accurate application of the Model was based on the quality of their reports. When a consultant wrote a report that offered a powerful description of the perpetrator's pattern of coercive control, I knew that consultant had applied the Model in the consultation with child protection workers. It also meant that I knew that the worker was getting habituated to the Model through the questions the consultant asked the worker. Since documentation is foundational behavior in diverse sectors, it made it easy to adapt the Model to different practice frameworks in different sectors because each system, despite the differences from system to system, depended on written documentation as a key aspect of the system's processes.

Now, let's take a look at the Critical Components alongside some of my own reflections about their development and design.

Critical Component 1— Perpetrator's Pattern of Coercive Control

I want to discuss this component's three aspects. First, the person engaging in domestic violence is front and center. There is no generic reference to domestic violence. Domestic violence is a behavioral problem. It is defined by those behaviors, and those behaviors belong to the person who acts abusively. There is no domestic violence without the person who chooses to abuse or coercively control. Period. This is where the Model starts. In lots of domestic violence education, including the omnipresent and much adapted Power and Control Wheel,[2] the person is absent, hidden behind the tactics. This may seem like a small thing, but it is a huge thing. The executive director of a major US domestic violence network once told me that **the domestic violence movement has made the perpetrator invisible**. I wanted the Critical Components to make clear whom those behaviors belonged to.

Next is the inclusion of the word "pattern." This was meant to combat the focus on incidents of physical violence that drive so many systems and fail to fully capture the reality of survivors. Any domestic violence-informed practice needs to be pattern-based, looking beyond any recent incident to wider patterns in this and other relationships. **When I utilize the Model in consultations, I will always ask, "What do we know about the perpetrator's pattern of coercive control and actions taken to harm the children, from all sources, across this relationship and other relationships?"**

Finally, the focus on coercive control reinforces the pattern-based thinking and ties domestic violence to deprivation of rights, entrapment, and the effects of domestic violence on functioning. This is the most accurate and comprehensive way to assess harm.

Critical Component 2—Actions Taken by the Perpetrator to Harm the Children

This Critical Component, which is part of the pattern-based assessment of the perpetrator, connects the dots between domestic violence perpetration and child maltreatment. Domestic violence perpetrators abuse and neglect children. They use them as weapons to control their partners. They attack and undermine their relationships with their mothers and their siblings. They physically and sexually abuse them. While not every domestic violence perpetrator engages in every form of child abuse or neglect, his very choice to control and hurt his partner has direct and indirect impact on his child's functioning and the overall functioning of the family.

Despite the obvious connections, in my early conversations about domestic violence with child protection workers, I was struck by how little they did to actively assess for direct child abuse and neglect by domestic violence perpetrators. The emphasis was usually on how the violence toward the other parent was "exposing" children to a harmful environment. Often the child protection worker had not assessed the parenting of the perpetrator, usually the father, so there was little to no information to tie him to any potential child abuse or neglect.

This Critical Component was designed to integrate a child maltreatment component into every domestic violence assessment by child protective services. It was also designed to create an expectation that child protection workers explore how domestic violence perpetrators are often engaging in multiple forms of family violence simultaneously. Statements like "I'm not going to give you a penny for the children if you leave me" are attempts at coercive control directed at the adult survivor *and* a direct threat to the children's basic needs. Perpetrator threats such as "I'm going to shove this fucking Christmas tree down your throat"—which was said to a mother in front her daughter—need to be seen as both a choice to abuse the mother *and* an action taken to psychologically harm the children. It is essential to see the connection between control directed at a mother and the grooming of a stepdaughter for sexual abuse. Every domestic violence assessment needs to include an assessment for physical and sexual abuse of children. And every assessment of physical and sexual abuse of children needs to include an assessment for coercive control.

I included "actions taken to harm children" as part of the perpetrator pattern-based approach to ensure that assessments more closely mirrored the nonsiloed reality of families. Mothers are not just worried about what the domestic violence perpetrators will do to them; their decisions are heavily shaped by their worries about what the perpetrators can do, will do, and will be *allowed* to do—by systems—to their children. Children are not only worried about what the perpetrator will do to them but also about what the perpetrator will do to their siblings and their mother.

In practice, the first and second Critical Components are often written together as part of the overall perpetrator pattern-based approach. The Model guides workers to produce statements that are more specific and useful than "the children were exposed to the domestic violence." Instead, the Model guides workers to document more like this: "The father has engaged in a pattern of behavior toward the mother and the children that includes multiple physical assaults, involving multiple punches to her head and breasts and kicking her in the stomach when she was on the ground. This has led the mother to be hospitalized on two separate occasions in the last five years. The father has also slapped his seven-year-old daughter in the face, thrown phones and dishes at both his children, and kicked his teenage son in the thigh and stomach on more than one occasion. The father has broken down each child's door at least once, each time using a hammer to slam through the door panels. The father regularly threatens the mother by telling her he's going to use family court to take the children. He regularly tells the children that they are "dumb idiots" just like their mother. Imagine what would change if information such as this was included in the standard format for documentation across multiple systems.

Critical Component 3—Full Spectrum of the Nonoffending Parent's Efforts To Promote Child Safety And Well-Being

The first two Critical Components help make visible the fathers' abusive behaviors, reflecting the idea that practice transformation requires paying more attention to their role in family functioning. The first two components also set the stage for the Third Critical Component, which is a direct attempt at unwinding mother-blaming practices. To fully understand and appreciate survivors' protective efforts, the worker first needs the context of the perpetrator's pattern of behavior. If the worker doesn't understand that the perpetrator has targeted a survivor's mother (the child's grandmother) for violence in the past when she has helped her daughter and grandchildren, the worker will judge the survivor in a negative way when

CHAPTER 10: CRITICAL COMPONENTS AND PRINCIPLES: A COMMON LANGUAGE

she doesn't want to go and stay with her mother, even when her mother has room for her and her children.

In a chicken-and-egg dynamic, high standards for mothers lead to mother-blaming. For example, the mother might be accused of not protecting her children if she won't drop everything and leave the relationship. At the same time, mother-blaming is a source of those high standards. For example, if children are doing poorly, the mother is blamed. This Third Critical Component interrupts this cycle by bringing a wide lens to the assessment of survivors' protective efforts. We cannot assess mothers' efforts through the narrow lens of only physical safety—for instance, making the assessment based on whether she called the police or took her children to refuge. We need to widen our gaze to include efforts that focus on day-to-day care, nurturance, and the stability of the home environment. It's absurd to only focus on physical safety as if this is all that matters to children. And it's absurd to ignore all the worry and work that mothers invest in daily parenting in the midst of coercive control and abuse. It's also absurd not to fully appreciate that survivors are often compensating for or fixing the physical and emotional damage the perpetrator has done to the children and their home even as they wrestle with their own harm and entrapment.

In fact, many of the actions taken by survivors are multifaceted. They are about safety, healing from trauma, stability, and nurturance all at once. For example, picture a home where the perpetrator regularly throws the household routine into chaos via his abuse, violence, and control. Now, imagine a survivor who puts her energy into ensuring that children have a normal bedtime routine every night, regardless of what the perpetrator did during the day or what he might do to her once the children are asleep. This commitment to a regular bedtime routine for her children, where she reads to them or lays down with them, can accomplish a lot at once:

> **She is managing her safety and their safety by making sure her partner doesn't hurt them when they fuss about going to sleep.**

> She is helping them heal from trauma by giving them healthy, connected, loving time with a caring adult.
>
> She is nurturing and educating them through reading.
>
> She is giving them stability through a regular nighttime ritual.

Protective mothers rarely get the full credit they deserve for how hard they are working to protect their children from the behaviors of the domestic violence perpetrator. In creating this Critical Component, I was trying to fix that. **This critical component was designed to give voice to every way that a domestic violence survivor is active in her efforts to shield the children from the perpetrator's harm. Resisting. Strategizing. Planning. Evading. Lying. Responding. Placating.** You name it, survivors do it to protect their children. I wanted to make visible to professionals—who were often looking for concrete and dramatic protective efforts like calling the police—how hard survivors need to work just to complete the most basic tasks of day-to-day parenting. Here are examples they might hear from survivors:

> "I can't leave him alone with the children when I go grocery shopping, so I need to take them all with me."
>
> "My back is hurting (from getting assaulted a few days ago), but I still need to get up and feed the children breakfast. Asking him to do it is not an option."
>
> "I still keep my asthmatic child up-to-date with his medical appointments even though my husband's violence has forced me to move out of the area where my child's doctor practices."
>
> "I don't scream when he hits me so that my children don't wake up and see what he is doing to me."

> "I'm going to send my kids to live with my sister on Country (traditional Aboriginal land) because they love her, and she'll keep them safe and connected to our culture."

Attention to this Critical Component can be transformational across systems by challenging both failure-to-protect and parental-alienation narratives about survivors. Unfortunately, in many systems, neither victim advocates nor mental health professionals are given the time, space, structures, and support to assess and document these strengths. By making this an expected part of domestic violence-informed assessment, it is more likely that survivors' strengths will help shape decisions related to children.

Critical Component 4—Adverse Impact of the Perpetrator's Behavior on the Child

Here is the meat-and-potatoes Critical Component when it comes to domestic violence and children. Who did what to whom and what was the result? You take the first two Critical Components (perpetrator's pattern) and answer the question: what harm has these behaviors caused the child? This Critical Component reinforces the responsibility of the perpetrator for the harm to children—an invaluable perspective for the different sectors that often ignore the perpetrator as parent or focus on blaming the mother for harming the children.

There are so many different ways to explore this bucket of information, but any possible version needs to name the person doing the behaviors, the behaviors themselves, and the specific harm these behaviors have caused the child. You can ask these questions: "How have the perpetrator's behaviors changed the child's day-to-day life? What is the child doing differently because of the perpetrator's behaviors? How did the perpetrator's behaviors contribute to or cause X (the children's missed days in school, behavioral problems, etc.)?" And then there's the most comprehensive question: "How did the perpetrator's behavior impact child, partner, and family functioning?" This can even include a focus on the damage that the perpetrator did to his own relationship with the child: "How did the perpetrator's behaviors harm the child's ability to have a loving, safe connection with the perpetrator himself?"

Clear documentation of harm in one system can help with decision-making in another system. Imagine child protective services sharing with family court this incomplete report: It indicates how child protective services "opened a case for the family for domestic violence," but it then closed the case when the "father was ordered out of the home on protection order." Yet the report provided no details about the specific pattern of behavior and its harm to the children.

Compare that to a report that was more detailed about the perpetrator's pattern and the adverse impact of those behaviors on the child:

"The father's pattern of coercive control and actions that he has taken to harm his child have created the following adverse impacts on his son, age seven:

> The son has missed two weeks of school after he and his mother were forced to flee to refuge due to the father's violence.
>
> The mother reports that her son, when he is mad at her, uses the same words that his father uses, such as "bitch" and "cunt."
>
> The mother reports that her son misses his maternal grandparents, whom he hasn't seen in a year because the father won't permit it, describing his son's grandparents to his son as "assholes" and "jerks."
>
> During the last incident of violence by the father toward the mother, after the father smashed the mother's cell phone, the son walked a mile, alone in the dark, to get help. He reportedly slept for twenty-four hours straight after that incident. After

CHAPTER 10: CRITICAL COMPONENTS AND PRINCIPLES: A COMMON LANGUAGE

> that, the mother reported he had trouble going to sleep for weeks, having nightmares that woke him up.
>
> The father failed to attend the recommended men's behavior change program and demonstrated no sense of responsibility for the impact of his behavior on his child.
>
> Part of the fathers' pattern when he was out of the house was to make false reports about the mother's mental health. Based on the social worker's assessment of the situation, the mother had no apparent mental health problems, and no referral was made."

From the perspective of a survivor, which report feels more supportive and reflective of her reality? From the perspective of a family court judge, which report offers more useful information? When information flows between systems, guided by a perpetrator pattern-based approach, it can create more accurate, efficient, and effective responses.

Critical Component 5—Role of Substance Abuse, Mental Health, Culture, and Other Socioeconomic Factors

Initially, I was conflicted about how to best reflect race, class, culture, substance use, mental health, sexual orientation, gender identity, and other socioeconomic factors in the Model. The other Critical Components spoke to defining aspects that were critical to every situation involving domestic violence and children. On the other hand, substance misuse and mental health issues were present in many, but not all, cases. Culture, income, educational level, and other social factors were highly relevant but different in every situation.

To make this discussion even more complex, professionals often approached those factors as the reason or the excuse for the abusive behavior. The thinking has been as follows: "The perpetrator was drinking when he got violent, so let's send him to a substance misuse program instead of a men's behavior change program. This will fix both things." Here's another example: "He has a mental health diagnosis of bipolar or intermittent explosive disorder. He needs counseling, not a behavior change program." You might even get this excusing explanation for the violence: "Well, he got violent because he was upset over the mother's addiction. He's trying to control her drinking." Or I'd hear statements like "Domestic violence is very common in that person's culture." as an inappropriate justification for shortchanging a conversation about accountability and change. It was all another way of saying that "it's not his fault" or "we cannot expect him to be any different." A perpetrator might have faced less or no accountability if he had a high status in his community, which might have meant that he was affluent, educated, or white. The perpetrator's status might have helped to keep the survivor trapped and isolated from support and resources. For example, how can you call the police safely when your partner, who is abusing you, is a police officer?

    I struggled with the tension between the prevalence, importance, and reality of these issues and how they were commonly used to excuse away perpetrator responsibility. I knew racism shaped the lives of many domestic violence perpetrators and survivors. I knew that the presence of weapons or the status and wealth of the perpetrator mattered. In the end, I created the Fifth Critical Component as a type of catchall for anything that was critical to understanding the overall context for the domestic violence but wasn't a specific behavior of the perpetrator or the survivor. For example, a threat to kill a partner would be captured in the perpetrator's pattern of coercive control. But the perpetrator's ownership of a weapon (even when he hadn't made an explicit threat to use the weapon to kill her) is relevant as a factor that may increase dangerousness, fear, and entrapment. This type of information would have its home in the Fifth Critical Component.

A survivor's chronic illness and dependence on her partner for care might not fall neatly into any of the other Critical Components but is important to keep in focus when partnering with her. A perpetrator's pattern of substance misuse might not cause his violence, but his continued use is likely to make it harder for him to stop his abusive behavior. Religious notions of patriarchal authority, regardless of the community, might be a factor that increases entrapment, and it is not reliant on overt actions by the perpetrator. The role of extended family members, as part of the perpetrator's network of control, could also be placed here.

This Critical Component is especially important for creating the common framework across sectors because it helps deflect the challenges to perpetrator accountability that arise in the mental health and substance use fields. It addresses racism, colonization, and other forms of oppression that perpetrators leverage across sectors. It also embraces diversity, including creating room for discussions of how different cultures can play diverse positive roles in intervening with perpetrators and supporting survivors.

Principles

While it may seem counterintuitive, I developed the Model's Principles after the Critical Components. My initial focus was on defining the key information practitioners needed to engage in domestic violence-informed practice. But eventually I realized I needed to offer more guidance around practitioner behavior. I wanted these practice Principles to touch on children, survivors, and perpetrators—a whole-of-family approach. Like the Critical Components, these Principles challenge the siloing that often guides traditional service-driven domestic violence practice, a practice in which there are mostly separate services and practices for adult survivors, child survivors, and perpetrators. The Model's Principles lay out overarching practice directions for all the family members. By doing this, the Principles help create a common framework that can be used by multiple sectors. Whether a practitioner is working with a high-risk team in

Australia, or the Army Welfare Service in the United Kingdom, or Child Protection in Canada, that practitioner can be reflecting on how to be partnering with survivors or intervening with perpetrators to reduce risk and harm to the child.

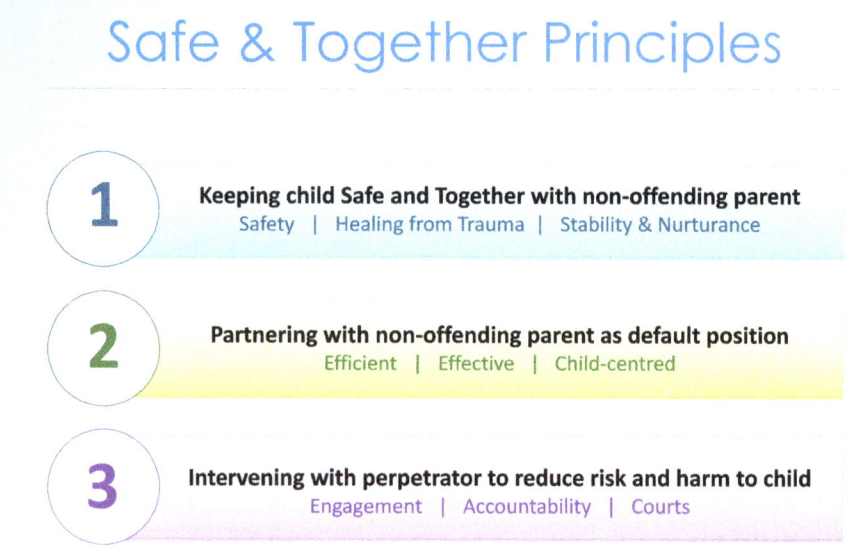

Principle 1: Keeping Children Safe and Together with the Nonoffending Parent: Safety; Healing from Trauma; Stability and Nurturance

The name and the overarching goal of the Model are derived from this First Principle. It was very important to me that the Model, at its highest level, acknowledged the importance of maintaining the child's connection with the domestic violence survivor, usually the mother. And it was important to make an argument for that connection from a focus on the children's important needs: safety, stability, nurturance, and healing from trauma. I wanted to show systems—such as child protective services—that were child-centered in their mission that keeping children with the nonoffending parent was consistent with their mission, not some form of ideologically driven charity to mothers. I wanted to combat the assumption that the mother's safety and well-being could easily be separated from the child's safety and well-being. Beyond that, I wanted to show that, in key areas of a child's needs, the nonoffending parent was the natural ally of systems focused on child safety and well-being.

Placing the child in the first Principle of the Model differentiates the Model from other family violence approaches in which children are not mentioned or are treated as secondary to the adult survivor. This makes the Model valuable to any sector in which children are part of the practice equation. Keeping children safe and together with their protective parent, usually the mother, is in the child's best interest. This is a point of view that is essential to domestic violence-informed practice. It is not ancillary. Domestic violence-informed practice has as an ideal the goal of maintaining the child's relationship with the mother. This is backed by clinical observations and research. We know that children's safety often correlates with the safety of the adult survivor. On the trauma front, even one strong connection with an adult can help buffer a child from the emotional and psychological harm of violence and abuse. Domestic violence-informed practice requires connecting the child's interests (safety, well-being) to the interests of the mother.

The subheadings of safety, stability, nurturance, and healing from trauma are meant to delineate key aspects of the protective bond between mothers and children. They guide practitioners to explore the mother's behavior in each of these areas. What had she done to promote the child's physical and emotional safety? What had she done to promote healing from the perpetrator's violence? What had she done to provide stability and nurturance? The tone behind each of these questions is curiosity, supported by a starting assumption that these efforts were occurring and needed to be named—the opposite of accusation and judgment.

This expanded focus on stability, nurturance, and healing from trauma reinforces the message that mothers' efforts in these areas and their value to child safety and well-being cannot be taken for granted. It can be argued that while all children need stability and nurturance, children impacted by domestic violence perpetrators need these things more—to help with their healing. The extraordinary efforts of mothers who engage in the parenting that helps children's stability and nurturance is often overlooked. This Principle helps counteract this tendency.

The Model starts from the presumption of protective behaviors by the nonoffending parent.

What justifies this? When we have domestic violence, we can assume that the perpetrator's behaviors are problematic for the children. But there is no reason to automatically assume any problems with the adult survivor's parenting. This simple concept may appear radical to many. But if we really lean into a perpetrator pattern-based approach, then there should be no a priori presumption of the survivor's failure to protect or poor parenting. Now this presumption doesn't mean that every protective parent is the same. Nor does it assume that every child is safe. It just means that our starting point for our assessment is clear:

> Presume the perpetrator's behavior is the source of the harm to child, partner, and family functioning.
>
> Presume, until proven otherwise through a domestic violence-informed assessment lens, that the survivor is engaging in meaningful protective behaviors.
>
> Then check all this out on a case-by-case basis using a behavioral, child-centered lens.

Each area identified in the First Principle was selected to address key concerns related to domestic violence and children and to capture the width and breadth of survivors' protective efforts. Embedded gender bias and pinched views of what constitutes protective behaviors have made huge areas of mothers' protective efforts invisible. The consideration of safety, stability, nurturance, and healing from trauma ensures that mothers get full credit for a wide array of efforts, including mundane daily tasks such as taking the children to doctors or getting them ready for school or bed, which the perpetrator is often making more difficult.

The practice Principle of keeping children safe and together with the nonoffending or protective parents is grounded in the children's experience. It is not an ideological or polemical position. If it is in a child's interest to stay with the nonoffending parent, we should be able to show it versus just simply resolving child safety by saying that "if you keep the adult survivor safe, you keep the child safe." Children's experiences are different. Their needs and perspectives diverge from those of the adult survivor. As postseparation abuse has shown us, an adult survivor may be able to separate herself from the bulk of the perpetrator's direct harm while children remain squarely in the control of the perpetrator through custody and visits. Domestic violence-informed practice honors the efforts and experience of adult survivors while listening to the voices of children.

The Principle invites practitioners to consider this question: "What has the practitioner done in this case with this family to keep the children safe and together with the protective parent?"

The concept of "safe and together" is broad enough that it encompasses children remaining with the protective parent in their own home (most ideal) and also safe and together somewhere else, such as a refuge or a new home. It includes children remaining "safe and together" with the protective parent *and* remaining in contact with the perpetrator as long as that contact includes safety. By defining the positive benefits of keeping children "safe and together" with their protective parent, the Model allows practitioners to focus on the real needs of the child versus the simplistic solutions to child safety and well-being—leaving and ending the relationship—associated with the myths of the child witness or the domestic violence incident. By setting this Principle as the north star of domestic violence-informed practice—whenever possible, we should work to keep children safe and together with the protective parent—the Model is setting the intention to reduce unnecessary removals of children from domestic violence survivors, especially Black and other marginalized families that are overrepresented in the child protection caseload.

Principle 2: Partnering with the Nonoffending Parent as a Default Position: Efficient, Effective, Child-Centered

I began my work with child protective services as the "perpetrator guy," the one who trained professionals to work with fathers who used violence. But as the only domestic violence expert for an entire child protection agency, I was quickly drawn into conversations about survivors. I realized the mother-blaming practices I witnessed were connected to the gaps in practice with perpetrators. I came to understand a perpetrator pattern-based approach had the potential to shift child protective services workers (and eventually other professionals) from the inefficiencies and ineffectiveness of failure to protect and other mother-blaming approaches to a more effective and efficient partnering relationship with survivors.

Out of these experiences, partnering with survivors became a central concept in the Safe & Together Model. Partnering refers to how professionals should behave toward survivors—as their partners in their efforts to achieve better outcomes for themselves and their children. It implies respect and collaboration. It offers professionals—who are in a different role than specialists on family violence or domestic violence victim advocates—the language for describing how to relate to protective parents, who are their natural allies around child safety and well-being when domestic violence is a factor. The term "partnering" assumes that professionals and survivors share similar interests: stopping domestic violence and improving outcomes for the children.

The language of the Second Principle is also consistent with the idea that professionals have an obligation toward survivors—that instead of blaming domestic violence victims, they need to have a constructive, collaborative orientation toward them. Eventually, the Safe & Together Model spelled out six specific steps associated with partnering:

The Six Steps of Partnering with Survivors

1. **Affirming (the perpetrator's, not the survivor's, responsibility for being the source of the harm to the children)**

2. **Asking (about the perpetrator's pattern of behavior)**

3. **Assessing (the survivor's protective capacities)**

4. **Validating (the survivor's strengths as a parent)**

5. **Collaboratively planning (around the survivor's safety and the safety and well-being of the children)**

6. **Documenting (the perpetrator's pattern, the survivor's strengths, and the safety plan)**

"Partnering" offers practitioners benefits as well. If your interactions with survivors are guided by the concept of "partnering," your work will be more objective, neutral, efficient, effective, and child-centered. The "partnering" principle in the Model contains an implicit promise to practitioners: if you approach survivors as potential allies in the safety and well-being of children (see the First Principle), you will be more successful in your work than if you approach survivors from a failure to protect perspective.

> *Child protection was always the enemy. They were always the people that you did not want in your life. And then they became partners in keeping my children safe. They became people that I actively sought out. After a while, I would pick up the phone and say, 'Hey, what do you think about this?' I would never have done that before. I would never have been honest with them. I would have just been evasive and given them the very bare minimum that they needed and gotten them the hell out of my life. Whereas in the most recent interaction, I was actively seeking them out towards the end to ask them for their advice. And I guess, you know, they became my cheerleaders—they didn't have rose-colored glasses, and they weren't ignoring the real risks that we faced. They were being realists and being positive, though, around my capacity to get through it. I think at that point, I developed enough trust and faith in them that I believed them when they said, 'You'll get through this.' And I did. Maybe I would have without them. But I just think they made it so much more possible.*

—Jane, survivor, Australia

CHAPTER 10: CRITICAL COMPONENTS AND PRINCIPLES: A COMMON LANGUAGE

A partnering approach offers survivors a dramatically different experience from mother-blaming. **Instead of putting blame and shame on the survivor, which she already gets from the perpetrator and perhaps others, partnering offers an alternative narrative, a message of validation and support.** It's validation that the perpetrator is solely responsible for the harm to the children. It's validation of active efforts to protect the children. And it's support for steps that will make the situation better.

To make this clearer, let me tell you a story to illustrate how "partnering" helps both the worker and the survivor. Imagine you are a child protection worker responding to a report of child abuse and neglect related to domestic violence. Your job is to go to the home and begin an assessment of the status of the child. The family doesn't know you are coming or that a report has been made. You ring the bell of the apartment. The mother, who was identified in the report as the domestic violence victim, opens the door. Now I'm going to offer you two different options, a kind of "choose your adventure" approach, about how you introduce why you are there:

> **Option 1:** "I'm here from child safety because we received a report that alleges you and your husband got into a fight last night in front of your eight-year-old son, who called the police because he was so scared. Domestic violence is bad for children, and I'm here to make sure your child is safe."

> **Option 2:** "I'm here from child safety because we received a report that alleges your husband assaulted you in front of your eight-year-old child. It appears that your husband's behavior scared your son enough that he called the police. I'm here because we are worried about your husband's behavior and its harm to you and your son. We see domestic violence perpetration as a parenting choice, meaning even if it's only directed at you, it still reflects on your husband as a parent. We want to make sure both you and your son are safe, get a sense of how serious your husband's behavior is, and see if we can help make the situation better."

So, pick the option, as the social worker, that is more efficient, effective, and child-centered. Hopefully you picked option 2. What is better about that option from the point of view of the social worker? While both options raise the issue of domestic violence with the mother, the second example replaces mutualizing language with a clear identification of the husband as the source of the danger to both the mother and the son. The subtle but critical shift achieves a number of things. It avoids the implicit blame of the mother that is expressed in option 1. Instead, it opens the door to a partnership around the son's safety. It also is inclusive of concern for the mother's safety. Instead of framing the mother as a potential impediment to child safety, the child protection professional is communicating the mother's value as a person by saying she is worried about the mother's safety as well. The language, with its clear focus on the person using the violence as the source of the danger and of his behavior as a parenting choice, communicates to the mother that she is not the target of the investigation.

As a survivor, which approach are you more likely to respond to positively? While there are many factors that might inhibit a mother's openness and trust with child protective services, such as the cultural history of removals of children from First Nations women, the second option increases the likelihood that the mother would engage and share meaningful information about the situation.

In a small study,[3] domestic violence survivors who acted as peer support for other parents navigating the child protection system felt that the Safe & Together Model would improve the experience of domestic violence survivors moving through that system. The study participants identified how, in the past, they had withheld information about domestic violence from workers who were not trained in the Model. However, after workers had received training in the Model, they witnessed survivors being more open about the violence when a worker used the Safe & Together Model partnering approach.

Why does the mother's reaction matter so much to the social worker, and what does it have to do with efficiency and effectiveness? Which option is likely to produce more information about the child's situation? If the mother is more open with you, you are more likely to learn more about the perpetrator's pattern, its impact on the mother, child, and functioning of the family, and also what the mother has already tried to do to protect the child. Every bit of this information is going to make your assessment more accurate, and any plan that evolves from these conversations is likely to be more effective and help improve the situation for the mother and the child.

To some, the power of the partnering principle is not always obvious at first. But it really comes alive in dialogues about practice. Asking the question, "what did you do to partner with the survivor?" is one of the most efficient ways to evaluate the quality of the domestic violence practice. I remember asking a supervisor what her worker did to partner with the survivor. She responded by saying, with some energy, "My worker explained to this mother (translation: lectured her) about how bad the domestic violence was for the children." From the answer, it was clear the approach was judgment and blame stemming from failure to protect culture rather than partnering.

By focusing the conversation on the practice of the professional as opposed to the behavior of the survivor, it became abundantly clear that the social worker was not setting up the best conditions for the mother to disclose to her information about the abuse. Bringing this victim-blaming practice into the open allowed me to name it, challenge it, and offer up suggestions for a partnering approach.

Partnering with survivors helps child protective services do its job (minus the mother-blaming).

Principle 3: Intervening with the Perpetrator to Reduce Risk and Harm to the Child: Engagement, Accountability, Courts

The Third Principle directs practitioners to take steps with the perpetrator as a parent. The thinking behind it is pretty simple: if the perpetrator is the source of the harm to the children, then systems should try to intervene with him to improve outcomes for children. It's not that complicated. However, intervening with perpetrators as parents historically has not been the norm for systems focused on domestic violence. In a world in which most children remain in contact with a violent father postseparation (one study reported that 70 percent of children remained in contact with a father who had abused the mother [4] and domestic violence perpetrators are involved in the majority of deaths of children known to child welfare (around two-thirds of child deaths known to child protective services were associated with domestic violence) [5, 6], systems had developed very few intervention strategies to deal with perpetrators as parents.

In fact, in many instances when a father's violence triggered a family's involvement with child protective services, much of the social work focus and scrutiny was on the adult survivor. In countless cases, referred from law enforcement as a result of a father's violence, most or all of the casework ended up being focused on the mother's parenting, mental health, and substance use. Even when he was the legal parent and the direct source of the harm to the children, child protective services did not intervene with him. Violent fathers, especially ones who were no longer in the home, were almost always ignored by social workers. When I would make the suggestion that child protective services should more actively engage with the parent who perpetrated the harm, the answer often was that criminal court was "dealing with him" or that he was "no longer living in the home." These were the answers even when he was having ongoing contact with the children, continued to have parental rights, and was not engaging in any behavior change efforts.

In training, I would often do a thought experiment to highlight the limitations of the criminal justice response to perpetrators as parents.

Here is a pared-down version of that thought experiment:

1. Imagine a family: mother, father, and three children under the age of ten.
2. The father, who has a pattern of coercive control, is arrested and forced out of the home after a particular incident of violence. This would be considered a successful action in "accountability" by the standards set by the system.
3. A referral is made from law enforcement to child protective services, which sends a professional to the home, and that worker meets with the mother and tells her to ensure the children are no longer exposed to any violence and to not "violate" the order by having contact with the father. The worker does not meet with the father because he is "being handled by the criminal justice system," is no longer in the home, and is no longer having contact with his children.

Now follow along as I ask (and answer, since this isn't a training event) a few questions about this very common scenario:

1. **Did the arrest and stay away order change the father's legal responsibilities for the children?** Answer: Living outside the home or an arrest for violence does not change a parent's legal responsibilities for his children. These legal responsibilities usually include keeping children safe from harm, medical care, basic needs like food and shelter, financial support, and education. He is still a legally responsible parent.
2. **Did the accountability strategies hold the perpetrator accountable as a parent?** No. Rarely do criminal justice processes and related court orders demand the perpetrator continue to pay for rent or mortgage, food, or other basic needs. This is true even when it is possible within the scope of the law.

3. **Does this failure to address the perpetrator as a parent in the criminal and civil "accountability" processes have an impact on the adult and child survivors?**
Yes. Without the coercion of the courts, perpetrators can immediately stop providing any financial support for the children and the household. The urgency of the moment around the violence that led the mother to call the police gives ground to the urgency of maintaining a household and a routine that might have been heavily reliant on the perpetrator's financial contribution or child caregiving time. Rent, mortgage, food, and utility bills don't stop coming. Transport to daycare and doctor's appointments become harder if the perpetrator takes the family car (whose possession is usually not covered under any court order). Work shifts might be missed because the perpetrating parent is no longer around to care for the children while the mother works. Even without any overt threat by the perpetrator to withhold financial support, it becomes clear that no support will be forthcoming until he's back in the house. Homelessness and inability to pay basic needs for the adult and child survivors may loom. Behind that is the fear of losing the children due to the inability to care for them.

4. **Is there a connection between failing to intervene with the perpetrator as parent (as outlined above), and the survivor's recanting to both child protective services, and criminal court?** You tell me . . .

The subtitle to this Third Principle is "Engagement. Accountability. Courts." This is an attempt to outline a wide range of interventions, especially ones that are usually not a major component of the dominant carceral approach to perpetrators. Engagement by professionals—with the exception of men's behavior change practitioners—is often left out of the practice equation. Conversations can be considered a type of intervention if they are with men who choose violence and if they are about their violence, its impact on others, and its impact on themselves. By themselves, these types of conversations do not guarantee behavior change. But if we don't teach social workers, therapists, children's attorneys, and others the skills and confidence to have meaningful conversations with their clients about their violence, negative consequences will ensue. The perpetrator doesn't hear the message that his behavior is a problem. Practitioners don't document a perpetrator's lack of concern for his children or his partner. Adult and child survivors feel (and are) abandoned. She thinks practitioners are just as scared of the perpetrator as she is (and she may be right). Watching professionals avoid speaking directly to the perpetrator about his behavior (or speaking to him at all) reinforces the message that she is to blame and that she's alone in needing to figure out the situation, including the safety of the children. Imagine what would change for survivors if every mental health, social work, addiction, and legal professional was trained in engaging, and holding accountable, domestic violence perpetrators as parents.

The Safe & Together Model expands the concept of "accountability" beyond the traditional carceral definition. It explicitly includes accountability as a parent. It also considers microaccountability in the day-to-day activities of practitioners. Accountability begins with the practitioner's clarity in framing domestic violence through a perpetrator pattern-based lens. Accountability gets operationalized in how the practitioner affirms the perpetrator's responsibility for his choices in the practitioner's conversations with the survivor, with the perpetrator, and even with colleagues. Accountability comes alive in documentation that clearly names the perpetrator's behaviors and ties them to the harm to child, partner, and family functioning.

Accountability doesn't only live in the big-ticket items such as arrest and incarceration. It lives in the small interactions, such as when a social worker says to a father who used violence, "I want to talk to you about your behavior and how it has harmed your child." Accountability lives in the "how" of the work. On the negative side, a police officer can arrest a father for domestic violence but at the same time say to the mother, "Why do you let your children keep living with this violence?" (True story.) On the positive side, the police officer might say, "Mate, you're hurting your kids when you get violent with their mother." Accountability comes alive when a judge says to an abusive father's lawyer, "If your client comes into my court and denies the violence and can't talk about his responsibility for it, it will cost him in my ruling about custody and access." (This was based on a real statement from a judge.)

Finally, the role of courts in accountability needs to be broadened within and beyond the criminal courts. While fines, incarceration, probation, and referrals to men's behavior change groups can be important interventions, they often do not specifically address perpetrators as parents. I was chatting with a friend who was a domestic violence prosecutor about the failure of criminal courts to hold perpetrators accountable as parents. He gave the standard response: This is not our job, and there are other systems such as family court and child protective services to deal with the children's needs. But when I made the connection between this failure and the recantation of survivors in domestic violence criminal cases, he suddenly realized that he had seen his judge, in other types of cases, enter financial orders as part of criminal court cases. He vowed to begin asking for financial orders in pretrial motions for domestic violence perpetrators. A few months later, he reported that, while the judge didn't grant his financial order requests every time, he was able to get financial orders against the perpetrator some of the time. Just by asking for them. No laws needed to be changed. In addition to considering how criminal courts consider perpetrators as parents, family and children's courts also need to consider how they intervene with perpetrators as parents to reduce risk and harm to children.

Final Thoughts

The Safe & Together Model, despite its firm roots in the child protection sector, is an approach that has value for many other sectors. **New child protection workers who are taught the Safe & Together Model from their first day are shocked to learn that any other approach has ever been used.** It makes that much sense to them. Their shock often increases when they hear about how mother-blaming and father-ignoring has been the norm. It is my hope that this becomes true for many other sectors and that a perpetrator pattern-based approach becomes the standard of practice across every sector that interacts with perpetrators and survivors.

CHAPTER 11

Developing Evidence for the Model

Everyone wants to know the results the Model produces. What changes does it make? The positive evidence is strong and growing. A building body of evidence shows the value of the Model to different sectors, to cross-sector collaboration, and to survivors. Positive feedback from practitioners is overwhelmingly positive. For example, in one project, 96 percent of the participants reported that the Model helped them improve their practice.[1] This kind of data is repeated over and over again from different sources. In this chapter, I'm going to cover this evidence about the Model's effectiveness from a few different angles, including the most recent data from the Safe & Together Institute training evaluations and recent projects from across the globe.

Early Child Protection Results

The earliest feedback on the Model involved small studies that offered evidence of promising outcomes. In one project, which was focused on enhancing skills of child protection workers to work with domestic violence perpetrators, anecdotal feedback suggested that increasing child protective services' capacity to intervene with perpetrators might translate into outcomes becoming less punitive toward survivors.[2] In the same jurisdiction, supervisors trained in the Safe & Together Model found that 66 percent of the respondents identified specific positive changes in their supervisory practice, including "greater understanding of the dynamics of coercive control and its impact on the family; increased understanding of survivors' strengths and safety planning; and more specific questions and directives to workers."[3]

An early, third-party study of the impact of the Safe & Together Model in Ohio reinforced the potential benefit of a perpetrator pattern-based approach for improving child protective services' orientation to survivors. The data produced strong evidence that supervisors were less victim-blaming. It also produced findings that documentation of harm to children improved, showing that "the proportion of cases that documented the effect of domestic violence on children jumped from 50 percent during the period before training to 80 percent after the training had been completed."[4] In focus groups run by the Department of Psychiatry at the Yale School of Medicine, researchers found positive results in interviews with child protection practitioners trained in an investigations protocol that focused on perpetrator accountability and partnering with survivors. The participants noted that the content and phrasing of the questions in the domestic violence protocol decreased defensiveness on the part of family members being interviewed, increased the level of detail of the information obtained, and facilitated talking with children about domestic violence. They noted that the reduced defensiveness led to a more open dialogue, and the increased detail helped them with their report writing."[5]

On a systems level, the Safe & Together Institute's work has been correlated with significant reductions in out-of-home placements of children. In one region of Florida, the statutory child protection agency repeatedly engaged in Safe & Together Model training for its staff after initial interest in only one round of training. When I asked why the agency had increased its commitment to Safe & Together training, I was told that after the training, there was a significant decrease of out-of-home placements of children, saving the government hundreds of thousands of dollars in foster care costs. These results appeared to be supported by correlative data from this and one other location in Florida where the Model's introduction was associated with a 50 percent drop in removals

CHAPTER 11 : DEVELOPING EVIDENCE FOR THE MODEL

of children due to domestic violence allegations.[6]

Outside the United States, an audit of child protection case files in Edinburgh showed significant changes in case documentation after Safe & Together Model training.[7] In Queensland, Australia, children's legal services attorneys are changing their practice as a result of Safe & Together Model practice. New strategies for partnering with survivors include applying for domestic violence protection orders in children's cases, helping "child protection practitioners advocate with parole boards about parole conditions and police to tailor bail conditions that enhance the safety of the children and nonoffending parent," and "redacting evidence that might place a parent in danger."[8]

Improving Cross-System Collaboration

The first evidence of the Model's capacity to improve collaboration between sectors was a survey conducted with practitioners who were a part of a Connecticut multiagency team focused on child physical and sexual abuse cases. The survey found that domestic violence-informed training improved safety for families, increased positive relationships with nonoffending parents, and improved perpetrator accountability.[9] The Model has also demonstrated the power to help child protective services' relationship with domestic violence victim advocates. This makes sense as it offers an approach that resonates with both advocates and professionals within child protective services—increased focus on the accountability of the perpetrator as parent and partnering with the adult survivor. A few years ago, Rutgers University found that the Safe & Together Model was the most common collaboration framework used by US-based victim advocates working alongside professionals with child protective services.[10]

A more recent control group evaluation[11] of a project focused on how implementation of Safe & Together Model tools could specifically improve collaboration between child protection workers and domestic violence victim advocates. It found the following results:

- Participants from child protective services and domestic violence victims advocates describe their preproject relationship with the following words: fractured, rocky, minimal, and adversarial. After the six-month project, they used these words: mending, improved, partnership, and collaboration.

- The participants self-reported on key variables before and after the project:
    - Trust: 17 percent before; 67 percent after
    - Communication: 8 percent before; 83 percent after
    - Information sharing: 0 percent before; 67 percent after
    - Role clarity: 54 percent before; 92 percent after
- After participating in the project, the majority of victim advocates and child protection staff reported that they "'agreed' or 'strongly agreed' that they worked closely with the other agency to support child protection-involved survivors and families (59 percent, compared to 17 percent before) and that they were informed as often as they should be about what was going on with a survivor/client at the other agency (67 percent, compared to 0 percent before)." In contrast, the control group showed no or negative change in these measures over the test period.
- After participating in the project, nearly all (92 percent, compared to 67 percent before) child protection and victim advocate staff reported they "'agreed' or 'strongly agreed' that both agencies shared a high level of commitment to survivors and families' well-being. In contrast, the (control group) showed a negative shift in perceived commitment of both agencies over the test period."

In Victoria, Australia, the Multi-Agency Triage Project, a two-year, multiagency triage pilot program that used the Model as a framework for its processes, was able to divert almost 90 percent of child welfare domestic violence referrals from the police away from statutory child protection to the nongovernmental sector, allowing for more collaborative and less punitive approaches to domestic violence survivors. The report noted, "Participants commented on the importance of the shift from focus on the woman to 'pivoting to the perpetrator,' their patterns of behavior, and how they can be held accountable." One participant said, "My understanding of the Safe & Together Model has assisted me greatly in the development and documentation of referral rationales. I have initiated questions in my rationales as to the perpetrator's parental capacity, roles, and expectations. There has been a huge shift from the available protective factors for adult survivors to the perpetrator parental deficits."[12]

Collaboration with the University of Melbourne

One of my most rewarding professional collaborations has been with Professor Cathy Humphreys of the University of Melbourne (Australia) and her team of researchers. The Safe & Together Institute has collaborated with Professor Humphreys's team of researchers for numerous national and state projects using the Safe & Together Model. These projects have explored how the Model can be used to assess and shape various aspects of systems responses to domestic violence. These projects have involved multiple sectors, including specialists in family violence, child protection services, law enforcement, mental health, substance use, and others. Each project had a different focal point, ranging from enhancing skills for practitioners to being able to engage perpetrators to exploring how to increase the capacity of health workers to respond to domestic violence.

The research projects offered insight into the value of the Safe & Together Model and domestic violence-informed practice. The following are just some of the results:

- The PATRICIA Project, an Australian multistate study that used the Safe & Together Model Case-reading Tool and found that it was "potentially an important enabler for improving competencies in risk assessment, case decision-making, complex case planning, and in cross-system collaboration." In an example of the feedback from the project, one participant said the tool "made us really talk about the practice and that behavioral stuff because we couldn't fall into the jargon of the safety. It really delved down to what we actually do with families. I liked that." [13]

- The multistate Safe and Together Addressing Complexity (STACY) Project involved research on how the Safe & Together Model might improve practice at the intersection of domestic violence, addiction, and mental health. The project design was heavily influenced by the Model's Principles. The results showed that the Model can be used "in informing worker practice where children and families are living with domestic and family violence (DFV) and where there are parental issues of AOD (alcohol and other drugs) and/or MH (mental health) issues." The results highlight the importance of "pivoting to the perpetrator" along with partnering with survivors. One participant commented that the Safe & Together Model focused on "partnering with non-offending parent and changing practice; not doing our usual thing of swooping in and saying Mum's not protective so the kids need to come into care. We are committed to using the framework."[14]

- The ESTIE Project (Evidence to Support Safe & Together Implementation and Evaluation) was an action research project run by the University of Melbourne in collaboration with the Safe & Together Institute and New South Wales Ministry of Health. The ESTIE Project took an action research approach to the question of improving the collaborative and holistic service provisions for children and families living with domestic and family violence (DFV), where perpetrators use alcohol and other drugs (AOD) and/or mental health (MH) as part of their coercive control. Here again, the Safe & Together Model was the organizing framework for practice improvement. Ninety-six percent of the community of practice participants involved with the project reported the Model helped them improve their practice. The project, because of its interdisciplinary nature, focused heavily on systems change. The final project report highlighted the importance of the Model's perpetrator pattern-based approach: "This shift toward pattern-based thinking is both a more effective way to explore use of violence and control and a stronger foundation for informed safety assessments across disciplines and contexts of practice."[15]

While the results from each individual project are important, the consistency of results across multiple projects that involve different areas of focus and are across multiple states speaks to the stability, versatility, and power of the Safe & Together Model. The cross-sector nature of the projects reinforce the value of the Model as a transformational framework.

Kirkpatrick Training Evaluation Data

In the mid-2010s, the Safe & Together Institute started focusing its training efforts on its four-day CORE training. This twenty-two-hour training is focused on skill development: interviewing, assessing, documenting, and case planning, using the Model's perpetrator pattern-based approach. To ensure fidelity and measure effectiveness, the Institute invested in tracking the results of this training across the globe using the Kirkpatrick training evaluation model.[16] The Kirkpatrick training evaluation approach considers four levels of outcomes: reaction, learning, behavior, and results. The Safe & Together Institute has created structures to measure the first three levels. The fourth level is more complex and costly to study and has been outside the Institute's current capacity.

Here are some of the highlights from those surveys of global training participants in our CORE training:

Scope of CORE training delivery:

- From 2019 to mid-2022, Safe & Together Model certified trainers delivered 475 CORE trainings for a total of 167,000 participant training hours.
- Of those trainings, 44 percent were delivered in the Asia-Pacific region, with the remaining trainings split evenly between North American and the United Kingdom.

Reaction results:

- In 2019, when all the CORE training was in-person, 93 percent of the participants said their training "expectations were met" and 87 percent said they were "engaged throughout the training."
- In 2020, when a significant portion of this training moved online, the numbers remained high: 88 percent of the participants said their training "expectations were met" and 83 percent said they were "engaged throughout the training."

Learning:

- In 2020, knowledge related to domestic violence-informed practice leaped by about 66 percent as a result of the training, from 56 percent (average pretest score) to 93 percent (average posttest score).

Behavior:

In follow-up surveys several months after the training was completed, participants reported high levels of confidence and effectiveness related to behaviors associated with the Model.

- In 2022, 79 percent of the participants indicated that they were adding perpetrator patterns and their impact to their interviews and that they were adding partnering with survivors

CHAPTER 11 : DEVELOPING EVIDENCE FOR THE MODEL

to both their interviews and case plans.
- Quotes from practitioners help fill out the story of behavior change:
    - "Shortly after completing the training, I was allocated a young seventeen-year-old Aboriginal woman who had a high-risk pregnancy. She experienced significant DV such as strangulation, hitting, punching, dragging. There was also coercive control, financial abuse, and emotional and verbal abuse. I was able to map the perpetrator behaviors and convey these to other agencies to create safety, work with the young woman to plan for her safety and the safety of her unborn baby, as well as advocate with confidence on her behalf with child protection and accommodation providers. I felt so empowered, armed with knowledge to be confident in my work."—J.D., Australia, CORE, Summer 2021
    - "We have taken two cases before the judge and through use of documentation and articulation by the worker (we prepped and worked hard for it), the judge authorized the petitions and ordered the perpetrator out of the home."—B.H., US, CORE training, Fall 2021
    - "It's been encouraging to see that the more staff we have who are trained in and familiar with the material, that we have a shared language in undertaking a holistic and balanced assessment of risk and safety."—J.S. Australia, CORE training, Winter 2020

This chart outlines other behavioral results from 2019 through part of 2022.

Safe & Together Model Kirkpatrick Level III Behavior Change Evaluation Results

Very Much + Completely (combined top answers on a Likert scale)	Confidence		Effectiveness		Enthusiasm	
	Pretraining	3-6 months later	Pretraining	3-6 Months Later	Pretraining	3-6 months Later
Assessing for perpetrator patterns of abuse	17 percent	60 percent	13 percent	55 percent	-	73 percent
Identifying the impacts of the perpetrators' patterns of abuse on child and family functioning	11 percent	65 percent	19 percent	62 percent	-	78 percent
Partnering with the adult survivor	28 percent	70 percent	26 percent	65 percent	-	82 percent
Identifying the adult survivor's strengths	32 percent	73 percent	31 percent	67 percent	-	83 percent
Safety planning with the adult survivor	27 percent	62 percent	25 percent	57 percent	-	77 percent
Developing case plans to intervene with the perpetrator	12 percent	37 percent	11 percent	34 percent	-	61 percent
Domestic violence-informed documentation	15 percent	62 percent	14 percent	57 percent	-	76 percent

The Model is demonstrating that it not only increases learning but that it also makes significant and lasting changes in professional behaviors.

CHAPTER 11 : DEVELOPING EVIDENCE FOR THE MODEL

Final Thoughts

The positive data on effectiveness of the Safe & Together Model continues to grow. We continue to work toward a better understanding of its impact and ways to improve its effectiveness. As the global network of practitioners trained in the Safe & Together Model grows, I'm excited to see what can be learned and what is possible. In the next chapter, you'll hear the voices of practitioners and survivors and their experiences of the Model.

CHAPTER 12

Honoring the Voices of Survivors and Practitioners

When I speak publicly on the Model, my most cherished feedback comes from survivors. After almost every live, in-person event, at least one survivor, who is usually also a professional, comes up to me and shares how validated she feels by the Model. The very first practitioner awarded a Safe & Together Model Champion Award, Jennifer Sosniak, shared that her "aha" moment as a survivor first came when the Model, and its clear language of partnering, helped her to realize that she was living under coercive control. This realization and the tools she acquired in training helped her to heal and move forward both personally and professionally. This is the kind of feedback that keeps me and my team moving forward in our work.

For this book to feel complete, I knew I wanted to include the voices of survivors like Jennifer, whose lives have changed because of their exposure to practitioners trained in the Safe & Together Model. Just like survivors were the intended ultimate beneficiaries of my early men's behavior change work, similarly, survivors are the intended ultimate beneficiaries of the Model's focus on practitioner and system change. Any success with practitioners doesn't mean a lot if it doesn't translate into transformed outcomes for adult and child survivors.

At the same time, the Model is just words on a piece of paper without the practitioners who champion it in their day-to-day practice. Without their passion, skill, and commitment to improve outcomes for families, no transformation would be possible. I knew that I wanted to include their experiences of applying the Model—what they learned and how it changed them—as part of this book.

While qualitative research has been conducted on the Model before, it felt important to do a fresh set of interviews specifically for this book. I wanted to find out what the Model meant for survivors who had experience working with practitioners trained in the Model and whose organizations were applying it across their systems. I also wanted to find out more about practitioners' experiences of using the Model and its impact on them as professionals and sometimes even as survivors themselves. While the sample size is small, I believe it offers valuable insight into the power of the Model as it reflects what the Safe & Together Institute sees in its own evaluation efforts, third-party research, and the anecdotal feedback we receive daily. The interviews were coordinated, conducted, and analyzed by Deb Nicholson, my assistant, based on questionnaires I developed, so when I use the word "we" in this chapter, it acknowledges the collaborative nature of the process.

Survivor-Only Voices

Identifying survivors who felt safe enough, ready in their own process, and available to be interviewed for the book was challenging. Despite starting with a wider potential pool, we ended up with two survivors who were ready and willing to share their story of the Model's impact on their lives and their children's lives. Both survivors' feedback was made more valuable by the fact that they had "before and after" experiences. Each could contrast how their cases were handled by practitioners unfamiliar with the Safe & Together Model with practitioners trained to use the Model. These side-by-side experiences added to the poignancy and power of their comments. As you'll see, their positive experience with the Model was also echoed in the experiences of practitioners speaking from their own perspective as survivors.

The first question we asked each survivor was simple: "How is your life better as a result of the Model?" Both women responded that they might not have their children with them if not for the Model.

> I genuinely believe that me and my two kids . . . wouldn't have been together if it wasn't for the Model because the Safe & Together-trained social work department approached it in an entirely different way to how it was before—I think my life is much better. My children are thriving, and everybody in my family is quite happy. We don't have any domestic abuse around us. So, yeah, it's changed my life massively. Otherwise, I don't believe that I'd have my children anymore.
>
> —Naomi, survivor, Scotland

> "I guess if we're looking at specifically what my life looks like now as a result and what it might have looked like otherwise, I think it enabled my children to live with me. And that's something that, you know, could potentially have been at risk if the child protection workers who were involved in the most recent investigations hadn't been domestic violence-informed and using the Safe & Together Model. I don't know whether they would still be with me. I don't know."
>
> —Jane, survivor, Australia

When we asked the women to describe how practitioners had partnered with them or intervened with the perpetrator, they highlighted a range of strategies used, including helping to recognize the perpetrator's behavior as abuse; reflecting back protective efforts; actively supporting efforts to seek protection; advocating for safe contact with the perpetrator; listening; advocating for medical, financial, and housing support, and advocating when trauma symptoms presented as anger or rage. For instance, the survivor in Scotland, Naomi, said that practitioners not trained in the Model "thought I was a psycho." In contrast, the survivor in Australia, Jane, said that practitioners trained in the Model mapped the abuse being perpetrated against her and were able to tell how the perpetrator "used systems and how he used coercive control."

As part of partnering with survivors, practitioners trained in the Safe & Together Model played a role in translating social work jargon. "It was almost like I spoke Spanish and they spoke English, and the Safe & Together-trained social worker was a translator in the middle," said Naomi. Jane said that her relationship with child protective services changed from adversarial to collaborative.

> "It genuinely felt like a partnership, not a relationship of this massive power imbalance that is characterized by any relationship with a statutory body like child protection. I think it was quite remarkable that they could turn the reality of that into something that even remotely looked like a partnership. I thought that was pretty skillful. Absolutely."
>
> —Jane

Naomi likened her previous experience with child protective services to the abuse she was experiencing at the time, and she said it was an example of how *not* to partner with a survivor.

"I think the way of social work at the time was really abusive. I remember saying to them, 'You tell me that it's not OK that someone is saying horrible things to me when I report the abuse. Even though I am constantly pointing out the things I'm doing right, you never bring up anything I'm doing right. It's all about what I'm doing wrong. I don't see how you think that this is any different from domestic abuse.' I remember thinking at the time that this is mirroring what he's doing, but it's OK for you because you're qualified. I genuinely found it as abusive as that."

—Naomi

When we asked both women about the impact of Safe & Together on them and their children's situation, their testimony was compelling.

"The impact of Safe & Together was massive. It was the difference between separation and togetherness. It was the difference between safety and harm. It was the difference potentially between life and death. I don't think I'm being dramatic when I say that it's the potential between perpetual litigation and systems abuse and a prompt stop to that behavior. I can't overstate the impact. It was amazing. We had a situation where we had actual threats of murder-suicide and guns and my pets being shot, and like every red flag you could wave, you know, it was there. All of the frustrating experiences I've had in the past and then the relief of domestic violence and trauma-informed practitioners in this last interaction. And it's just a world of difference."

—Jane

Jane's experience with the Safe & Together Model-trained professionals stands starkly against her previous experience of reaching out to a national domestic violence helpline for support to plan her escape:

CHAPTER 12 : HONORING THE VOICES OF SURVIVORS AND PRACTITIONERS

"Once I mentioned to them what was going on, they started with the 'failure to protect' talk. They told me, 'We're going to have to notify child safety, and we're going to have to intervene.' And I ended up just saying, 'Sorry, that was a joke. I made it up. I'm not really seeking help. I'm fine. It's fine. Everything's fine.' And I hung up, and I stayed four years longer than I should have. I guess that's the difference. That very first moment I reached out should have been the moment that somebody said to me, 'You are not to blame for your ex's behavior. I can see that you're doing these protective things.'"

—Jane

It was very interesting to see how Safe & Together helped both women when they were involved with more than one system. Jane and Naomi both reported that their support workers helped to navigate across systems, made links where they were needed, and provided support in specific ways, such as making a complaint against a worker.

"She helped guide me through their complaints systems . . . because it's not as easy as it looks to complain to these people and to get them to take you seriously as well. When we were having meetings, there was a child protection consultant involved who I knew was telling lies. My Safe & Together-informed social worker helped defend me against that. It's almost like my social worker gave me a voice—because I could say something to the child protection social workers, and it was like banging my head on a brick wall. But the minute my social worker said the same thing, they were willing to listen. It was mad."

—Naomi

Jane spoke of the "domino effect" of having informed practitioners working with other workers across the sector and being able to influence their practice and attitudes, consciously or unconsciously:

> "When child protection workers finally 'got' Safe & Together, when they finally put it into words and named it—all the other systems I was involved with started to get it. It was kind of a domino effect. It was really obvious to me, as the person in the middle of it all, through all of these discussions that were being had, that the way that child safety was representing my situation (using the Safe & Together Model) was having a demonstrable impact on these other places in my life—statutory systems, other people who were making decisions about what my future will be like and what my children's future would be like. They were being influenced kind of by osmosis because these people were embodying this very empowering framework. The people around them just fell into step because I think people naturally want to do right by victims. I think it feels intuitive in some way, and they just need that leadership, someone to go, 'Hey, I'm taking the lead here. I'm going to map the perpetrator's behavior. I'm going to notice and celebrate all of the protective efforts of this mother.'"

—Jane

We also asked the survivors about their experiences of the Safe & Together Model's key goals to stop mother-blaming, stop ignoring fathers, and help keep children safe. Naomi talked about the important role of her own social worker in ensuring the perpetrator's actions were kept in view.

CHAPTER 12 : HONORING THE VOICES OF SURVIVORS AND PRACTITIONERS

"My Safe & Together-informed social worker would listen to the list of issues presented by the child protection social workers, and say, 'Actually, that wasn't her, that wasn't her, and neither was that.' Being blamed or held responsible for my perpetrator's behavior happened all the time, and it constantly felt like I was having to defend myself."

—Naomi

Jane spoke of the need to ensure that stopping mother-blaming, stopping ignoring fathers, and helping to keep children safe was something that must be done *all at the same time*:

"In the most recent experience I had with child protection, they did all three of these things, and it was the combination of them all that helped. I think if you were to do one to the exclusion of the others, you wouldn't have the same profound impact. It's the combination of all three that's really important for practitioners to know. You can't just cherry-pick bits of the Model that you like. You need to really do justice to it by focusing on all of these things—on children's safety, obviously first, and putting the focus back on the person who's actually perpetrating the harm, and then supporting the parent that is protecting and keeping the kids safe."

—Jane

When asked whether the Model, and the practitioner using the Model, changed the way they thought about themselves and their situation, both women answered with a resounding "absolutely."

"When they were intervening with the perpetrator, my Safe & Together-informed social worker was helping me see what was happening. At the time I was saying, 'No, it's not that bad. This is not domestic violence.' And my social worker was able to get me to see it from a completely different perspective. I don't know how she managed to do that because the child protection workers were saying one thing about me and something else about my perpetrator. So, it was very easy for the perpetrator to say to me, 'Oh but look what they're saying about you.' I was believing everything he said. But my social worker was always saying to me, 'That's abuse.' She was able to get me to look at it for what it actually was. Nobody else in that room would have been able to do that because I didn't trust any of them. I was able to keep my children safe through that, through my own knowledge, because I understood what was going on. And every time it was hard, there was knowledge I could fall back on—I understood myself more than I ever had because of my Safe & Together-informed social worker."

—Naomi

Jane's testimony reinforces the idea the Model has the potential to change survivors' self-perceptions, counteracting the negative impact of the perpetrator and systems:

"It completely changed how I looked at myself. They just were so effective at noticing what was going on. And I think that's what had previously been missing in all my interactions with helping agencies—is that they just didn't notice. And it was so frustrating. I was like, 'Did you not see what he's doing? Do you not see that he's using your system to get to me? Do you not see that this is part of his plan? That you're just a pawn in this ridiculously convoluted game of his?' Once these

CHAPTER 12 : HONORING THE VOICES OF SURVIVORS AND PRACTITIONERS

practitioners that were well-versed in Safe & Together noticed what was going on, they helped make it more clear to me. So that's the important step for me around how I feel about myself—is if they just noticed it and popped it in a case note, that wouldn't have had the same impact as it did when they sat me down and they said, 'I've observed this. I see that you do that. I see that you've tried to keep your kids safe through these very specific actions.' For me, that made a world of difference because I was well and truly beaten and bruised in every possible way, and I didn't think that I was much good as a parent. I felt like I was failing on all fronts. They gave me the opportunity to reframe that and say, 'No, actually, I've taken extraordinary efforts to keep my kids and myself safe.'"

—Jane

The final interview question gave Jane and Naomi the opportunity to tell us what they'd like to say to other survivors about the Model:

"I would say that if you're ever in a situation of having to deal with child welfare agencies or workers, ask them outright if they have heard of or if they used the Safe & Together Model. I think so often we're afraid to challenge the people—especially statutory bodies that are in our life to judge us and potentially intervene in ways that we don't want them to. I think even if they say no, ask them why. Ask them why they believe that their theoretical and practical approach is going to result in increased safety for you and your kids."

—Jane

"I would say that it is a really positive model to work with.

I would say that it is really productive.

I would say that you're given a voice where normally you don't have one.

Safe & Together does what it says on the tin. I think it is so important."

—Naomi

Practitioner Voices

I also wanted to include the voices of the practitioners who are using the Model in their day-to-day work with adult and child survivors, perpetrators, and their professional colleagues. Eleven practitioners in the United Kingdom, Australia, and North America volunteered to answer a series of questions about their experience applying the Model, its effectiveness, and even their personal transformation as a result. Some of them were even willing to share their personal perspective as survivors. Most were still working in the field in roles where they could apply their Safe & Together Model knowledge, skill, and experience. Their training, methods of applying the Model, and sectors were diverse. In many ways, they are representative of the wider group of practitioners applying the Model globally every day.

Major Themes

When we asked practitioners to reflect on why they became interested in the Model and what about it propelled their use of it, most responses fell under these themes:

> Becoming more skilled and confident working with perpetrators—holding men accountable as parents and pivoting to the perpetrator
>
> Understanding the impacts on parenting—recognizing the strengths and protective efforts of mothers
>
> Having the language and tools that enabled improved practice
>
> Improving systems—sometimes through improved coordination and other times through gaining confidence to challenge other agencies—and having the tools and framework to back this up
>
> Transforming personal and professional lives as a result of involvement with the Model

Becoming More Skillful and Confident Working with Perpetrators as Parents

All the practitioners said the Safe & Together Model helped them become more skillful and confident in working with perpetrators as parents. Some even acknowledged that prior to Safe & Together Model training, perpetrators as parents were not even on their professional radar. Several of the practitioners had never worked with perpetrators before—and did not want to—but they realized that it was necessary work to make the changes needed to keep kids safer.

"[What attracted me to the Model] was definitely working with the person using family violence, and how important that work was to keep children safe and to work with the adult survivor. I think there was an understanding within the sector . . . that to create change you work with children, women, and mothers. But you can't create change unless you work with the perpetrator. How do we go about doing that when we don't have the skills? The Model gives you the confidence and the skills and the framework to do that work."

—Karen, child and young person practice lead, Australia

"I didn't know about accountability for perpetrators. I think that has transformed my practice in working with fathers and father figures—talking to them about their abuse to their loved ones and the impacts. That's really given confidence across the sector to do that. Safe & Together has brought that to the sector, and it was so important. In some ways Safe & Together has given us hope"

—Emma R., domestic and family violence principal project officer, Australia

All the practitioners talked about being able to influence colleagues inside and outside their agencies by raising awareness about a father's parenting choices, his patterns of coercive and controlling behavior, and mapping that behavior as a source of information. In some instances, the changes were both personal and professional.

CHAPTER 12 : HONORING THE VOICES OF SURVIVORS AND PRACTITIONERS

"I talked to my male colleague—whose primary client was the perpetrating father—about shifting the responsibility and choice for the behavior to making him aware of his parenting choices to abuse the mother. He had a "light bulb moment," and I've since heard from him that he found it such a helpful process in his own development and own work with clients. He's also a father. He said to me he wants to integrate and intersect his experiences in a positive way to support men around their parenting choices, which has been fantastic. In terms of impact, he is bringing some of those conversations around fathering into his practice."

—Emma S., specialist family violence adviser, Australia

Becoming Better at Partnering with Survivors

All the practitioners said the Model transformed their thinking and ability to partner with survivors. This was true regardless of sector and background. In many cases it gave them language to articulate what they already felt and knew. Beth Ann, a very experienced domestic violence advocate, shared the following:

"The first thing that happened was I saw the Domestic Violence-Informed Continuum of Practice, and I looked at it, and I was able to see my community scattered throughout the examples—my county's child protection system. I saw their policies and protocols and ways of working with women and their children. So, I was blown away to actually see this in black and white. And to see labels such as domestic violence destructive and neglectful and then looking at the goal of proficiency. So, I was extremely excited about and interested in that."

—Beth Ann, S&TI faculty, independent consultant, US

"The Multiple Pathways to Harm transformed my practice. When I write a report, I'm clear—I know that I'm talking about harm and stopping that harm. Then I can bring in intersections and have positive discussions with child protective services about intersections and intersectionality. Using Safe & Together is quite liberating because you move away from being negative about women's lives, about children's lives."

—Catriona, independent social worker, Scotland

How Practitioners Used the Model's Tools to Help Improve Practice

When the practitioners spoke about the transformation of their own practice and the practice of those around them, they often referred to specific Safe & Together Model tools and the Multiple Pathways to Harm assessment framework or the Perpetrator Pattern Mapping Tool. Many of their comments reflected how the Model focused on the behavioral basics of practice, including improved documentation and more focused risk assessments. Consistent with the Model—and this book—they also said they were "pivoting to the perpetrator" by talking more to other agencies about perpetrators' harmful behaviors and survivors' protective efforts. This held true across different sectors. Emma, an experienced child protection practitioner spoke about how the Model had become pivotal in her work:

"The Perpetrator Pattern Mapping Tool has changed the way we do our child safety assessments. Now we have such a solid, comprehensive assessment that it also helps the domestic violence sector."

—Emma R., domestic and family violence principal project officer, Australia

Another practitioner spoke of what pivoting to the perpetrator meant in terms of multiagency management of domestic abuse:

> "I was drawn to the Model because of the pivot from victim to perpetrator. It spoke to me because I had just gone through a process with the police in establishing a multiagency tasking and coordination group that, despite initial resistance, meant that we had a perpetrator-focused intervention that made perpetrators visible. Before, it felt like our agency was managing the victim, but nobody was managing the perpetrator."
>
> —Mhairi, violence against women and girls consultant, Scotland

Improving Systems

Throughout the interviews, all the practitioners said the Model helped them improve the way the system responded to adult and child survivors and to perpetrators. While we often think of "improving collaboration" as an easy process, some of the practitioners underscored how the Model helped them become stronger advocates for survivors by becoming better at challenging other systems to do better. More than one victim advocate spoke about how the Model helped them strengthen their ability to advocate for survivors by highlighting their protective capacities:

> "I challenge every single assessment that I come across with the goal to really highlight the need and the importance of identifying protective factors."
>
> —Eloise, independent consultant, child-adult survivor, US

"Oh, it has completely transformed my thinking and my practice. I challenge every assessment that I come across, whether it is with the domestic violence agency, a human trafficking agency, law enforcement, educators. I challenge every single assessment with the goal of highlighting the need and the importance of identifying protective factors."

—Mhairi, violence against women and
girls consultant, Scotland

Another victim advocate spoke of the Model's focus on information gathering and processing—one foundational aspect of the Safe & Together Model's approach. In this quote, Carol talks about how the application of the Perpetrator Pattern Mapping Tool helped challenge perpetrators' ability to control and influence practitioners through manipulation and victim-blaming.

"It's always bothered me how child protection workers get their sources of information—they are not the most accurate. We hear things like 'Dad said she's crazy and she's a drunk and she does this, and she was upset, and he had to hold her around the throat because she was throwing herself all over the place.' The workers treat that as though that's an accurate source of information. And so, the mapping process really focuses on the facts of what happened—who did what to whom."

—Carol, advocate, The Domestic Violence Project, US

Many of the practitioners spoke about how the Model offered a powerful common language and framework that improved the ability to work together across sectors. Karen, an experienced child and family agency practitioner, said this:

One of the learnings for me that came from the Safe & Together framework was the absolute importance of collaboration. What the framework taught me was that to truly bring about change, you must work collaboratively across the sector—you can't work in silos."

—Karen, child and young person practice lead, Australia

A specialist family violence adviser in an Australian alcohol and other drugs agency said the Safe & Together Model had transformed all the agency's multiagency work.

"When we have a case where we have a high-harm, high-risk perpetrator, we bring it to the table to everybody who's speaking the same language. We arrive at the same risk assessment because we're using the mapping, understanding the impacts of the behaviors on the mother and the children. It's so conducive to a better working relationship. It helps build trust between the agencies."

—Emma S., specialist family violence adviser, Australia

Other practitioners highlighted "aha" moments that led to changes in collaborative processes like this one:

"A team leader in social work who chairs the case conferences came to a Safe & Together an overview training we offered over two mornings. After the first morning, she chaired a case conference in the afternoon and looked through the notes of a case where she'd already made a decision. The child was probably going to be put on the child protection register, and the mum was going to be held accountable. She completely overturned her thinking, and in fact, decided instead to hold over the review—

which is unheard of—and insist on her team gathering the information on the perpetrator's pattern of behavior. She hadn't yet done the second half of the overview training."

—Debbie, practice development coordinator, Scotland

The interviews also raised the potential for improved coordination in historically challenging areas. More than one practitioner spoke to how the Model can help improve the fraught relationship between the domestic violence victims advocates and child protection.

"Safe & Together has meant child protection has now got a really good working relationship with domestic violence services. It has helped build trust because they then could see the framework that we were working on. We don't train child protection services unless we're training their partner agencies too."

—Emma S., specialist family violence adviser, Australia

"The Model has the potential to close the gap between family court and child protection—a critical need for survivors who often feel caught between these two very powerful systems. Shared training leads to really detailed discussion with child protection using the same language because we were having the same Safe & Together training."

—Joanna, senior family court child expert, Australia

One of my favorite quotes from a domestic violence victims advocate speaks to the viral nature of the Model and how it can pass from a Safe & Together Model-trained practitioner to survivors, who then are better-equipped to challenge the system to better protect them and their children.

CHAPTER 12 : HONORING THE VOICES OF SURVIVORS AND PRACTITIONERS

> "The true accountability to change I see is when we provide training for survivors. Survivors then begin to hold systems accountable to say, 'Hey, I didn't hear you name my protective factors today in court' or telling their attorney, 'Make sure that we start off with my protective factors today in court.' You start hearing the survivors using that language"
>
> —Eloise, independent consultant, child-adult survivor, US

Personal and Professional Transformation

Over the years, I've learned that the Model doesn't just improve practitioners' skills but that it also has deeply transformational aspects for some. This may be the most important benefit of the Model but perhaps one of the hardest to capture and quantify. Many of the practitioners we interviewed spoke eloquently about how the Model impacted the way they viewed themselves, their work, and the world. Eloise, a US-based domestic violence victim advocate, equated the change brought about by the Model to rewriting one's professional genetics.

> "When you learn about the Safe & Together Model, you can't unlearn it—it becomes part of your professional DNA. The Model will make you think differently about women, children, and the men that use violence. It changes your attitude, and it's not just professionally—it's personally as well. It will impact your life."
>
> —Eloise, independent consultant, child-adult survivor, US

Carol, another US-based victim advocate, spoke to the paradigmatic change of "pivoting to the perpetrator," which often has not been part of the traditional definition of victim advocacy. The Model not only allows her to increase her ability to advocate for perpetrator accountability but also builds better partnerships to support survivor safety.

> "It's transformative in how we're using pivoting to bring dad into the conversation to make him part of the case. We're asking if child protection has mapped his patterns. We're looking at the Multiple Pathways to Harm. We're having conversations with partner agencies that aren't judgmental of workers or clients. We're talking about all the ways that mom has kept the family safe and stable despite having to leave in the night, or moving house, or being without housing for the kids, or changing schools. We're talking about how moms have been able to maintain their grades or play sports or be in an activity or be up-to-date at the doctor's or just get them fed and clothed without resources. We're talking about these strengths and highlighting them."
>
> —Carol, advocate, The Domestic Violence Project, US

Others spoke to how the Model supported their identity as activists and change agents. It was clear that for many practitioners, the Model supported their embodiment of deeply held beliefs about social justice and helped facilitate positive alignment with those values in their professional world.

Voices of Practitioners Who Identified as Survivors

The transformation resulting from involvement with the Model was very personal for the practitioners who also identified as survivors. This group was made up of more than half of the practitioners interviewed, and they were diverse in their experiences of abuse. Some were able to provide insights into how their childhood experiences could have been different if the Safe & Together Model had been around at the time. The adult domestic violence survivors spoke of how their own training and practice in the Model influenced the way they dealt with ongoing relational and legal issues within their personal lives while increasing the amount

CHAPTER 12 : HONORING THE VOICES OF SURVIVORS AND PRACTITIONERS

of empathy they had with their clients. It was wonderful to see in their responses how they had reframed their own experiences of being protective parents—how they did their best for their kids despite what they were hearing from professionals.

One childhood survivor of domestic violence said she believed her life would've been different if professionals who responded to her situation had been trained in the Model.

> "The police came when I was a child and did nothing. There were shelters, but there wasn't any kind of serious capacity for anyone to understand. From my perspective, [the Model] would have created a safer childhood for me, created the capacity for intervention as well—some level of protection. Nobody would have dreamt of talking to me about family violence when I was a child. It just wouldn't have happened. Even though there were quite serious incidents that involved police, I have no recollection of anyone ever finding out what my experience was like, and this would have helped if schools or shelters or police were aware of its impact on me. That would have been amazing."

The practitioners who were adult domestic violence survivors could look back on their lives using the lens provided by the Safe & Together Model and imagine a different outcome for themselves and their children. One practitioner-survivor envisioned a past in which her child might have been safer.

> "Oh my God, it would have made so much difference to have Safe & Together back then. The things that were in my head, his behaviors at the time I couldn't make visible. If workers or police had the Safe & Together language and understanding at the time, it would have made such a huge difference. My child probably would not have had to spend so much time with her father."

Others spoke to real, powerful current changes that resulted from their immersion in the Model. One survivor discussed in detail how the Model helped her set new expectations for her ex-partner as parent.

"A part of my healing has been the pivot in the accountability piece for the person who uses violence. When my former partner was released from prison after many years, he wanted to reestablish a relationship with our two children. I was able to help my children to have that hard conversation with their dad, for him to really own the responsibility, the outcomes, the reality of things that had happened. And I had one conversation with him where I said, 'If you want to do this, you have to own what you did. You have to be able to say, "I did this" without saying, "because she made me," or "because I was under the influence."' Since then, my ex and my children have been reestablishing their relationship. It takes me back to—even if they're an absent father, they're always a father."

More than one practitioner said the Model helped empower her as a woman, mother, and survivor.

"I know from my professional experience that survivors don't really sit and think about how we are protective. Keeping our children safe is automatic, instinctive. Often helping a survivor to understand how protective they are is very difficult because they don't know they've done it. It's been so automatic. Nobody's ever told them or given them credit. It was empowering for me in realizing through my work with Safe & Together that it was not my fault; it was the perpetrator's fault. That is incredibly empowering because living under the guilt of thinking it was my fault, particularly if you're a parent, is dreadful."

In these instances, it helped shake off the weight of internalized mother-blaming.

> "The impact of my transformation has been my healing. This cloak of guilt and shame that I held against myself came off. And I was able to say, 'Hey, I didn't fail my kids.' I did some things that were right in the process and started identifying my own protective factors. I also see a shift in how I do my work. The outcomes for adults and child survivors have, in some cases, determined the difference between life and death."

FINAL THOUGHTS

The results of these interviews moved me profoundly, and I hope they have moved you as well. While the sample is small, the results are mighty. One of the key takeaways from the interviews is how the positive results are reflected from multiple perspectives. Survivors and practitioners are using the same language and seeing the same effects. Practitioners who are also survivors are seeing the value of the Model from both their personal and professional perspectives. The results span vast distances and diverse sectors.

I was especially touched by how the Model empowered survivors. I cried as I read about how survivors, because of the Model, are demanding more attention paid to their protective efforts. This is what keeps me going; this is what motivates me. Supporting survivors in voicing their own protective efforts and giving them better practitioner allies is the system transformation children and families need.

CHAPTER 13

Change Starts Now

This book is a call to action. It is my hope that after reading this book, you are going to use the information included here to do something different. While there is no substitute for the full training and resources offered by the Safe & Together Institute, this book explores the thinking behind the approach. Whether you are a survivor or a practitioner, I hope this book is transformational for you.

The Safe & Together Model offers a predictable and dependable method for changing how systems respond to domestic violence in which children are involved. A Safe & Together Model-trained child protection practitioner recently shared with me how her articulation of worries about a domestic violence perpetrator, using a perpetrator pattern-based approach, had a profound impact on a family court case. Her letter about the perpetrator led the judge to reverse her decision, returning children to the protective parent. The judge even apologized to the mother for the earlier decision to place the children with the perpetrating father. Sharing the story on Twitter, someone referred to it as a "miracle." While the outcome is momentous and sorely deserved for that mother and her children, it is not a miracle in the sense of an unexpected and unexplainable event. It is a predictable result from the application of an approach that has been years in the development. It involves concrete, specific steps that can be replicated over and over again across sectors by practitioners. It is the result of a shared language and framework being used over and over again. It is the transformation that children and families need.

The Safe & Together Model's perpetrator pattern-based approach is changing practice and saving lives. From our military colleagues, I hear stories of service women who are being abused and receiving the support they need and deserve from counselors trained in Safe & Together. The pivot to the perpetrator, who is also often a service person, changes the scenario from one in which the survivor is about to be discharged for poor performance resulting from her subjection to abuse to her being protected, turning around, and achieving promotions because she is now safe and supported. I hear the same story from victim advocates who use the Model to keep their clients safe and mental health practitioners who help keep children safely with protective parents.

These changes are dependable and predictable when practitioners, and the systems they work in, take steps to dismantle mother-blaming and end the systemic ignoring of fathers' behaviors. The Model's behavioral approach works because it moves systems past the myths that have constrained them from being aligned with the reality of survivors. It's a Model that offers a pathway to tackle the underlying gender bias with a transparent behavioral approach that honors the need for objectivity and nonprejudicial practice.

I hope this book inspires you and provides some building blocks for your own powerful work. I wish you the best of luck in your journey and look forward to the legacy of transformation we are all creating together.

What are the steps you can take right now after reading this book?

Here are some specific suggestions for actions.

Action Steps for Professionals

Pivot to the Perpetrator as a parent by

- talking about the fact that domestic violence perpetration is a parenting choice.

Stop using language that is victim-blaming, mutualizing, or ignoring of the perpetrator by

- talking about how the domestic violence perpetrator's *behaviors* harm children instead of how "domestic violence harms children" or instead of talking about how the children "were exposed to the couple's domestic violence."

Make sure you always start your discussion of domestic violence using a comprehensive, behavioral framework by

- describing the perpetrator's pattern of coercive control and actions taken to harm the children.

Focus on Multiple Pathways to Harm, not just "witnessing," by asking

- how the perpetrator's pattern of behavior has harmed child, partner, and family functioning.

Set high expectations for all fathers by assessing their contributions to family functioning using questions probing

- how the father's choices have made the family functioning stronger or weaker.

Set a high bar for perpetrator behavior change by expecting the perpetrator to
- admit to his behavior.
- claim the harm it has caused.
- stop his abusive and controlling behaviors.
- repair the harm caused by his behaviors.

Support diverse interventions with perpetrators as parents by
- assessing for domestic violence perpetration in multiple situations, including mental health, substance misuse, and primary health care settings.
- supporting the creation of diverse vectors of accountability, including public health campaigns or faith-based initiatives.

Don't allow mental health or substance use issues to be used to deflect interventions related to coercive control and violence by
- seeing coercive control, mental health, and addiction as separate issues that need their own assessments.
- not assuming that treating a perpetrator's mental health and/or substance use will automatically stop the abuse.
- mapping the relationship between the perpetrator's abusive behavior and his substance use and mental health issues.

Give mothers credit for the full spectrum of their protective efforts by
- identifying and validating the day-to-day ways the survivor tries to keep the home environment safe, stable, and nurturing in the context of coercive control.

Partner with survivors by
- listening to what they say about what will make their situation better instead of prejudging what is the "right" thing they need to do.

Be curious by
- making the effort to learn what the survivor was doing to protect herself and her children before systems ever got involved.

Commit to antiracist and anticolonization practice by
- remembering that survivors from marginalized groups are likely to be mistrustful of mainstream services.
- honoring survivors' desire to be both safe and connected to culture.
- assessing how certain perpetrators will attempt to manipulate privilege to increase their control over a partner from a minority group.
- integrating into assessments of the perpetrator's harm to children any concerns about other forms of adverse childhood experiences such as violence from the perpetrator undermining the child's ability to deal with societal racism.
- supporting both behavior change and healing trauma histories for perpetrators.

Consider intersections of domestic violence, mental health, and substance misuse by
- talking about a survivor's mental health and/or substance use issues in the context of the perpetrator's pattern.
- not talking about the perpetrator's substance use and/or mental health issues separate from the pattern of coercive control.

Pay attention to postseparation coercive control by
- Asking specific questions about how the perpetrator continued his pattern of control postseparation.

Assess postseparation coercive control by
- not assuming the abuse ends after the relationship ends.
- understanding how perpetrators target and manipulate

practitioners and systems to extend their control postseparation.
- considering how a survivor's experience of family court is being shaped by her fears of being punished by the perpetrator for standing up for what she wants.
- setting high expectations for accountability for perpetrators as part of family court processes.

Challenge your own gender bias by
- validating the extra work involved in mothers' everyday caregiving efforts in the context of domestic violence perpetrators' behaviors.
- approaching the families with which you work with the attitude that fathers' choices and behaviors matter to child and family functioning.

Take care of yourself by
- understanding how perpetrators' harm of children can produce some of the strongest reactions among professionals.
- making sure you are getting the emotional support you need when dealing with perpetrators' behaviors, especially if you have experienced abuse yourself.
- asking for support with regards to emotional and physical safety when working on domestic violence cases.
- owning your reactions to and judgments about survivors.

Action Steps for Survivors

Make the perpetrator as a parent visible by
- telling professionals how the perpetrator's behaviors have changed your, your children's, and your family's day-to-day functioning. Be specific. For instance, you might say, "We were forced by his

behavior to move in order to be safe. As a result, my children lost regular contact with their best friends. They don't ever see them. They tell me regularly how much they miss their friends. The youngest doesn't really understand why they can't go back and visit and gets mad at me when I say, 'You just can't.'"
- keeping records of how the perpetrator is or isn't doing the following:
    - engaging in postseparation coercive control.
    - acknowledging his behavior that harmed you and your children.
    - taking responsibility for the harms that those behaviors have caused.
    - making it safe for your children to talk about their feelings.
    - safely parenting your children.
    - supporting your relationship with your children.

Trumpet your own protective efforts by

- clearly explaining to professionals about all the actions you are taking to keep your kids on track and how you compensate for the perpetrator's behaviors.
- sharing what you are doing to keep your children physically and emotionally safe. Talk about how you nurture them, keep the home structured and stable, and help them heal from trauma.

Help professionals understand the relationship between any of your own mental health or substance use issues and the perpetrator's behavior by

- talking about how the perpetrator's behavior caused or exacerbated your substance use or mental health issues.
- citing examples of threats to use your mental health and/or substance use issues to take away your children.
- citing examples of the perpetrator interfering with your access to services and/or sabotaging your recovery.

Action Steps for Perpetrators

Take responsibility for your behavior by

- admitting your abusive actions and how they were wrong.
- acknowledging the harm those actions have caused others.
- stopping those behaviors.
- seeking out help from professionals trained in working with men who use violence and coercive control.
- supporting your children's relationship with the other parent.
- becoming a more emotionally supportive and engaged parent (where safe and desired by your children and the other parent).
- engaging in behaviors that help repair the damage you've caused, supporting the rights of others to safety and autonomy, and providing a healthy, stable, nurturing environment for your children.

ACKNOWLEDGMENTS

As often is true in my life, when in doubt, I default to more words, not less. This acknowledgment is not any different. It feels important to speak to both the immediate supporters who helped produce this book and also speak to the longer arc of my career.

Many people helped make this book possible. First, I want to acknowledge the across-the-board, every day, in every way support of my partner, Ruth Reymundo Mandel. She has always believed in my work and has supported this book on every possible level—from taking our son to school in the morning so I could write, to reading drafts and offering feedback, to helping develop the marketing plan in her role as communications manager at the Institute. Our life together nourishes me on so many levels.

I want to thank Deb Nicholson for her stalwart and talented assistance every step along the way. She kept me on track with timelines, provided excellent editing, and conducted the interviews with the survivors and practitioners cited in this book. Deb was my ally, my cheerleader, confidante, creative consultant, editor, and project manager. Thank you to Awele Emili for taking my scripts and turning them into fabulous graphic images that bring alive scenarios, making them more accessible for the reader. I want to acknowledge Amanda Miller and the great team at My Word Publishing for guiding us through the publishing process. Amanda gathered together a wonderful group of book professionals—Laura Kaiser, our thoughtful editor; Asya Blue, our fabulous designer; and Tom Locke, our meticulous proofreader. A special thanks to Polly Letofsky, My Word

Publishing owner, for her generous guidance around marketing and communications.

I also want to acknowledge my team at the Safe & Together Institute, who support and carry out our mission every day. Their passion and commitment make the Institute's impact possible and have supported me in the publishing of this book.

I would very much like to acknowledge the practitioners and survivors (and those who identified as both and shared their stories), who contributed to this book in such a profound way.

List of contributor voices

1. "Jane"—victim survivor, Australia
2. Naomi Fleming—victim survivor, Scotland
3. Beth Ann Morhardt—Safe &Together Institute faculty and founder of Beth Ann Morhardt Collaborations, US
4. Carol Fallon—advocate, The Domestic Violence Project, US
5. Catriona Grant—independent social worker, Scotland
6. Debbie Willett—practice development coordinator, East Ayrshire Council, Scotland
7. Eloise Sepeda—national independent consultant, Harmony One Restorative Justice, child-adult survivor, US
8. Emma Rogers—domestic & family violence principal project officer, Australia
9. Emma Shaw—specialist family violence adviser, Odyssey House Victoria, Australia
10. Joanna—senior court child expert, Court Children's Service, Federal Circuit and Family Court of Australia
11. Karen Piscopo—practice lead, Victoria, Australia
12. Melody—court child expert, Court Children's Service, Federal Circuit and Family Court of Australia
13. Mhairi McGowan—violence against women and girls consultant, Scotland

ACKNOWLEDGMENTS

Now to that larger arc. As a man working against male violence against women, I try to move thoughtfully, constantly working to understand and unlearn my own sexism. My early personal journey was jump-started by listening to and learning from the experiences of women, reading feminist theory, and reflecting on masculinity. Over thirty-five years, my commitment to ending male violence against women has never wavered. This longevity sometimes startles even me. Along the way, different relationships and experiences impacted the development of the Model, its implementation in the world, and what you've read in these pages.

I'm uplifted by remembering all the people whose own individual choices made a difference in my journey. While it is impossible to name every single person who supported me in my journey, it feels important to name a few whose contributions stand on their own and also represent the support of those not explicitly named here. I think about Patricia Weel, a child protection planner in Connecticut, who, in 1996 fought against institutional resistance to hire me to train my first-ever group of child protection workers about perpetrator engagement. I think about Laureen Sheehan, a long-time domestic violence victim advocate, who overcame her skepticism about working with perpetrators to fund some of my earliest work to change child protection systems. I think of Neil Blacklock, a UK leader in addressing domestic violence, whom I met at a batterer-intervention conference in the US. Blacklock then recommended my work to Rodney Vlais, an Australian expert in perpetrator interventions. And I remember how, after a year of trying and almost giving up, Rodney finally found a partner, Dr. Heather Nancarrow, to cosponsor my first trip to Australia in 2014. It was Rodney who then set up a thirty-minute meeting in a hotel lobby with Professor Cathy Humphreys, one of my heroes and a leader in the research on domestic violence and child protection. Cathy and I have now been collaborating for years. Each of these people shared a belief in change, saw value in the work I was doing, and helped advance my mission. They each provided a piece in the support of the Model and its global impact. The journey has not been made alone.

GLOSSARY

accountability—A term of art in the domestic violence sector that has historically applied to carceral approaches to interventions with perpetrators. In this book, I explore different "vectors of accountability" in an attempt to widen the approach to perpetrators. You will also see the term "microaccountability," which refers to how micro practices of language, documentation, and interviewing support accountability for perpetrators.

child protection—The government agencies entrusted with statutory responsibility for the safety and well-being of children. Their primary tasks are investigating or assessing reports of alleged child maltreatment, developing plans with families to safeguard children in their own homes, or placing children in foster care or adoptive homes.

child protection practitioner—A social worker, welfare officer, or other professional working in child protection.

coercive control—A term made popular by Evan Stark's book *Coercive Control: How Men Entrap Women in Personal Life*. He defines coercive control as "a pattern of behavior which seeks to take away the victim's liberty or freedom, to strip away their sense of self. It is not just women's bodily integrity which is violated but also their human rights."

criminal court—The court structures concerned with hearing criminal matters in the various jurisdictions discussed in this book.

domestic violence—There is no universal term for the issue of abuse of a partner or ex-partner. Across the globe, different terms are used. "Intimate partner violence," "family violence," "domestic abuse," "battering," and "domestic and family violence" are just a few of the terms that refer to a pattern of behavior that encompasses both physical and nonphysical forms of control and abuse in intimate relationships. The phrase "domestic violence" is the one embedded in the Safe & Together Model and used in this book. It is used interchangeably, at times, with the terms "coercive control," "domestic abuse," and "domestic and family violence." For the purpose of this book, all the terms encompass the range of physical and nonphysical perpetrator behavior or patterns of behavior—including financial, psychological, spiritual, reproductive, and other forms of abuse. In practice, globally, the Institute uses local terms when working in specific jurisdictions. For example, "domestic abuse" is commonly used in the UK and "domestic and family violence" is used in Australia. Some of these terms are used throughout the book in testimony from practitioners and survivors from the countries where the Safe & Together Model is applied.

domestic violence advocate—A professional working in domestic violence victim survivor services.

domestic violence-informed continuum of practice—A term of art developed by the author for categorizing practitioner and system responses to domestic violence cases involving children. Modeled after Continuum of Cultural Competence developed by Dr. Terry Cross[1], and later continuums around trauma-informed practice, the domestic violence-informed continuum of practice identifies five stages of professional and systems development. Each stage is associated with different types of practice, some more positive than others, based on its alignment with a perpetrator pattern-based approach and outcomes for families. From negative to positive: domestic violence destructive, domestic violence neglectful, domestic violence precompetent, domestic violence competent, and domestic violence proficient.

domestic violence perpetration as parenting choice—A term of art associated with the Safe & Together Model. It is a catchphrase that encapsulates the

---

[1] Terry L. Cross *et al,* "Towards a Culturally Competent System of Care: A Monograph on Effective Services for Minority Children Who Are Severely Emotionally Disturbed," *Georgetown University Child Development Center,* (1990) https://eric.ed.gov/?id=ED330171 Accessed 28 February 2023.

connection between intimate partner violence, child maltreatment, and perpetrators' responsibilities as parents. It is also a term that helps hold fathers who are violent to their family to higher standards as parents. You may also encounter this variation: *Domestic violence perpetration is a parenting choice.*

family court—The court structures concerned with hearing child custody, parenting time, and property matters related to the dissolution of marriages and other relationships.

father—Any male-identified person who is in a fathering role whether he is the biological father, stepfather, or adoptive father. This label can also refer to other male biological or social relatives such as uncles or grandfathers who are in a caregiving role. For the purposes of raising expectations on men as parents, this label is inclusive of boyfriends or partners who may have no formal legal or biological relationship to a child but are a force and factor in a child's development and daily life. This applies whether the father is custodial or noncustodial.

First Nations—The original inhabitants of different countries where Safe & Together operates—Canada, the United States, New Zealand, and Australia. While no one term is accepted everywhere, "First Nation" is a commonly used term for the diverse groups and peoples who have been or are still subjected to genocide, land appropriation, and cultural destruction at the hands of settler groups. It includes but is not limited to Native Americans in the United States, the Maori in New Zealand, Aboriginal and Torres Strait Islander peoples in Australia, and First Nations peoples of Canada.

historically marginalized groups—Populations that have been subjected to systemic discrimination, exclusion, or oppression on the basis of their social identities such as race, ethnicity, religion, gender, sexual orientation, or disability. (See also the "intersectionality" entry.)

intersectionalities—Plural of the term coined by African American scholar Kimberlé Crenshaw and refers to the interconnected nature of social categorizations that may lead to discrimination or oppression such as race, class, gender, disability, or identity (among other "categories") as they apply to an individual or group. For example, an affluent African American heterosexual man or a poor white gay woman may experience different privilege and vulnerability based on their race, class, gender, and/or sexual orientation. In the Safe & Together Model, it is often paired with the term "intersections" as both concepts are part of the fifth Critical Component. While they reference different dynamics, they are similar in that neither intersections or intersectionalities are causal—none of the associated factors cause domestic violence perpetration.

intersections—The interplay between domestic violence and other issues such as the role of substance misuse, mental health, culture and/or other socioeconomic factors. This term replaces the outdated and inadequate term "co-occurrence."

men's behavior change program—Therapeutic and/or educational programs for perpetrators of domestic violence. The primary goal of such a program is the cessation of abusive behaviors. Such a program is known by different names around the world, such as "perpetrator intervention program" or "batterer intervention program." These programs usually differ from anger management programs in their prioritization of the safety and well-being of the victim; their length (twenty-six or fifty-two weeks is common); and their focus on wider patterns of abuse and control.

Multiple Pathways to Harm (MPH)—A term of art within the Safe & Together Model. It refers to an assessment framework for harm to child, partner, and family functioning that is much more comprehensive than the child witness framework.

nonoffending parent—Term in the Safe & Together Model that refers to the parent in child protection cases who has *not* been alleged to have maltreated her child. In the context of domestic violence cases, it refers to the survivor. The term is used interchangeably here with the term "protective parent" and "survivor."

partnering—Term of art associated with the Safe & Together Model. It refers to a type of domestic violence-informed practice with survivors. It is one of the Model's Principles and involves six specific steps: affirming, asking, assessing, validating, collaboratively planning and documenting. It is strongly correlated with a perpetrator pattern-based approach.

perpetrator/person using violence—The Safe & Together Model uses the term "perpetrator" to describe a person of any background, sex, sexual orientation, or gender who engages in patterns of coercive control and actions taken to harm children. It is similar to other terms, such as "batterer," "person who uses violence," or any other language that refers to a person who engages in coercive control and actions taken to harm children. I originally selected the term "perpetrator" for the Model because I eschewed terms such as "offender," which have strong associations with criminal justice systems. I wanted a term I considered more neutral, descriptive, broad, and useful across different systems, like child protection. In recent years, terms such as "person using violence" or "person causing harm" have been advanced as preferable over terms like "perpetrator." The explanation is that "person using violence" separates the person from the behavior, which underlines the potential to change and moves away from reductionistic, one-dimensional characterizations of domestic violence perpetrators. This is particularly useful as a way to combat stereotyping and vilifying perpetrators who belong to historically marginalized groups. When I present in person, I use these terms interchangeably. For the sake of brevity and consistency with the Model, the book uses the term "perpetrator."

Perpetrator Pattern-Based Approach—Term of art associated with the Safe & Together Model. It is used as a high-level descriptor for the Model. For example, "The Safe & Together Model uses a perpetrator pattern-based approach." It also refers to a specific assessment process that starts with a description of the perpetrators' behaviors. It is central to the Safe & Together Model tools and training.

pivot to the perpetrator—Term of art associated with the Safe & Together Model. It describes how practitioners and systems need to shift their attention away from blaming survivors for the harm to children caused by domestic violence and toward holding perpetrators accountable for the harm their behavior causes children. It is also a reflection of this book's title and major theme since often this shift is associated with a cessation of mother-blaming and a greater focus on the impact of fathers' behaviors on the functioning of their children, their partner, and the family.

police officer-involved domestic violence (OIDV)—Situations in which police officers perpetrate domestic violence against a partner or family member. It is also referred to as "police perpetrated domestic violence."

practice-generated resistance—Survivors' understandable resistance to professionals when they are approached with mother-blaming or other practices associated with the negative end of the domestic violence-informed continuum of practice.

primary caregiver—The adult primarily responsible for the day-to-day care and welfare of a child or children.

refuge—Emergency safe houses for domestic violence survivors and their children. They are also known as shelters.

reparations—The responsibility that perpetrators have to repair the harm caused to their children, partner, and family by their behavior. It's not enough to stop coercive control, especially for a perpetrator who is a parent. The definition of meaningful change needs to include the expectation that perpetrators will support their children's healing.

Safe & Together Model—The suites of tools and concepts designed to promote a "pivot to the perpetrator" in domestic violence cases involving children. The name of the Model refers to the concept that children are best served when they can be kept "safe and together" with the nonoffending parent, usually their mother.

Safe & Together Critical Components—Categories of information that are required to make good decisions related to domestic violence and children. They form one of the key pillars of the Safe & Together Model.

Safe & Together Model Principles—Practice principles that guide domestic violence-informed practice.

survivor—For the purposes of this book, the term "survivor" is used to denote adults or children who have experienced or are *currently* experiencing domestic violence. For clarity, there is no differentiation between past and current victimization. It is considered more strengths-based than the term "victim." Hence, it is used as part of the Safe & Together Model. Many people use the term interchangeably with the term "victim." You may also see the combined terms "victim survivor."

term of art—Terms that have a very specific meaning associated with a discipline or an approach such as the Safe & Together Model.

ABOUT THE AUTHOR

David Mandel is the founder and executive director of the Safe & Together Institute and creator of the Safe & Together Model. In a career spanning almost four decades and three continents, David has counseled men who have been violent to their partners and children; consulted at the highest level on issues involving child protection, family court, and related matters; contributed to numerous research studies; and addressed domestic violence as an invited speaker and trainer across the globe. Through the Safe & Together Institute's growing network of hundreds of trainers, David's Safe & Together Model has improved the practice of thousands of professionals and impacted tens of thousands of children and families. David lives in rural Connecticut with his partner and collaborator, Ruth Reymundo Mandel, their three children, and an assortment of much-loved pets. When not changing systems, David is a keen traveler and home chef.

THE SAFE & TOGETHER INSTITUTE'S OFFERINGS

David's Safe & Together Institute is a global organization dedicated to domestic violence-informed systems change. The Institute offers individual practitioners, governments, non-governmental organizations and private sector companies online learning, practice tools, data services and consultation, in-person and remote training, and more. The Institute's work is utilized by diverse sectors including child protection, substance use, mental health, family court, the military, and beyond.

To learn more about the Institute's offerings, go to **safeandtogetherinstitute.com**. To access the Institute's online learning portal, go to **academy.safeandtogetherinstitute.com**. To learn how to become a Safe & Together Institute Partner Agency or a certified trainer, visit **safeandtogetherinstitute.com/what-we-offer/trainer-certification-program/**

To book David to speak either in person or online, visit **safeandtogetherinstitute.com/home/keynote-speaking/**

ABOUT THE ARTIST

The cartoon graphics in this book were designed by Awele Emili, who is from Lagos, Nigeria. She is an award-winning illustrator and animator. She illustrates books and content for brands and organizations such as Facebook and the World Bank. She is the author of the book *Growing up African*. You can find her work at **aweleemili.com**. Or purchase her book at **aweleemili.com/project/growing-up-african**.

ENDNOTES

Introduction:

1   U.S. Department of Justice: Office of Justice Programs, *Extent, Nature and Consequences of Intimate Partner Violence: Findings from the National Violence Against Women Survey*, Research Report, USDJ, July 2000.

2   Stark, Evan, *Coercive Control: The Entrapment of Women in Personal Life*, (Oxford University Press, 2009)

Chapter 1:

1   Thiara, Ravi and Humphreys, Cathy. "Absent presence: The ongoing impact of men's violence on the mother-child relationship." *Child & Family Social Work*. Volume 2, Issue 1 (January 2015): 137-145, https://doi.org/10.1111/cfs.12210

2   Humphreys, Cathy, *et al* "More present than absent: Men who use domestic violence and their fathering" *Child & Family Social Work*. Volume 24, Issue 2 (November 2018): 321-389, https://doi.org/10.1111/cfs.12617

3   Ernest N Jouriles, *et al*. "Child abuse in the context of domestic violence: Prevalence, explanations, and practice implications." *Violence and Victims*, 15(2), (2000): 137-160. https://doi.org/10.1891/0886-6708.23.2.221

4   Anne E Appel, & George W Holden. "The co-occurrence of spouse and physical child abuse: A review and appraisal," *Journal of Family Psychology*, 12(4), (1998): 578-599. https://psycnet.apa.org/doi/10.1037/0893-3200.12.4.578

5   NSW Family & Community Services, *Child Deaths 2012 Annual Report: Learning to improve services*, Government of New South Wales, Sydney, 2012.

6   University of East Anglia, United Kingdom Department for Children, Schools, and Families, *Analysing child deaths and serious injury through abuse and neglect: what can we learn? A biennial analysis of serious case reviews 2003-2005* Marian Brandon *et al*, University of East Anglia, Research Report Number: DCSF-RR023, 2008

Chapter 2:

1   The Consultation Center, The Department of Psychiatry of Yale School of Medicine, *et al Assessment of DCF/DV Protocol Project*, Report by Bridgeport Safe Start Initiative, 2005.

2   Bloom Paul. 2016. *Against Empathy: The Case for Rational Compassion* First ed. (New York NY: Ecco, an imprint of HarperCollins)

3   Marianne Hester, "The three planet model: Towards an understanding of contradiction in approaches to women and children's safety in the context of domestic violence," *British Journal of Social Work*, (July 2011): 41, 837–853, https://doi.org/10.1093/bjsw/bcr095

4   Radford, Lorraine and Hester, Marianne. 2006: *Mothering Through Domestic Violence*, (Jessica Kingsley Publishers, London)

Chapter 3:

1. GBD 2019 Police Violence US Subnational Collaborators, "Fatal police violence by race and state in the US, 1980–2019: a network meta-regression", *The Lancet*, Volume 398, Issue 10307, (October 02, 2021): 1239-1255, https://doi.org/10.1016/S0140-6736(21)01609-3

2. Australian Law Reform Commission, "Pathways to Justice—Inquiry into the Incarceration Rate of Aboriginal and Torres Strait Islander Peoples," Final Report No 133 (2017): 93, https://www.alrc.gov.au/publication/pathways-to-justice-inquiry-into-the-incarceration-rate-of-aboriginal-and-torres-strait-islander-peoples-alrc-report-133/

3. Jean-Denis David and Megan Mitchell, "Contacts with the Police and the Over-Representation of Indigenous Peoples in The Canadian Criminal Justice System," *Canadian Journal of Criminology and Criminal Justice*, Volume 63 Issue 2 (April 2021): 23-45

Chapter 4:

1. "Domestic Abuse Act 2021" United Kingdom Government, accessed December 10, 2022, https://www.legislation.gov.uk/ukpga/2021/17/contents

2. "Domestic Abuse (Scotland) Act 2018" United Kingdom Government, accessed December 10, 2022, https://www.legislation.gov.uk/asp/2018/5/section/5

3. "Family Violence Protection Act 2008" Government of Victoria, Australia, accessed December 10, 2022, https://content.legislation.vic.gov.au/sites/default/files/2022-06/08-52aa060%20authorised.pdf

4. The United Nations Children's Fund (UNICEF), *The State of the World's Children 2006: Excluded and Invisible*, New York, UNICEF, 2005.

5. "What is child trauma?", National Child Traumatic Stress Network, accessed 10 December 2022, https://www.nctsn.org/

6. "Adverse Childhood Experiences (ACEs)", Centers for Disease Control and Prevention, accessed 10 December 2022 https://www.cdc.gov/violenceprevention/aces/index.html

7. "Enhancing Law Enforcement Response to Children Exposed to Violence and Childhood Trauma," International Association of Chiefs of Police, accessed 10 December 2022 https://www.theiacp.org/projects/enhancing-law-enforcement-response-to-children-exposed-to-violence-and-childhood-trauma

8. Jeffrey L Edleson, "Children's Witnessing of Adult Domestic Violence", Journal of Interpersonal Violence, Vol. 14 No. 8 (August 1999): 839-870 https://doi.org/10.1177/088626099014008004

9. "Publications," Centre for Response-Based Practice, accessed 10 December 2022, https://www.responsebasedpractice.com/

10. Katz, E, *et al*, "When Coercive Control Continues to Harm Children: Post-Separation Fathering, Stalking and Domestic Violence", Child Abuse Review, Vo 29, Issue 4, (July/August 2020): 310-324, https://doi.org/10.1002/car.2611

11. Queensland Government, *A Child's Disability: Risk and Vulnerability Factors*, Child Safety Practice Manual, September 2022, https://cspm.csyw.qld.gov.au/practice-kits/disability/risk-assessment/a-child-s-disability-risk-and-vulnerability-factor Accessed 22 February 2023.

12 David Mandel, "The value of Multi-Disciplinary Teams reviewing serious domestic violence cases. One Connecticut team's experience," (Report, April 2011)

13 Humphreys, C, *et al*, "Children Living with Domestic Violence: A Differential Response through Multi-agency Collaboration," Australian Social Work, Vol 71, Issue 2 (2018), 162-174, https://doi.org/10.1080/0312407X.2017.1415366

Chapter 5:

1 Stark, Evan, *Coercive Control: The Entrapment of Women in Personal Life*, (Oxford University Press, 2009)

2 Katz, Emma, *Coercive Control in Children's and Mothers' Lives*, (Oxford University Press, 2022)

3 Walker, Lenore, E, *The Battered Woman*, (William Morrow & Company, 1980)

4 Janet K Wilson, "Cycle of Violence" The Encyclopedia of Women & Crime, (August 2019): 1-5 https://doi.org/10.1002/9781118929803.ewac0083

5 Bonomi, A., Martin, D. "Jail Calls: What Do Kids Have to Do with It?" *J Fam Viol* (33, 2018): 99–102, https://doi.org/10.1007/s10896-017-9919-2

6 Edward Gondolf, "Cautions About Applying Neuroscience to Batterer Intervention," *Court Review*, Volume 43, Issue 4 (2007): 178-181 https://www.biscmi.org/wp-content/uploads/2015/05/Neuroscience-and-Batterers-EF-Court-Review.pdf

7 "What are Disruptive Impulse Control and Conduct Disorders?" American Psychiatric Association, Diagnostic and statistical manual of mental disorders (5th ed.) accessed 23 February 2023. https://www.psychiatry.org/patients-families/disruptive-impulse-control-and-conduct-disorders/what-are-disruptive-impulse-control-and-conduct

8 "The Web-based Perpetrator Pattern Mapping Tool" Safe & Together Institute, accessed 23 February, 2023, https://safeandtogetherinstitute.com/tools-for-systems-change/practice-toolkits/mapping-tool/

9 "How to be an Ally to a Loved One Experiencing Domestic Violence," Safe & Together Institute, accessed 23 February, 2023, https://safeandtogetherinstitute.com/how-to-be-an-ally-to-a-loved-one-experiencing-domestic-violence/

10 "Organizational and Systems Assessment," Safe & Together Institute, accessed 23 February, 2023, https://safeandtogetherinstitute.com/tools-for-systems-change/organizational-systems-assessment/

11 Stark, *Coercive Control: The Entrapment of Women in Personal Life*.

Chapter 6:

1 Elaine Arnull and Stacey Stewart, "Developing a theoretical framework to discuss mothers experiencing domestic violence and being subject to interventions: A cross-national perspective," *International Journal for Crime, Justice and Social Democracy* 10(2): (2021) 113-126. https://doi.org/10.5204/ijcjsd.1561

2 Colleen Henry *et al*, "Substantiated allegation of failure to protect in the child welfare system: Against whom, in what context, and with what justification?" Children and Youth Services Review, 116, (2020): 1-9

3   Christina Risley-Curtiss and Kristin Heffernan, "Gender Biases in Child Welfare," AFFILIA, Vol. 18 Issue 4, (2003): 395-410. https://doi.org/10.1177/0886109903257629

4   Alex Campbell, "Enabling Child Abuse" And Why Oklahoma Imprisons So Many Women, *Buzzfeed News*, December 16, 2014, https://www.buzzfeednews.com/article/alexcampbell/enabling-child-abuse-and-why-oklahoma-imprisons-so-many-wome

5   Humphreys, C. and Absler, D., *History repeating: child protection responses to domestic violence,* Child & Family Social Work (Vol 16, Issue 4, 2018): 464-473, https://doi.org/10.1111/j.1365-2206.2011.00761.x

6   Mona Eltahawy, *The Seven Necessary Sins for Women and Girls,* (Beacon Press, 2017)

7   Children's Commissioner for England, "PreBudget Briefing 2018" accessed 20 February 2023, https://www.childrenscommissioner.gov.uk/report/pre-budget-briefing-autumn-2018/

8   The National Child Traumatic Stress Network, *Facts for Policy Makers. Complex Trauma and Mental Health of Children Placed in Foster Care,* NCTSN, December 2011, https://learn.nctsn.org/ Accessed 22 February 2023.

9   "Ohio Needs Assessment for Child Welfare Services," Ohio Department of Jobs and Family Services, accessed 22 February 2023 https://jfs.ohio.gov/PFOF/PDF/NeedsAssessment.stm

10 Black, T., *et al. Intimate Partner Violence Investigations in Ontario in 2018.* (CWRP Information Sheet #200E Toronto, ON: Canadian Child Welfare Research Portal): 1-7, https://cwrp.ca/publications/intimate-partner-violence-investigations-ontario-2018

11 Congressional Research Service, *Child Welfare: Purposes, Federal Programs, and Funding,* Emilie Stoltzfus, IF10590, January 2023, https://sgp.fas.org/crs/misc/IF10590.pdf Accessed 23 February 2023.

12 Australian Institute of Health and Welfare, *Australia's welfare 2017. 2.5 A stable and secure home for children in out-of-home care,* No 13 AUS 214, Canberra, 2017. https://www.aihw.gov.au/getmedia/e84b6721-7ea0-4688-8eac-59353cfb4452/aihw-australias-welfare-2017-chapter2-5.pdf.aspx Accessed 22 February 2023.

13 Nico Trocmé and Nicholas Bala, "False allegations of abuse and neglect when parents separate," *Child Abuse & Neglect*, Volume 29, Issue 12, (December 2005): 1333-1345 https://doi.org/10.1016/j.chiabu.2004.06.016

14 *ibid.*

15 Katie Lamb, et al. "Your behaviour has consequences: Children and young people's perspectives on reparation with their fathers after domestic violence," *Children and Youth Services Review*, (Vol 88, 2018): 164-169, https://doi.org/10.1016/j.childyouth.2018.03.013

Chapter 7:

1   Donna Chung, *et al,* "Improved accountability: The role of perpetrator intervention systems," *ANROWS* Research report, Issue 20/2020. https://anrowsdev.wpenginepowered.com/wp-content/uploads/2020/06/Chung-RR-Improved-Accountability.pdf

2   U.S. Department of Justice, *Intimate Partner Violence, 1993-210,* Shannon Catalano, Special Report, Office of Justice Programs, Bureau of Justice Statistics, revised September 2015, https://bjs.ojp.gov/content/pub/pdf/ipv9310.pdf Accessed 22 February 2023.

ENDNOTES

3   Lawrence Sherman, "Increased homicide victimization of suspects arrested for domestic assault: A 23 year follow-up of the Milwaukee Domestic Violence Experiment (MilDVE)," *Journal of Experimental Criminology* 9(4), (December 2013): http://dx.doi.org/10.1007/s11292-013-9193-0

4   Kathleen Oriel, *et al*, "Screening Men for Partner Violence in a Primary Care Setting: A New Strategy for Detecting Domestic Violence," *The Journal of Family Practice*, Vol 46, No. 6 (June 1998): 493-498, https://pubmed.ncbi.nlm.nih.gov/9638114/

5   State of Victoria (Australia), "The Victorian Expert Advisory Committee on Perpetrator Interventions," *Final Report*, (2018), Retrieved from *Analysis & Policy Observatory* website, accessed 30 January 2023 https://apo.org.au/node/268781

6   Leigh Goodmark, *Law Enforcement Experience Report. Domestic violence survivors' survey regarding interaction with law enforcement,* National Domestic Violence Hotline, accessed February 2023, https://www.thehotline.org/wp-content/uploads/media/2022/09/2209-Hotline-LES_FINAL.pdf

7   Johnson, L. B. "On the front lines: Police stress and family well-being." *Hearing Before the Select Committee on Children, Youth, and Families House of Representatives*: 102 Congress First Session May 20, U.S. Government Printing Office, Washington, DC, (1991): 32–48.

8   Neidig, Peter H., Harold E. Russell, and Albert F. Seng. "Interspousal aggression in law enforcement families: A preliminary investigation." *Police Stud.: Int'l Rev. Police Dev.* 15 (1992): 30.

9   Ryan, Andrew H. "The Prevalence of Domestic Violence in Police Families." in Sheehan, ed., Domestic Violence by Law Enforcement Officers (2000): 297-308

10   Heather Dorries & Laura Harjo, "Beyond Safety: Refusing Colonial Violence Through Indigenous Feminist Planning," *Journal of Planning Education and Research*, Vol. 40(2) (2020), 210-219. https://doi.org/10.1177/0739456X19894382

11   David Mandel, "A National Study of Batterers' Perceptions of Their Children's Exposure to their Violence and Abuse," MA diss. Goddard College, Vermont, 2003.

12   Lisa Jane Wood, et al, "Freedom from Fear Domestic Violence Campaign Review," *Department for Community Development, Western Australia* (November 2006)

13   The Consultation Center, The Department of Psychiatry of Yale School of Medicine, *et al Assessment of DCF/DV Protocol Project*, Report by Bridgeport Safe Start Initiative, 2005

14   Liz Kelly and Nicole Westmarland, "Domestic Violence Perpetrator Programmes: Steps Towards Change. Project Mirabel Final Report," *London and Durham, London Metropolitan University and Durham University* (2015) https://www.dur.ac.uk/criva/projectmirabal

15   Katie Lamb, et al. "Your behaviour has consequences: Children and young people's perspectives on reparation with their fathers after domestic violence," *Children and Youth Services Review*, (Vol 88, 2018): 164-169, https://doi.org/10.1016/j.childyouth.2018.03.013

Chapter 8:

1   Meier, Joan S., "Denial of Family Violence in Court: An Empirical Analysis and Path Forward for Family Law." *GW Law Faculty Publications & Other Works*. (2021) 1536. https://scholarship.law.gwu.edu/faculty_publications/1536

2   Richard Garnder, "Parental Alienation Syndrome" (article based on keynote address presented to International Conference on Parental Alienation Syndrome (PAS) held in Frankfurt/Main, Germany, 2002) http://richardagardner.com/ar22

3   Janet R. Johnston and Joan B. Kelly, "Rejoinder to Gardner's 'Commentary on Kelly and Johnston's 'The Alienated Child: A Reformulation of Parental Alienation Syndrome'", *Family Court Review*, Volume 42, Issue 4, (October 2004): 622-628, https://doi.org/10.1111/j.174-1617.2004.tb01328.x

4   Jennifer J. Harman, *et al*, "Parental Alienating behaviors: An Unacknowledged Form of Family Violence," *Psychological Bulletin*, Vol. 144, No. 12, (2018): 1275–1299, http://dx.doi.org/10.1037/bul0000175

5   Meier, Joan, "U.S. child custody outcomes in cases involving parental alienation and abuse allegations: what do the data show?". *Journal of Social Welfare and Family Law*. 42(3). (January 2020): 1-14. https://doi.org/10.1080/09649069.2020.1701941

6   "Friends of the Court Handbook" Oakland County, Michigan, accessed 30 January 2023, https://www.oakgov.com/courts/foc/Documents/forms1/FOC%20Handbook.pdf

7   The Leadership Council on Child Abuse and Interpersonal Violence, *Overview of Dr Richard Gardner's Opinions on Pedophilia and Child Sexual Abuse*, 2005 http://www.leadershipcouncil.org/1/pas/RAG.html

8   Kelly Musick and Ann Meier, "Are both parents always better than one? Parental conflict and young adult well-being," *Social Science Research*, Volume 39, Issue 5 (September 2010) 2010): 814-30. https://doi.org/10.1016/j.ssresearch.2010.03.002

9   "Perpetrator Intervention Program Completion Certificates are Dangerous," David Mandel, Safe & Together Institute, accessed 24 February, 2023, https://safeandtogetherinstitute.com/wp-content/uploads/2020/03/CertsAreDangerous_paper2142020_web.pdf

Chapter 9:

1   Haroon Chowdry, "Estimating the prevalence of the 'toxic trio' : Evidence from the Adult Psychiatric Morbidity Survey," Vulnerability Technical Report 2, Children's Commissioner, UK (July 2018), https://www.drugsandalcohol.ie/30255/1/Vulnerability-Technical-Report-2-Estimating-the-prevalence-of-the-toxic-trio.pdf

2   Children's Commissioner for England, "PreBudget Briefing 2018" accessed 20 February 2023, https://www.childrenscommissioner.gov.uk/report/pre-budget-briefing-autumn-2018/

3   "Ohio Needs Assessment for Child Welfare Services," Ohio Department of Jobs and Family Services, accessed 22 February 2023 https://jfs.ohio.gov/PFOF/PDF/NeedsAssessment.stm

4   "Stress and Trauma," Australian Institute of Health and Welfare, accessed 30 January 2023, https://www.aihw.gov.au/reports/mental-health-services/stress-and-trauma

5   "Trauma," UK Trauma Council, accessed 30 January 2023, https://uktraumacouncil.org/trauma/trauma

6   "Effects" The National Child Traumatic Stress Network, accessed 30 January 2023. https://www.nctsn.org/what-is-child-trauma/trauma-types/refugee-trauma/effects

7   Vincent. J. Felitti, *et al* "Relationship of childhood abuse and household dysfunction to many of the leading causes of death in adults: The Adverse Childhood Experiences (ACE)

study," *American Journal of Preventive Medicine*, Vol. 14 Issue 4, (May 1998): 245-258 https://doi.org/10.1016/S0749-3797(98)00017-8

Chapter 10:

1. Radford, Lorraine and Hester, Marianne. 2006: *Mothering Through Domestic Violence*, (Jessica Kingsley Publishers, London)

2. "Understanding the Power and Control Wheel," Domestic Abuse Intervention Programs: Home of the Duluth Model, accessed 30 January 2023, https://www.theduluthModel.org/wheels/faqs-about-the-wheels/

3. "'It has empowered me': Domestic violence survivors' reflections on applying the Safe & Together Model in their role as Parent Partners", Safe & Together Model Systems Assessment, Safe & Together Institute, accessed 22 February 2023, https://safeandtogetherinstitute.com/wp-content/uploads/2018/11/Iowa-ST-PP-Assessment3.pdf

4. Hunter, E. C., & Graham-Bermann, S. A., (2013). "Intimate Partner Violence and Child Adjustment: Moderation by Father Contact?" *Journal of Family Violence*, 28(5), 435–444. http://doi.org/http://dx.doi.org/10.1007/s10896-013-9517-x

5. Brandon, M. et al. (2008) "Analysing child deaths and serious injury through abuse and neglect: What can we learn? *Biennial Analysis of Serious Case Reviews 2003-2005*. Department for Children, Families and Schools. http://webarchive.nationalarchives.gov.uk/20130401151715/https://www.education.gov.uk/publications/eorderingdownload/dcsf-rr023.pdf

6. New South Wales Government Department of Family and Community Services, *Child Deaths 2012 Annual Report: Learning to improve services*. 2012, https://www.facs.nsw.gov.au/__data/assets/file/0019/313408/child_deaths_report_2012.pdf Accessed 1 July 2023.

Chapter 11:

1. ANROWS, *ESTIE: Evidence to support Safe & Together implementation and evaluation*, Cathy Humphreys, Sydney, ANROWS, 2022 https://www.anrows.org.au/project/estie-evidence-to-support-safe-together-implementation-and-evaluation/ Accessed 22 February 2023.

2. Sheri Chaney Jones and Kenneth Steinman, "Ohio Intimate Partner Violence Collaborative: Final Evaluation Report of the Safe & Together Training Program" (Evaluation Report, Safe & Together Institute, 2014).

3. David Mandel, "Supervising Domestic Violence Cases: A training for child welfare supervisors and managers," (Report, Domestic Violence Consultation Initiative, September 2009)

4. Chaney Jones and Steinman, *Ohio Intimate Partner Violence Collaborative*.

5. Department of Psychiatry at the Yale School of Medicine *et al*, "Bridgeport Safe Start Initiative: Assessment of the DCF/DV Protocol Project" (Report, August 2005)

6. David Mandel, anecdotal data received from primary sources

7. Anna Mitchell, "Safe & Together Edinburgh," (Report, 2017)

8. Tracey de Simone, et al, "Evidencing better Child Protection practice: why

representations of domestic violence matter," Current Issues in Criminal Justice, 32(4) (December 2020): 1-17, https://doi.org/10.1080/10345329.2020.1840957

9 David Mandel, "The value of Multi-Disciplinary Teams reviewing serious domestic violence cases. One Connecticut team's experience," (Report, April 2011)

10 Brittany diBella, et al, "From Research to Practice: An Overview of Systems Collaboration Efforts to Address the Co-occurrence of Domestic Violence and Child Maltreatment," Rutgers University (Research to Practice Brief, Rutgers University, School of Social Work, May 2017)

11 Safe & Together Institute, "The Safe & Together Model Collaboration Kickstarter Project: Dona Ana, New Mexico" (Project Report, October 2022)

12 ANROWS, Cathy Humphreys, et al, "Children Living with Domestic Violence: A Differential Response through Multi-agency Collaboration," Australian Social Work, Volume 71, Issue 2 (February 2018): 162-174, https://doi.org/10.1080/0312407X.2017.1415366

13 *The PATRICIA Project: PAThways in Research In Collaborative Inter-Agency working: State of knowledge paper*, Michelle Macvean et al, Landscapes Issue 14/2015, Sydney, ANROWS, 2015 https://www.anrows.org.au/publication/the-patricia-project-pathways-in-research-in-collaborative-inter-agency-working-state-of-knowledge-paper/ Accessed 22 February 2023.

14 University of Melbourne, *Working at the intersections of domestic and family violence, parental substance misuse and/or mental health issues*", Lucy Healy, Research Report of the STACY Project: Safe & Together Addressing ComplexitY, University of Melbourne, 2020, https://psplearninghub.com.au/wp-content/uploads/STACY-working-with-complexity-Final-Report.pdf Accessed 22 February 2022.

15 ANROWS, *ESTIE: Evidence to support Safe & Together implementation and evaluation*.

16 James D. Kirkpatrick and Wendy Kayser Kirkpatrick, Kirkpatrick's Four Levels of Training Evaluation, ATD Press, New Orleans, 2016